THE BEST
IN TENT
CAMPING

NEW ENGLAND

SECOND EDITION

Other titles in this series:

THE BEST IN TENT CAMPING

A GUIDE FOR CAR CAMPERS WHO HATE RVs, CONCRETE SLABS, AND LOUD PORTABLE STEREOS

NEW ENGLAND

SECOND EDITION

LAFE LOW

MENASHA RIDGE PRESS
BIRMINGHAM, ALABAMA

This book is for my son, Devin, my best camping buddy ever.

Library of Congress Cataloging-in-Publication Data

Low, Lafe, 1962—
    The best in tent camping, New England : a guide for car campers who hate RVs, concrete slabs,
and loud portable stereos / Lafe Low.—2nd ed.
        p.   cm.
    ISBN 0-89732-622-9
    1. Camping—New England—Guidebooks.   2. Camp sites, facilities, etc.—New
England—Guidebooks.   3. Automobile travel—New England—Guidebooks.
4. New England—Guidebooks. I. Title.

GV191.42.N3L69 2005
917.404'44—dc22

                                                                        2004061131

Cover and text design by Ian Szymkowiak, Palace Press International, Inc.
Cover photo by Robert Harding Picture Library Ltd./Alamy
Cartography by Steve Jones

Menasha Ridge Press
P.O. Box 43673
Birmingham, Alabama 35243
www.menasharidge.com

917.404
L 11/5

TABLE OF CONTENTS

NEW ENGLAND CAMPGROUNDS KEY

MAPS ON PAGES VIII–IX

MAINE

1 BAXTER STATE PARK
2 BLACKWOODS CAMPGROUND
3 BRADBURY MOUNTAIN STATE PARK
4 CAMDEN HILLS STATE PARK
5 COBSCOOK BAY STATE PARK
6 LAMOINE STATE PARK
7 LILY BAY STATE PARK
8 MOUNT BLUE STATE PARK
9 MOUNT DESERT CAMPGROUND
10 ORR'S ISLAND CAMPGROUND
11 PEAKS–KENNY STATE PARK
12 RANGELEY LAKE STATE PARK
13 SEAWALL CAMPGROUND
14 SEBAGO LAKE STATE PARK
15 WARREN ISLAND STATE PARK

NEW HAMPSHIRE

16 BEAR BROOK STATE PARK
17 BIG ROCK CAMPGROUND
18 BLACKBERRY CROSSING CAMPGROUND
19 COVERED BRIDGE CAMPGROUND
20 CRAWFORD NOTCH STATE PARK
21 DOLLY COPP CAMPGROUND
22 DRY RIVER CAMPGROUND
23 HANCOCK CAMPGROUND
24 JIGGER JOHNSON CAMPGROUND
25 LAFAYETTE CAMPGROUND
26 MOUNT MONADNOCK STATE PARK
27 PASSACONAWAY CAMPGROUND
28 PAWTUCKAWAY STATE PARK
29 PILLSBURY STATE PARK
30 WHITE LEDGE CAMPGROUND

VERMONT

31 ALLIS STATE PARK
32 BRANBURY STATE PARK
33 CHITTENDEN BROOK RECREATION AREA
34 COOLIDGE STATE PARK
35 EMERALD LAKE STATE PARK
36 GIFFORD WOODS STATE PARK
37 GROUT POND RECREATION AREA
38 HALF MOON STATE PARK
39 JAMAICA STATE PARK
40 MOUNT ASCUTNEY STATE PARK
41 MOUNT MOOSALAMOO CAMPGROUND
42 QUECHEE GORGE STATE PARK
43 SMUGGLERS NOTCH STATE PARK
44 UNDERHILL STATE PARK

MASSACHUSETTS

45 BEARTOWN STATE FOREST
46 CLARKSBURG STATE PARK
47 GRANVILLE STATE FOREST
48 HAROLD PARKER STATE FOREST
49 MOHAWK TRAIL STATE FOREST
50 MOUNT GREYLOCK STATE RESERVATION
51 NICKERSON STATE PARK
52 SAVOY MOUNTAIN STATE FOREST
53 WAQUOIT BAY NATURE PRESERVE

CONNECTICUT

54 DEVIL'S HOPYARD STATE PARK
55 HOUSATONIC MEADOWS STATE PARK
56 MACEDONIA BROOK STATE PARK
57 SELDEN NECK CAMPGROUND

RHODE ISLAND

58 BURLINGAME STATE PARK
59 FORT GETTY RECREATION AREA
60 GEORGE WASHINGTON MANAGEMENT AREA

ATLANTIC
OCEAN

MASSACHUSETTS
BAY

PROVINCETOWN

CHATHAM

SOUTH
YARMOUTH

NANTUCKET

BRUNSWICK 10

3

KENNEBUNKPORT

PORTLAND

PORTSMOUTH

95

PLYMOUTH

51

6 53

FALMOUTH

MARTHA'S VINEYARD

WHITE MOUNTAIN NATIONAL FOREST

14

18 NORTH CONWAY

30

GLOUCESTER

SALEM

BOSTON

FALL RIVER

NEWPORT

BUZZARDS BAY

LAKE WINNIPESAUKEE

24

28

CONCORD

16

MANCHESTER

19

METHUEN 48

PROVIDENCE

RHODE ISLAND

59

BLOCK ISLAND

27

17

33

29

NEW HAMPSHIRE

26

495

90

WORCESTER

190

60

58

25

23

HANOVER

89

MASSACHUSETTS

2

395

CONNECTICUT

NORWICH

54

CONNECTICUT RIVER

42

41

91

AMHERST

SPRINGFIELD

84

NEW LONDON

31

36

34

35

39

BRATTLEBORO

49

NORTHAMPTON

47

HARTFORD

57

95

MIDDLEBURY

33

37

46

52

95

97

WATERBURY

32

40

RUTLAND

45

55

NEW HAVEN

BRIDGEPORT

38

GREEN MTN. NATIONAL FOREST

BENNINGTON

50

PITTSFIELD

1

56

84

STAMFORD

95

LONG ISLAND SOUND

NEW YORK

ALBANY

90

GREAT BARRINGTON

87

LONG ISLAND

MAP LEGEND

WHITE WOLF

Campground name
and location

 24 ▲ 🚐

Individual tent and RV
campsites within
campground area

Table Rock
△

Other nearby
campgrounds

NATIONAL | STATE
FOREST | PARK

Public lands

══ **64** ══   Interstate highways

══ **19 219** ══   US highways

325 ◇ **219** **SR-219**   State roads County roads Service roads

MAIN ST.
════════   Other roads

▪▪▪▪   Unpaved or gravel roads

▪▪▪▪▪▪▪▪   Boardwalk

▫▫▫▫   Political boundary

++++++++   Railroads

– – – –   Hiking, biking, or horse trail

Swift Creek
〰〰〰   River or stream

Asheville
◉

City
or town

N

Indicates North

Ward Lake ⬭

Ocean, lake,
or bay

╍ Bridge or tunnel		🛝 Playground		⊼ Picnic area	
📶 Amphitheater		🚗 Parking		⛺ Sheltered picnic area	
🎣 Falls or rapids		⛴ Marina or boat ramp		💧 Spring/well	
🍴 Food		🔥 Fire ring		♨ Dishwater disposal	
🚻 Restroom		☎ Telephone		🔺 Summit or lookout	
🚰 Water access		🧺 Laundry		🛁 Bathhouse	
⬛ Gate		✝ Cemetery		🚽 Dump station	
🗑 Trash		🏊 Swimming		🏊 No swimming	
♿ Wheelchair accessible		🐴 Horse trail		🏇 Stables	

ABOUT THE AUTHOR

A LIFELONG NEW ENGLANDER, Lafe Low spends nearly all of his free time outside—skiing, camping, skiing, mountain biking, skiing, kayaking, and skiing. He first started camping in grade school, when he and his best friend Dan Quagliaroli would head off into the southern-Connecticut woods every Saturday afternoon with lofty ideals, indomitable spirit, and ridiculously heavy backpacks.

On the professional side, Lafe earned a Bachelor of Arts degree in journalism from Keene State College in 1984. From there, he immediately went to work in the magazine world. After working for a variety of computer magazines, he decided to launch his own magazine, *Explore New England*, in 1995. This was truly the crossroads of his personal and professional passions. After *Explore New England*, he went on to be the editor of *Outdoor Adventure* and an acquisitions editor for The Globe Pequot Press. He is now an editor with *Redmond* magazine. *The Best in Tent Camping: New England* is his first book, but probably not his last. He currently lives in the Boston area.

ACKNOWLEDGMENTS

W HILE I WROTE THE WORDS and drove the miles in preparing this book, I enjoyed the tremendous benefit of support and inspiration from many people. Most of all, I would like to thank my family and my parents (all three of them!), Douglas and Linsey Low, and Larry Howard, for their endless encouragement, understanding, love, and patience, especially while I dragged them around to these campgrounds.

To the innumerable state park rangers and volunteers I chatted with at campgrounds all over New England, as well as the friendly folks at the private campgrounds I visited: I tip my hat to you. I'll be back soon, when I can stay a few days and relax!

PREFACE

NEW ENGLAND IS A REMARKABLE REGION. Nowhere else in the United States are you simultaneously so close to the ocean, the mountains, lakes, and rivers. Drive a few hours, and the landscape and the scenery change as rapidly and dramatically as the weather.

I have lived in New England all my life, moving around and experiencing almost all of the six New England states. (Rhode Island is the only New England state whose license plate hasn't graced my vehicle at one point or another.) I am also somewhat of a creature of habit. Over the years, I have found spots where I can experience the solitude, wonder, and awesome beauty of the wilderness, and I keep going back to those same spots. There's a comfortable cloak of familiarity, but in cruising back to familiar territory, I've inadvertently blown by some incredible areas.

By traversing New England to research this book, I discovered some magical spots I might never have found otherwise, and for that I am thankful. The absolute solitude of camping on the shores of Benedict Pond at Beartown State Forest, the isolation and deep wilderness beauty at several Pillsbury State Park campsites, the natural cathedral of site 21 at Branbury State Park—these are places that gave me chills when I first found them. Now, I'll return to these spots for longer visits. When you have the chance to visit here, I hope you have an equally memorable experience. Enjoy the ride.

—Lafe Low

THE BEST IN TENT CAMPING

A GUIDE FOR CAR CAMPERS WHO HATE RVs,
CONCRETE SLABS, AND LOUD PORTABLE STEREOS

NEW ENGLAND

SECOND EDITION

INTRODUCTION

THERE ARE LITERALLY HUNDREDS of campgrounds in New England. Winnowing down the list to 60 was no easy task. That said, this book is a guide to 60 of the best for tent camping. In this second edition, there are five new campgrounds that capture the solitude and sense of wilderness that define the very best in tent camping. There are also plenty of wonderful campgrounds and campsites out there that didn't make it into the book, but are still well worth checking out. In developing the list of campgrounds to explore here, I took into account numerous factors, one of which was accessibility. I wanted to profile campgrounds that offer a peaceful wilderness experience and are also accessible enough for a quick escape. Of course, there are some pristine, incredibly remote campsites carved out of the wilderness of northern Maine, northern New Hampshire, and tucked away on islands in several New England lakes that aren't included in this book—yet. They may be in future editions, so stay tuned.

One other thing you'll no doubt notice is that most of the campgrounds profiled here are either state park or national forest campgrounds. That's no accident, as these campgrounds tend to provide much more of a wilderness experience. It's probably a simple matter of economics. Many private campgrounds cater to the RV crowd because, quite frankly, they spend more money when they visit. RV campers need hookups, which cost money, and they tend to stay for long periods of time. Simple economics, really.

There are some notable exceptions, however. The Mount Desert Campground leaps to mind. While it neither excludes nor bends over backwards to bring in the land yachts, the simple factor of its rugged, waterfront topography will limit the size and quantity of RVs. The Orr's Island Campground is another tent-friendly, private campground. There is an interesting dichotomy here. There are certainly rows of RVs that you can't help but notice as you enter the campground. Keep driving over to the tent-only area, and you'll know why I chose to profile these beautiful, windswept, secluded campsites.

I hope you'll be able to visit many of the campgrounds profiled in this book and will agree that they are among the region's best.

THE RATING SYSTEM

For each campground, there's a rating from one to five for each of the following categories: beauty, privacy, spaciousness, quiet, security, and cleanliness. This was often a tough call, as there are different sections within the campgrounds that may warrant different ratings. So the ratings you'll see at the beginning of each profile are representative of the campground as a whole. While you may see a three or four for privacy overall, you can probably bet on a couple of sites tucked off in the far reaches of the campground that clearly rate at least a five.

BEAUTY

This factor may seem obvious, but is often elusive, or at the very least, subjective. What appeals to one camper may not appeal to another. I prefer campgrounds and campsites that are set deep within the woods. The greater sense of natural solitude a campsite provides, the better it is, at least in my view.

Speaking of views, many of the campgrounds profiled here, and certainly many of the individual sites within these campgrounds, are perched right along the shores of a lake, a pond, or even the ocean. These campsites are off the charts when it comes to site beauty. If there was a six-star rating, sites like those situated along the waters of Moosehead Lake, Half Moon Pond, and Somes Sound would easily deserve it. There are also many sites at campgrounds in close proximity to the water that, while they may not be right on the shore, provide dramatic water views. These sites too are among some of the most spectacularly scenic.

PRIVACY

When you set up your campsite, the last thing you want is to feel as if you're piled up on top of your neighbors. Even in campgrounds where the sites aren't huge, if they are encircled by a relatively dense forest and arranged with a sensitive eye toward privacy, you can find a site that puts you in your own slice of the woods.

SPACIOUSNESS

Some of the campsites I've seen in New England are just barely big enough for your tent, a picnic table, and a fire ring. Others are large enough to accommodate a house. I don't typically need a lot of room when I'm camping, but I don't want to pitch my tent right next to the picnic table. This rating will give you an idea of how much elbow room you can expect when you set up camp.

QUIET

This is another factor that is particularly important to me. I like campsites that are very well isolated, secluded from neighboring sites and the rest of the campground. So I find it especially distracting if there is a persistent drone of cars and trucks blasting by on a nearby road, the steady whine of powerboats zipping by on a lake, or (worse yet) the sounds of portable TVs and radios.

You can rest assured I paid close attention to the noisiness of these campgrounds. In some cases, there are parts of a campground that are close to a main road, while the rest of the campground is separated by enough distance and enough forest to block out the road noise.

SECURITY

It's a shame that this even has to be a factor, but you have to be practical. I've never had anyone steal or rummage through my stuff at any of the campgrounds mentioned here, but there are some that feel "safer" to me than others. The size of the campground and proximity to urban areas are the primary aspects I considered when making my security determinations. Be prudent, even when it looks like there's no one around. It's not a bad idea to lock up your car and your bike when you retire to your tent for the night. A little bit of precaution can go a long way toward making sure you return home with all your gear.

CLEANLINESS

Most of the campgrounds profiled here scored highly on the cleanliness scale. This is true for a couple of reasons. First, I think that most people who enjoy the idea of spending a night in the woods are also inclined to take good care of the forest and their campsites. Second, many state parks make extraordinary efforts to keep their campsites well maintained. When you see the park rangers or other staff about the campground, take a moment to say "Hi" and thank them for keeping the campground clean.

Of course, all of this depends on you doing your part as well. Even though campgrounds are heavily traveled and well-worn spots, do what you can to leave no trace. Pack out everything you packed in (and even a little more). Please don't pile your trash in the fireplace, or try to burn things that won't burn or that emit dangerous fumes.

Even at the cleanest of campgrounds and campsites, whenever I find a stray piece of paper, bottle cap, or cigarette butt (especially the latter), I always take a moment to reach down and pick it up to dispose of it properly. If everyone is mindful to be as gentle with the forest as possible, it will remain pristine for generations to come. Every time you pick up a bit of trash in the woods, consider it doing a favor for your children or grandchildren, even if you don't have any yet!

NEW ENGLAND WEATHER

Even during the summer, it's prudent to pack a fleece jacket and a waterproof jacket. It seems like on at least half of the occasions where I find myself camping outside, it rains. I think the camping gods start chuckling every time they see me grab my tent.

Anyway, it's a good idea to be prepared for any kind of weather. That doesn't mean bring your snowshoes in August, but by all means do bring a warm jacket and something water-resistant. The weather in New England can and does change faster than the scenery as you drive from Cape Cod to the Berkshires. Have something warm, have something dry. You'll be much more comfortable and safe.

Also, even if it has been a bright, sunny day, foul weather can blow in at any time, and frequently does. I've been tempted on many nights to ignore the rain fly on my tent and just leave it in the car. This can be a bad idea, especially if it starts raining at 2 a.m. Be ready and you'll be happy.

CANOE AND KAYAK CAMPING

Several of the campgrounds profiled here are accessible only by canoe or kayak. While this poses several logistical and packing challenges, the rewards of absolute solitude and camping right on the water are well worth the extra effort.

There are a few important safety factors to consider when canoe or kayak camping. First and foremost, you need to be comfortable with your paddling skills before you add the weight of camping gear to your boat. Don't plan a camping trip as your first experience paddling a canoe or kayak.

With a sea kayak, try to stow all your gear in the sealed bulkheads. It may be tempting to strap your tent or sleeping pad to the deck, but anything protruding above deck level will make your kayak less stable. Besides catching the wind, it also raises the boat's center of gravity. Keep all your gear below decks.

Most touring kayaks have a fore and aft storage compartment. Try to spread out your gear evenly. Even if all your gear will fit in the aft compartment, spread it out among both to ensure that your kayak floats level. Once you've packed your boat, take it for a test float. Get it into water deep enough that it floats freely. If it looks like you're riding a wheelie or about to do a nose dive, you need to redistribute your gear. The same goes for side-to-side balance. Keep those same principles in mind when stowing gear in a canoe. Try to balance to load in the center of the canoe, and evenly distributed fore and aft.

Having said all that, you can pack an amazing amount of gear in a canoe or kayak. Prior to packing up for the first group trip I ever went on, we divided the group gear. I stowed the group gear in my aft compartment and my personal gear in the forward compartment and still had plenty of room in each.

There are a few things you can do to make your canoe or kayak camping trip a bit more convenient. For your first dinner at your island campsite, prepare something in advance, freeze it in a Tupperware container, then when dinnertime arrives, all you have to do is heat it up and you're ready to eat. Also, any gear that you haven't been able to store in a dry bag, you should wrap tightly in a large, plastic garbage bag. Anything you store in the bulkheads or open in your canoe can and most likely will get a bit wet. There's nothing worse than reaching for a jacket or vest to wear and finding it damp and soggy.

THE CAMPFIRE AWAITS

There's nothing like a night spent outside. The soft crackle of a campfire, the flickering light thrown about the forest, the satisfaction of the day's travels, and the anticipation of tomorrow's adventures—it's a potent combination.

Hopefully, the camping tips provided here and the descriptions of the campgrounds that follow will steer you to a memorable experience. Pick a state, read the profiles, pack the car, and hit the road! New England is a vast and diverse region. There are campgrounds profiled here from the farthest northern reaches of Vermont, New Hampshire, and Maine to the seashores of Connecticut and Rhode Island, and everything in between. Some are familiar haunts, some are unexpected hidden gems; all are spectacular. Wherever you choose to go camping in New England—from the sandy bluffs of Nickerson State Park to the deep woods of Beartown State Forest, from the absolute solitude of Warren Island to the cool, crisp mountain air of Underhill State Park—you're in for a memorable and magical trip.

GET OUT AND GET ACTIVE WITH THE APPALACHIAN MOUNTAIN CLUB

With the AMC, you can participate in a wide variety of outdoor activities, connect with new people, and help to protect the natural world you love. Join us and each year you'll receive 10 issues of our member magazine, *AMC Outdoors,* which will keep you informed of environmental issues and outdoor recreation opportunities—including hiking, paddling, biking, and snowshoeing—across the Appalachian region. You'll receive discounts on AMC guided adventures and courses, lodging, and books. You can also join our Conservation Action Network (CAN) and help increase public influence on critical conservation issues today at **www.outdoors.org/conservation/can.**

LEARN SOMETHING NEW: AMC OUTDOOR ADVENTURES

Develop your outdoor skills and knowledge through AMC Outdoor Adventures! Learn to rock climb, snowshoe, or navigate by map and compass. From beginner backpacking and family canoeing to dogsledding and guided winter camping trips, you'll find something for any age or interest at spectacular locations throughout the Appalachian region, including the Maine Woods, White Mountains, Adirondacks, Catskills, and the Delaware Water Gap. For a full listing and to sign up, go to www.outdoors.org and click on Education.

BE OUR GUEST: AMC DESTINATIONS AND ACCOMMODATIONS

From the North Woods of Maine to the White Mountains to the Delaware Water Gap, AMC offers a wide variety of accommodations, from full-service lodges to backcountry huts, shelters, and campsites. Experience outdoor adventure at its best as our guest. Get trip suggestions, check lodging availability, and make reservations through our Web site, **www.outdoors.org.**

CONTACT US TODAY

Appalachian Mountain Club
5 Joy Street
Boston, MA 02108
www.outdoors.org

MAINE

BAXTER STATE PARK

" **FOREVER WILD**"—those are the words of Percival Baxter (1876–1969), former governor of Maine, and a philanthropist and conservationist who donated Katahdin and the land surrounding it to the state on the condition that it remain "forever wild." Those words perfectly describe Baxter State Park as well. The remoteness, size, and grandeur of the park are profound. Baxter's intent was to keep the park undeveloped. Today, the park is managed as a wildlife preserve first and a recreation resource second.

At more than 200,000 acres, Baxter State Park is a huge place. There are actually ten campgrounds within the park. Truth is, no matter where you end up in Baxter State Park, you're bound to have a remote wilderness experience. Eight of the campgrounds you can reach by driving; the other two are hike-in areas. Camping in these areas requires a bit of additional effort, but the solitude and splendor are well worth it. If you're camping in Baxter State Park, by all means enjoy the convenience of the car-camping areas, but try to spend at least one night at Chimney Pond or Russell Pond, or even one of the many truly remote wilderness campsites spread throughout the park.

Upon entering the massive park through the Togue Pond Gate along the park's southern border, the first campground you'll come to is Abol Campground. Abol has 9 tent sites and 12 lean-tos; each lean-to can accommodate four people. Abol Campground is situated at the trailhead for the Abol Trail, one of the routes to the summit of Katahdin, so this is one of several popular spots for hikers with designs on summiting the park's centerpiece peak.

Farther up the Nesowadnehunk Tote Road that encircles the perimeter of the park is Katahdin Stream Campground. This campground has 10 tent sites, 12 lean-tos that can fit three to five people, and a bunk-

A night spent camping in Baxter State Park, especially in one of the remote sites, is a true wilderness experience.

RATINGS

Beauty: ✿ ✿ ✿ ✿ ✿
Privacy: ✿ ✿ ✿ ✿ ✿
Spaciousness: ✿ ✿ ✿ ✿
Quiet: ✿ ✿ ✿ ✿ ✿
Security: ✿ ✿ ✿ ✿ ✿
Cleanliness: ✿ ✿ ✿ ✿ ✿

ADDRESS:	Baxter State Park
	64 Balsam Drive
	Millinocket, ME
	04462
OPERATED BY:	Maine Department
	of Conservation,
	Bureau of Parks and
	Lands
INFORMATION:	Baxter State Park,
	(207) 723-5140
OPEN:	May 15–October 15
	(some campgrounds
	have variable dates)
SITES:	97 tent sites, 84 lean-
	tos, 4 bunkhouses,
	and 23 cabins in 10
	campgrounds
EACH SITE HAS:	Fire ring, picnic
	table
ASSIGNMENT:	Reservations
	strongly recom-
	mended, accepted
	Monday–Friday,
	8 a.m.–4 p.m.; other-
	wise first come, first
	served
REGISTRATION:	At gatehouse and
	with ranger; check
	in after 1 p.m., check
	out by 11 a.m.
FACILITIES:	Pit toilets, water
	spigots
PARKING:	At sites
FEE:	$12 nonresident
	vehicle fee to enter
	park, $18 per night
	for tent spaces and
	lean-tos, $10 per per-
	son per night for
	bunkhouses
RESTRICTIONS:	Pets: Prohibited
	Fires: Fire rings only
	Alcohol: Prohibited
	Vehicles: Parking at
	sites only

house with room for six. From here, hikers can head to the summit of Katahdin on the Hunt Trail, which is part of the Appalachian Trail. You can also easily get to the Owl Trail and the Grassy Pond Trail heading east.

Just to the east of Katahdin Stream, you'll find Daicey Pond Campground. You get there by continuing north and west on the Tote Road, then heading south just before the Foster Field Picnic Area. You could also hike there from Katahdin Stream Campground (or vice versa) on the Grassy Pond Trail. The Daicey Pond Campground doesn't have any tent sites, but it does have a pair of lean-tos and 11 cabins with two to four beds each. The Appalachian Trail goes right through the campground. There's also a trail that encircles Daicey Pond and leads to the short Lost Pond Trail, which takes you out to the still and secluded waters of Lost Pond.

Continuing north on the Nesowadnehunk Tote Road along the western border of the park brings you to Nesowadnehunk Field Campground. Here there are 12 tent sites, 11 three- and four-person lean-tos, and two group sites. From here, you could easily get to the Doubletop Trail, a sturdy hike that takes you up and over Doubletop Mountain and offers some outrageous views of Katahdin.

Taking the Roaring Brook Road off to the right from the Togue Pond gatehouse brings you first to Roaring Brook Campground. There are 10 tent sites (four of which are walk-in sites), 12 lean-tos that accommodate anywhere from two to six people each, and a bunkhouse with room for 12. From here, you have plenty of hiking options. Follow the Sandy Stream Pond Trail to the Turner Mountain Trail to hike up Turner Mountain. You could also head west on the Helon Taylor Trail to reach Katahdin.

Head west on the Chimney Pond Trail from Roaring Brook Campground, and you'll come to Chimney Pond Campground. This is a remote and supremely beautiful spot. There are no tent sites here, but there are nine lean-tos that can each handle four people and a bunkhouse that can fit 12. At least your tent is one less thing to carry.

Besides being remarkably scenic, Chimney Pond Campground is a perfect base camp from which to

BAXTER STATE PARK CAMPGROUNDS

N

CAMPGROUND ▲

TROUT BROOK FARM CAMPGROUND

SOUTH BRANCH CAMPGROUND

ROARING BROOK CAMPGROUND

ROARING BROOK RD.

TRACY HORSE TRL.

POGY NOTCH TRL.

FREEZEOUT TRL.

S. BRANCH MTN. TRL.

TROUT BROOK RD.

RUSSELL POND TRL.

BASIN CHIMNEY POND CAMPGROUND

RUSSELL POND CAMPGROUND

NORTH PEAKS TRL.

ABOL CAMPGROUND

WASSATAQUIOK LAKE TRL.

NORTHWEST BASIN TRL

WASSATAQUIOK LAKE TRL.

WEBSTER LAKE TRL.

KATAHDIN STREAM CAMPGROUND

DAICEY POND CAMPGROUND

NESOWADNEHUNK TATE RD.

FREEZEOUT TRL.

NESOWADNEHUNK CAMPGROUND

KIDNEY CAMPS

MILLINOCKET RD.

GETTING THERE

summit Katahdin. You have your choice of the Saddle Trail, Cathedral Trail, or Didley Trail. Any of these hikes is steep and strenuous, so plan ahead and be prepared.

Also from the Roaring Brook Campground, follow the Russell Pond Trail to Russell Pond Campground, another incredibly remote and wild camping area. There are four tent sites, four lean-tos that can accommodate anywhere from four to eight people, and a bunkhouse for 12. This campground is also situated within a hub of trails. There are several long hiking trails, including the Russell Pond Trail and the Northwest Basin Trail (which leads to the North Peaks Trail) to the south, the Pogy Notch Trail to the north, and the Wassataquiok Lake Trail to the west. These are all fairly long hikes, so plan and pace yourself carefully, especially if you're doing a round-trip day hike from the campground. If you're looking for a shorter hike from Russell Pond Campground, try the Ledge Falls Trail, Grand Falls Trail, or Lookout Trail.

Entering the park from the northeast at Matagamon Gate Public Landing will get you close to the Trout Brook Farm and South Branch campgrounds.

To get to the Togue Pond gatehouse, follow the Baxter State Park Road northwest from the intersection of ME 11 and ME 157 in Millinocket. To get to the Matagamon Public Landing gatehouse, from Patten, take US 1 north to ME 159 north to Grand Lake Road. Follow Grand Lake Road to the gatehouse.

From the gatehouse, follow the road west to Trout Brook Farm Campground. This campground is set aside for tent campers, with 18 tent sites and no lean-tos or bunkhouses. From here, you can also hike in to a number of remote, wilderness campsites. To the south, follow Five Ponds Trail to sites spread out along Littlefield Pond, Billfish Pond, and Long Pond. To the north, the lengthy, multiday Freezeout Trail brings you to remote campsites and lean-tos along Second Lake, Webster Brook, and Webster Lake.

From Trout Brook Campground, continue west on the road to The Crossing picnic area. Then head south on South Branch Road to find South Branch Camp-ground, with 21 tent sites, 12 four-person lean-tos, and a bunkhouse for six. This campground is located at the northern tip of Lower South Branch Pond. From here, you can hike the short and sweet Ledges Trail or the Middle Fowler Trail.

There are also several excellent hikes to nearby peaks, including the North Traveler Trail, which leads up the mountain of the same name; the Howe Brook Trail, which follows its namesake brook past two dra-matic waterfalls; and the Center Ridge Trail, which brings you to the summit of the Traveler. To the west of Upper and Lower South Branch ponds, the South Branch Mountain Trail takes you up and over Black Cat Mountain. These hikes aren't very long, but they are very steep. Never underestimate the intensity of the hiking anywhere within Baxter State Park.

Baxter State Park is a popular destination, and there is a finite number of campsites in and around the park. You could wing it by not making reservations, but you might end up disappointed or driving way out of your way to find an open site. If you do get jammed, there are several private campgrounds just outside the park that provide a backup place to pitch your tent, but do yourself a favor and make a reserva-tion. The peace of mind will be well worth it.

BLACKWOODS CAMPGROUND

FOR SUCH A HUGE CAMPGROUND, most of the sites at Blackwoods still retain a cozy atmosphere. The three-lane paved road (two lanes in, one out) accessing the campground might make you wonder what you're getting into, but rest assured, this is a wonderful place to pitch a tent.

For one thing, Blackwoods Campground is situated just off the Park Loop Road that winds its way around Acadia National Park. Better still, from your campsite it's a short walk to the ocean, Sand Beach, Thunder Hole, Otter Cliff . . . the list goes on. Also, the campground rests on the mostly flat forest floor beneath a loosely spaced forest canopy of mixed pine, balsam, hemlock, and hardwoods. The open forest lets lots of light filter through to the campground floor on sunny days, and there's a near-constant, cool breeze blowing in from the nearby ocean.

Blackwoods is separated into two main loops. Loop A has 160 sites and Loop B has 154 sites, plus several group sites available by reservation only. The place is big! Blackwoods accepts reservations from June 15 to September 15. Making a reservation for an in-season trip is not a bad idea, as Acadia National Park receives hordes of visitors during the summer, and Blackwoods is likely to be full on most weekends.

Outside of those dates, it's first come, first served. About 50 campsites on Loop A are open year-round if you've come to Acadia to snowshoe or cross-country ski on the massive network of carriage roads that wind their way in and around the park. Camping during the winter is usually free, unless a ranger at the main station informs you differently. I've frequently visited Blackwoods in the off-season. There has never been a fee, and I've always felt like I had the place to myself.

Looking at the 160 sites within Loop A, there are several areas that are especially conducive to quality

> *This campground is set between the still of the forests and mountains of Acadia National Park and the thundering surf of the Atlantic Ocean.*

RATINGS

Beauty: ✩ ✩ ✩ ✩
Privacy: ✩ ✩ ✩
Spaciousness: ✩ ✩ ✩ ✩
Quiet: ✩ ✩ ✩ ✩
Security: ✩ ✩ ✩
Cleanliness: ✩ ✩ ✩ ✩

KEY INFORMATION

tent camping. The first sub-loop, with sites 3, 4, 5, 7, and 10 through 19, has loosely spaced sites beneath a rich forest canopy. The sites have a welcoming blanket of pine needles, which makes a soft, aromatic bed for your tent and sleeping bag.

The next loop contains sites 2, 6, 8, 9, 22, 27, 29, 32, 33, and 34, which are also loosely spaced. These two loops are quite close to the path leading down to the cliffs—an extra bonus. After the day crowds have cleared out, you've had your fireside dinner, and the campfire has died down, grab a flashlight and a mug of tea (or whatever suits your mood) and wander down the path and across the Park Loop Road to watch the surf crashing incessantly against the cliffs. That's a sight and sound combination of which I never tire.

Farther up the larger part of Loop A, the sites off to the left of the outer loop offer a nice sense of seclusion. Look for sites 104 through 108, 124 through 131, and 144 through 151. In truth, though, most of the sites within the sweeping expanse of Loop A will offer you a nice spot for your tent.

Over in Loop B, there are several areas where the sites are set apart from each other. The crossroad at the far end of Loop B sets off sites 141, 143, 147, 150, 153, and 154. These are the sites I'd look for first in Loop B.

Taking the second or third left from the main outer loop will bring you to sites numbered in the high 60s and low 70s. Sites 65 through 73 have a good amount of elbow room between one another. Site 45 is also stuck onto the far end of this loop. It's right on the main outer loop, but if you set up well within the site, you'll be fine.

There are also several group sites on the left side of Loop B. G4 and G5 offer the most space, although G5 is right across from the restrooms. Each of these reservation-only group sites has room for 15 to 20 campers. There's an amphitheater between Loop A and Loop B where rangers present evening slide shows and interpretive programs. Check the schedule at the campground entrance ranger station.

If you end up pitching your tent at the north end of Loop A, you'll be close to the South Ridge hiking

MAP

BLACKWOODS CAMPGROUND

ATLANTIC OCEAN

CHECK OUT BOX

To Bar Harbor

To Park Loop Rd.

OCEAN PATH

Park Loop Rd.

19–11

1–10

20–31

34–32

35–45

80–74

46–63

48–71

64–74

75–91

To Seal Harbor

81–92

93–107

108

136–138

92–107

109–135

109–131

132–151

139–152

Loop A

152–160

153   154

Loop B

RESTROOM
WATER ACCESS
PARKING
PUBLIC PHONE
AMPHITHEATER
DUMP STATION

CADILLAC MOUNTAIN SOUTH RIDGE TRAIL

N

trail, leading to the summit of Cadillac Mountain. Wherever you land at Blackwoods, or even if you stay elsewhere in or near Acadia National Park, a trip to the summit of Cadillac is one thing you won't want to miss. From the mountain, you'll have a sweeping, panoramic view that defies clichés, platitudes, and expletives! Here's a tip: The sunsets are phenomenal, so much so that one per day may not be enough. Situate yourself along the Park Loop Road to watch the sunset. The instant it dips below the horizon, hop in your car and boogie up to the summit of Cadillac Mountain and watch it again!

GETTING THERE

From Ellsworth, follow ME 3 onto Mount Desert Island. Follow ME 3 to ME 102/198. Stay on ME 198 when it turns left, and follow this to ME 233. Follow ME 233 to the entrance to Acadia National Park on the left. Enter the park and follow the Park Loop Road to Blackwoods Campground on the right.

BRADBURY MOUNTAIN STATE PARK

> *The cool breezes and sunlight filtering through the trees add to the peace of Bradbury Mountain State Park.*

DESPITE ITS LOCATION, Bradbury Mountain State Park is an exceptionally quiet campground. There's a bit of sporadic road noise from ME 9, but the fragrant evergreen scent wafting through the loose forest is constant. There's an open, airy character to the forest that lets sunlight brighten the campground floor and breezes blow through.

Pick your campsite, and the ranger will come by to register you. Sites 1, 7, 14, 26 through 29, 35, 36, 38, and 40 are first come, first served. You can reserve any of the other sites. There's a campground host site on the right as you enter the campground. On a map, it looks like sites 1 and 2 were thrown out into the forest and replaced by the campground host site.

All of the sites have a hard, sandy surface that holds on to tent stakes. Sites 6 and 7 are moderately spacious. There's an old stone wall running along the back of these sites, and one behind site 15. The open character of the forest here provides lots of light and nice breezes, but consequently not as much privacy as would a densely forested campground. Sites 8 and 9 are very spacious, but open to each other and to the road. Sites 15 and 16 are very open to each other; they almost look like one extremely large, sandy spot. They would make a good pair of sites for a larger group or family needing two sites side by side.

The individual sites differ in size and are marked as such on the campground's map. The sites at Bradbury Mountain, however, are similar when it comes to their level of privacy. There's only a mild sense of seclusion afforded by relatively light undergrowth.

If you're looking for site 1, you'll find it curiously cast off near site 15. It doesn't really matter how it got there, just that it did, because it is remarkably secluded. It's a hike-in site reserved only for tent campers. The trail leading into the site is located next

RATINGS

Beauty: ✿ ✿ ✿ ✿
Privacy: ✿ ✿ ✿
Spaciousness: ✿ ✿ ✿ ✿
Quiet: ✿ ✿ ✿ ✿
Security: ✿ ✿ ✿ ✿
Cleanliness: ✿ ✿ ✿ ✿

to site 15. It's about a 100-foot walk on a flat, sandy path to the site, which gives it a true wilderness sense of seclusion.

The site itself is set within loosely spaced, mixed forest with very little undergrowth. There's a very open, breezy character to the forest here as well, but you're so secluded from the rest of the campground that the sense of privacy is complete. From this site, you can look around 360 degrees, and all you'll see is the forest. Site 1 at Bradbury Mountain State Park offers a sense of seclusion equal to a backpacking site way off in the backcountry. Site 2 is another supremely secluded walk-in site. This site shares all the characteristics and accolades of site 1, although it is actually a bit farther into the woods.

You might want to avoid sites 17 and 18, as these sites are right next to the shelter. Site 19 is huge, but it also has a very open feel. Exposed on two sides to the campground's loop road, site 20 feels too open for me. Site 21 is a bit more secluded. It's set at the corner of the campground road with a decent amount of space between it and site 19. It looks like you could drive right through site 22. It's very open to site 20, as well as being on the inside corner of the campground road.

Sites 23 through 26 are all very spacious. These sites are set along the edge of an open, grassy area providing fire pits and picnic tables. It's a pleasant area, very open to the sky and framed by a dense wall of mixed deciduous and coniferous trees. The wall of woods at the back of the sites is also filled in with undergrowth, providing a dense barrier against ME 9.

If you're going to grab a site near this small field, go for site 27, which is set off from the field a bit within a dense grove. The only drawback to this cluster of sites is that this side of the campground is closer to ME 9, so there is some occasional road noise.

Sites 29 and 30 are tiny, but they are surrounded by a bit more undergrowth and feel more secluded. Site 31 is slightly larger and more open, but it's still set off by undergrowth. The forest on this side of the campground is denser and has thicker undergrowth.

The forest opens over sites 32 through 36. Site 37 is huge. It's very open to the sky and framed by loose

KEY INFORMATION

ADDRESS: Bradbury Mountain State Park 528 Hallowell Road Pownal, ME 04069

OPERATED BY: Maine Department of Conservation, Bureau of Parks and Lands

INFORMATION: Bradbury Mountain State Park, (207) 688-4712

OPEN: Year-round

SITES: 41 sites

EACH SITE HAS: Fire ring, picnic table

ASSIGNMENT: First come, first served or by reservation: (800) 332-1501, (207) 287-3824, www.campwithme.com (additional $2 reservation fee per site, per night)

REGISTRATION: At ranger station as you enter the campground; check-in after 1 p.m., check-out by 11 a.m.

FACILITIES: Pit toilets, water spigots, recycling station, playground, ball field

PARKING: At sites

FEE: Maine residents, $11; nonresidents, $14

RESTRICTIONS: Pets: On leash only
Fires: Fire rings only
Alcohol: Prohibited
Vehicles: Parking at sites only
Other: No visitors after sunset; quiet hours 10 p.m.–7 a.m.; 14-day maximum stay

MAP

To Bradbury Mountain Trails

DAY-USE AREA

BRADBURY MOUNTAIN STATE PARK CAMPGROUND

← To PORTLAND AND POWNAL

ROAD BLOCKED OFF

9

CAMPGROUND HOST SITE

RESTROOM	
WATER ACCESS	
PICNIC AREA	
CHECK-IN STATION	
GATE	
SHELTER	

GETTING THERE

Follow ME 9 north through Pownal. Continue heading north, following signs to the campground. You'll pass the other side of Bradbury Mountain State Park before you come to the campground on the right (left if you're heading south).

birch and maple trees. Set off from the other sites and surrounded by a bit more undergrowth, site 38 is close to the restrooms. Site 39 is quite spacious and covered by a canopy of maples for a shady feel, while 40 is tiny but still feels secluded, as it is set within dense pines.

Within a delightful maple and birch grove, site 41 is moderately spacious and looks like another scene from the 100 Acre Wood. This site is right next to—and I mean *right* next to—sites 20 and 22. This troika of sites is in a charming, loose grove of deciduous trees, but the sites are very open to each other.

Even though many of the sites here seem exposed to one another, you still won't feel as if you're piled on top of your neighbors. Although you'll certainly be able to see your fellow campers, the sites are generally spacious and spaced far enough apart to offer a modicum of elbow room.

You will have to drive a bit to get to the rest of Bradbury Mountain State Park and the hiking trails, but it's not too far, and it's definitely worth the trip.

CAMDEN HILLS STATE PARK

THE CAMPGROUND AT **C**AMDEN **H**ILLS State Park would make it into this book by virtue of its location alone. You know what they say about real estate. The campground is nestled at the foot of Mount Battie and on the shores of Penobscot Bay. The whole area is as fine a place as you could possibly hope to find for hiking, climbing, biking (both on and off the road), and sea kayaking.

Fortunately, the campground is also well worth a stay on its own merits. Camden Hills State Park is deceptively large. As you enter the park from US 1, all you can see is the ranger station, the Mount Battie Auto Road, and a large, open field off to the right. You may even spot a (gasp) RV! Don't back up the car—this place definitely deserves closer examination. Venture a bit farther into the park, and you'll find the wilderness atmosphere you seek.

There are two main loops and one miniloop within the campground. The first loop, home to sites 1 through 63, is just off to the right as you enter the park. This loop holds most of the sites at Camden Hills. Although the sites here are closer together, there are still quite a few that provide a sense of solitude. Within this primary loop, sites 3 through 10, 14, 20 through 24, 35, 37, 39, and 49 are some of my favorites. These seem best suited for pitching a tent. The sites themselves are slightly smaller, and make nice, cozy spots to camp. These tent-friendly sites are grouped together. Most of the larger sites, where the land yachts make safe harbor, are off on their own.

The miniloop that contains sites 103 through 105 also offers good tent sites. The next loop, just past the miniloop, has fewer sites than the first loop, with lots of space in between. When you first arrive at Camden Hills, drive this loop and check out sites 70, 74, 76 through 78, 84 through 86, and 91 through 93. The

> *Whether your taste in outdoor adventures tends toward hiking, biking, paddling, or climbing, you've come to the right place.*

RATINGS

Beauty: ✰ ✰ ✰ ✰
Privacy: ✰ ✰ ✰ ✰
Spaciousness: ✰ ✰ ✰ ✰
Quiet: ✰ ✰ ✰
Security:✰ ✰ ✰ ✰
Cleanliness: ✰ ✰ ✰ ✰

outer loop road that brings you to sites 71 through 81 also leads to the trailhead for the Mount Megunticook trail, a one-hour, moderate hike of about 1 mile.

The sites at Camden Hills are cut from fairly dense, mixed deciduous and coniferous forest. In spots where the pine needles outnumber the leaves, visitors are treated to an amazing olfactory gift. When the conditions are just right, you can smell the musty balsam perfume of the forest and the briny tang of the ocean in the same breath. And there's more Camden Hills State Park right across the street (that street being US 1, so be careful if you're walking across).

The town of Camden's slogan is "Where the Mountains Meet the Sea." Nowhere is that theme more concretely embodied than at the state park. To the west of US 1 are the campground and Mount Battie. East of US 1, you'll find a small network of hiking trails and a picnic area settled within the woods right on the shores of Penobscot Bay. Few things are more soothing than watching the waves crashing endlessly over the rocks.

When (or should I say "if") you tire of hanging around the campground or the ocean side of the park, there are numerous hiking trails right at your feet. Take your pick. There are trails for all abilities and interests, and virtually all lead to sweeping views of Penobscot Bay or nearby Lake Megunticook. Start off with a quick jaunt up Mount Battie. From the campground, the only way up is the paved auto road, but if you're heading into town anyway, you can go up the auto road, then down the Mount Battie Trail, which drops you off at a small trailhead and parking area. This trail is only a half mile long, but a steep section requires some hand-over-hand scrambling. It might be best to take another route if it has rained recently.

The Ski Shelter Trail is a hike everyone in your group can enjoy. An old fire road that leaves from the campground, it passes by a massive stone hearth—all that remains of an old ski shelter. This is a great spot to stop for a snack, a gulp of water, and perhaps a photo or two. You can follow the Ski Shelter Trail all the way to the Youngtown Road, a distance of about 3 miles. You could also head off on one of several bisecting trails.

MAP

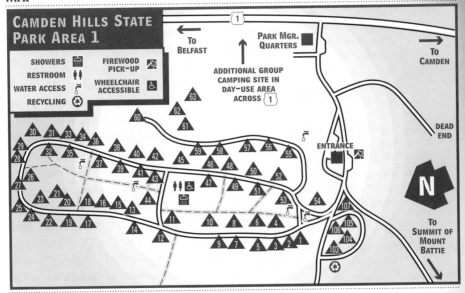

CAMDEN HILLS STATE PARK AREA 1

SHOWERS
RESTROOM
WATER ACCESS
RECYCLING

FIREWOOD PICK-UP
WHEELCHAIR ACCESSIBLE

1

To BELFAST

PARK MGR. QUARTERS

ADDITIONAL GROUP CAMPING SITE IN DAY-USE AREA ACROSS 1

To CAMDEN

DEAD END

ENTRANCE

N

To SUMMIT OF MOUNT BATTIE

For one such foray, try the Bald Rock Trail. After you've passed the stone hearth, keep walking for another 30 minutes or so until you see the trail heading off to the right. The Ski Shelter Trail will be going downhill at this point. The Bald Rock trail is short and a little steep, but it leads to a large, flat, rock outcropping with a commanding view of Penobscot Bay and the islands.

There's enough to do in and around Camden to fill an entire guidebook. Ask the cordial park rangers for a recommendation, or just take off on your own and explore. Just set aside plenty of time, because when it's time to leave, you'll swear you haven't been there long enough.

GETTING THERE

Follow US 1 north through Camden. Proceed another couple of miles to the state park on the left. There is a park entrance on the right (the ocean side), but the campground is on the left.

MAP

CAMDEN HILLS STATE PARK AREA 2

To Mount Megunticook

Host Site

SHOWERS	
RESTROOM	
WATER ACCESS	
RECYCLING	
WHEELCHAIR ACCESSIBLE	
DUMP SITE	

COBSCOOK BAY STATE PARK

COBSCOOK BAY STATE PARK comes the closest of any park in this book to providing the remote, oceanside, wilderness feeling of island camping without actually traveling to an island. There are numerous waterfront sites here, and all are spectacular and dramatically beautiful. Since there are so many of them, you have an excellent chance of scoring one of these pristine sites.

When you do get a waterfront site, you'll bear witness to the extreme tidal swing in this area. In fact, the name Cobscook is from the Maliseet and Pasamaquoddy Indian dialect for "boiling tides." The change in tidal depth runs from 24 to 28 feet! Be extremely careful if you venture out onto the mud flats at low tide to dig up some clams (which is perfectly legal, by the way, up to a peck a day). When the tide turns, it comes racing in.

There are several tent-only areas within Cobscook Bay State Park. As you may well imagine, these are the spots you want. Cobscook Point, Broad Cove, and the Harbor Point areas are reserved for our tent-bound brethren. The other areas here are fine, but the tent-only areas are superb.

Cobscook Point includes sites 40 through 74, all carved out of the dense forest of balsam and birch overlooking the waters of Cobscook Bay. These are extremely remote, quiet, and scenic campsites, especially the waterfront sites like 40, 41, 44, and 49. Site 43 is set up on a small hill with a dramatic view of the bay through the trees, and beautiful onshore breezes blow through the site.

There's a short hike into site 48, giving it an amazing sense of seclusion, but not much of a view of the bay. That's not a bad tradeoff—depends on what you're in the mood for. Sites 50 and 52 are also set deep within a dense forest of mostly spruce trees, for a cool, sylvan feeling.

> *A unique treasure, with its picturesque shoreline, waterfront sites, numerous inlets, and dramatic tidal surge.*

RATINGS

Beauty: ✩ ✩ ✩ ✩ ✩
Privacy: ✩ ✩ ✩ ✩ ✩
Spaciousness: ✩ ✩ ✩ ✩
Quiet: ✩ ✩ ✩ ✩ ✩
Security: ✩ ✩ ✩ ✩
Cleanliness: ✩ ✩ ✩ ✩ ✩

ADDRESS:	Cobscook Bay State Park RR 1, Box 127 Dennysville, ME 04628
OPERATED BY:	Maine Department of Conservation, Bureau of Parks and Lands
INFORMATION:	Cobscook Bay State Park, (207) 726-4412
OPEN:	May 15–October 15
SITES:	106 sites
EACH SITE HAS:	Fire ring, picnic table
ASSIGNMENT:	First come, first served or by reservation: (800) 332-1501, (207) 287-3824, www.campwithme.com (additional $2 reservation fee per site, per night)
REGISTRATION:	At ranger station as you enter park
FACILITIES:	Flush toilets, water spigots, pay showers, picnic area, public boat launch
PARKING:	At sites
FEE:	Maine residents, $14; nonresidents, $19
RESTRICTIONS:	**Pets:** On leash only **Fires:** In established fireplaces only **Alcohol:** Prohibited **Vehicles:** Parking at sites only **Other:** Quiet hours 10 p.m.–7 a.m.; 14-day maximum stay; check-in after 1 p.m., check-out by 11 a.m.; limit of 1 peck of clams per day

At the end of Cobscook Point is a short peninsula with sites 56 through 62 (which actually only includes sites 56, 57, 59, and 62, since a couple of sites must have been taken out of use to allow for regrowth). These are incredibly secluded. This area is reminiscent of the revered (at least by me) peninsula A at the Mount Desert Campground. There's about a 50-yard hike into site 56, the first site you'll come to. It is a very large site surrounded by dense woods, so this would be perfect for a larger group or family. The rest of the sites on the end of Cobscook Point—57, 59, and 62—are all set down at the water's edge. They are moderately spacious and extraordinarily secluded from each other. All these sites share a common parking area as you head out onto the peninsula.

Back on the campground loop road, sites 63, 64, and 65 are all set along the water's edge, and are far enough from each other for a decent sense of seclusion. Sites 66 and 67 are spectacularly secluded hike-in sites set on the water's edge about 50 feet from the road. Site 72 is set up on a hill off the inside of the road, so there's a nice sense of seclusion, but you miss the commanding view of the bay afforded by some of the other sites.

Farther along the main campground road heading toward Harbor Point and Whiting Bay, you'll find sites 33, 34, and 35, which are open to the road but next to a small pond that is quite scenic. These sites are also close to the day-use access for the clam flats. You won't find fresher seafood than clams that were deep in the briny mud just a couple of hours ago.

The cozy Harbor Point area is home to sites 29 through 32. Site 29 is at the end of a long, grassy driveway. It is a fairly open site with sweeping views of the bay. Site 30 is on a bluff overlooking the bay. Sites 31 and 32 are nicely private and set along the shore of the bay. All the Harbor Point sites are quite secluded from each other, so there really isn't a bad one here. Site 30 is the best, as it is extraordinarily isolated and affords a priceless view of Cobscook Bay.

The Broad Cove area is another of Cobscook Bay State Park's tent-only areas with a plethora of beautiful hike-in and waterside sites. Sites 75, 77, 78, and 79 are hike-in sites that are spectacularly secluded and give

MAP

you that feeling of being deep in the woods. Sites 83 and 84 are also nicely isolated hike-in sites that share a parking area. If you can't score a waterfront site, do what you can to land in one of these.

Sites 85 and 86 share a parking area as well, but these hike-in sites are set down on the water, so they are incredibly private and scenic. Site 89 has a short walk down toward the water, but the site itself is not as close to the water as sites 85, 86, and 88. Sites 90, 92, 95, and 96 are also spectacular waterside sites with short walks into them.

Then we come to site 101. This is one of those to-die-for campsites. It is a hike-in site, but the hike in is about 200 feet. This makes it a bit more challenging to haul in your gear, but the sense of solitude is worth it. You'll hike up and down the rolling terrain and over a short bridge to reach this profoundly secluded site. It's set within some fairly dense forest, but it's on a bluff overlooking the bay, so you'll get slivers of bay view and fantastic sea breezes.

Heading toward the day-use area, most of the sites include covered picnic tables, which would be nice on

Follow US 1 north for what seems like an eternity. Cobscook Bay State Park is on the right in the town of Dennysville.

a rainy day. Sites 102 and 103 are set off on their own, and also have covered picnic tables. Site 111 is another nice hike-in site in this area. Sites 114 and 115 are set off on their own. They are fairly close together but very secluded from the other sites. Site 116 stands alone, offering a deep sense of privacy. Site 119 sits at an intersection of the campground road and is open to the road, but there are no other sites around; it also overlooks a wildflower meadow that separates the camping area from the day-use area, so it's quite scenic. Sites 124 and 125 are very secluded with water views.

The Whiting Bay area, home to sites 1 through 27, is designated as the RV zone, but there are still some nice sites with good tent-camping potential. These sites are fairly large and private, so don't panic if you pick one and hear an RV lumbering toward you.

After you pass site 27, you'll come to the loops for sites 1 through 8 and 9 through 26. Site 2 is a medium-sized site on an open, grassy spot with an amazing view of the bay through loosely spaced spruce trees. Site 3 is very large and perched on a bluff overlooking the bay for gorgeous views and sea breezes.

Most of the sites on the outer edge of the loop have D-shaped driveways to facilitate egress for the land yachts. That also makes them very spacious for tent campers. Site 4 has awesome views, but it's quite open to the road. Site 5 is a pleasant, open spot set down from the road. It's very open to the bay for dramatic views and breezes, but it's also close to the rest rooms. Sites 6 through 8 are set in their own little loop. They are slightly open but have fantastic bay views.

There are some other sites here worth exploring. Site 17 is small and open to the road, but it's right next to a trail that leads down to the shore. Site 18 is very spacious and offers a decent sense of privacy, as it's secluded from the road and from neighboring sites. Site 22 is large and has that D-shaped driveway, so it's secluded from the road by the "island" of trees and shrubs that form the center of the D.

There's only one thing that bothered me about the Cobscook Bay State Park experience: I can't for the life of me figure out how many clams constitute a peck.

LAMOINE STATE PARK

WHAT **DO YOU DO WHEN** Acadia National Park is packed? Head a bit farther north to Lamoine State Park, which is just far enough away to escape the swarms of Acadia-area campers and travelers during the summer. There's a very open sense to most of the sites at Lamoine State Park, overlooking the waters of Frenchman Bay toward Bar Harbor.

The view of the ocean and its cool breezes, even on the muggiest summer afternoons, give Lamoine State Park an easy combination of pastoral serenity and seaside appeal. The whole gestalt here is that of being on a wind-swept, coastal bluff—which you are! It's a bit different than the wooded campgrounds to which I usually gravitate, but wild and beautiful nevertheless.

The campground loop road encircles the campground and is intersected by several short roads that run parallel to the seashore. The sites on the outer edge of the loop as you enter the campground, including sites 21 through 29, are spacious, open sites set on a grassy surface and separated by short stands of trees and shrubs. There's a sunny, breezy, open sense to these sites, but not much privacy. On the other side of the campground road, even-numbered sites 20 and up are a bit more secluded, but still have an open feel. The only trouble here would be if an RV settled in nearby—you would have it right in view. Otherwise, the sites themselves are exposed but comfortable.

A big beech tree grows right up through the center of site 19. This proud old guardian gives the site a comfortable feeling and a canopy of shade. This is a beautiful, medium-sized site encircled by a dense wall of undergrowth. Sites 16 through 18 are open, but they are also secluded from each other by short stands of deciduous trees and solid undergrowth. The backs of these sites open to a huge field and the group camping area—a great spot for stargazing on a clear night.

> *During the thick of summer when Acadia is mobbed, head north to Lamoine State Park to reclaim the solitude for which Maine is renowned.*

RATINGS

Beauty: ✿ ✿ ✿ ✿
Privacy: ✿ ✿ ✿
Spaciousness: ✿ ✿ ✿
Quiet: ✿ ✿ ✿ ✿
Security: ✿ ✿ ✿ ✿
Cleanliness: ✿ ✿ ✿ ✿

KEY INFORMATION

ADDRESS:	Lamoine State Park 23 State Park Road Ellsworth, ME 04605
OPERATED BY:	Maine Department of Conservation, Bureau of Parks and Lands
INFORMATION:	Lamoine State Park, (207) 667-4778
OPEN:	Mid-May– mid-September
SITES:	61
EACH SITE HAS:	Fire ring, picnic table
ASSIGNMENT:	First come, first served or by reservation: (800) 332-1501, (207) 287-3824, www.campwithme. com (additional $2 reservation fee per site, per night)
REGISTRATION:	At ranger station as you enter campground, check-in after 1 p.m., check-out by 11 a.m.
FACILITIES:	Hot showers, flush toilets, water spigots
PARKING:	At sites
FEE:	Maine residents, $15; nonresidents, $20
RESTRICTIONS:	**Pets:** On leash only **Fires:** Fire rings only **Alcohol:** Prohibited **Vehicles:** Parking at sites only **Other:** Quiet hours 10 p.m.–7 a.m.; 14-day maximum stay

Moving down this side of the campground, there's more of a sense of solitude to sites 13, 14, and 30. These sites are set along the outer edge of the campground loop road. Site 14 is a bit close to the restroom building but is encircled by dense, deciduous forest.

Set within a loose grove of spruce and backed into the mixed forest, site 12 is an open site with a delightful wooded-grove feel. It's situated right at a campground road intersection, but it has a comfortable, charming character. Site 30 is small, but also tucked off the road and nicely isolated by virtue of its location.

Heading back toward the campground entrance on one of the intersecting roads brings you to the lower-numbered sites, including sites 11 and 10, which have an exposed feel but are secluded on the sides. Site 10 abuts a small field and is near the restrooms, so it feels a bit too open for me. Sites 7 through 9 are moderately spacious and isolated from each other. However, site 6 is wide open and right at the corner intersection of the campground road. It's right across from site 5, which also lacks privacy.

The dense, low forest isolates sites 3 and 4 on the sides, but they are open to each other across the road. Site 1 is in an open field and not secluded enough for me, but if you want to catch the strongest breezes, this is the spot. Site 2 is right across the road from Site 1 and is somewhat isolated by a patch of dense woods and undergrowth, but it is open in front to the road.

There are a number of wide-open field sites in the center of the campground at Lamoine State Park, including sites 35 through 39 and site 60. These sites don't provide much of a sense of privacy. Although site 36 is somewhat isolated on the sides, the others aren't. They're also fairly close to (and within view of) the shower building.

It may be small, but site 33 is nicely secluded, despite being situated on the corner of the campground road. The site is carved out of a mixed deciduous forest of maples, birch, and dense undergrowth. Site 32 is a great site. It's very secluded and set off from the other sites, as well as being surrounded by dense, low forest. There's a scraggly spruce hanging over the site, providing shade and companionship.

MAP

LAMOINE STATE PARK CAMPGROUND

ENTRANCE TO GROUP CAMPING

TO PARK MANAGER'S QUARTERS

N

HOST SITE

LOOP TRAIL

LOOP TRAIL TO DAY AREA

PATH TO PLAYGROUND

SHOWERHOUSE
RESTROOM
WATER ACCESS
PARKING
WHEELCHAIR ACCESSIBLE
PUBLIC PHONE
RECYCLING BIN
PICNIC AREA
BOAT LAUNCH
PLAYGROUND
CHECK-IN STATION

Even though it's on a corner of the campground road, site 31 is spacious and nicely set off. It's surrounded by dense woods and separated from the road by a narrow stand of trees. Site 40 is tiny, but cozy and very secluded. This site is carved out of very dense forest of short deciduous trees and dense undergrowth.

Site 41 is wide open to the road but secluded from its neighbors. You're getting closer to the water here, so there are tantalizing views of the bay through the trees. Site 42 is way too exposed and right behind the restroom building. Site 43 opens to site 42 and the restrooms, but it's secluded on the sides and offers views of the bay to balance the view of the restroom. Sites 46 and 45 are rather open, while sites 47, 59, 38, and 60 are another set of wide-open field sites.

You're getting closer to the water at sites 55 through 58. These are open to the road and each other, but they're very sunny and breezy. You'll feel what is practically a constant breeze easing in (and sometimes rushing in) off Frenchman Bay.

The sites that open to the water are where you really want to be at Lamoine State Park. Sites 48 through 54 are set along the campground road facing

GETTING THERE

Follow US 1 north through Ellsworth. At the junction of US 1 and ME 184, follow ME 184 south to the park.

the open view of the ocean. These are views of Frenchman Bay and its islands worthy of the Rockefellers.
The view from sites 51 through 54 is through loose
crabapple and maple trees growing in the picnic area.
From 50, 49, and 48, you view the bay through a
majestic stand of spruce.

All these sites are spacious and open to the road,
but they're also open to the view, and they're fairly well
secluded from each other. Sites 49 and 50 probably feel
the most isolated and farthest from their neighbors.
Each is surrounded on three sides by dense undergrowth and shrubs. They open to the bay view through
a grove of loosely spaced spruce and pines, trees of
hardy stock that stand up to the steady salty breezes.
There's a short path down to the water right across
from site 49. You can also get to the 1–mile Loop Trail.

Site 48 is oddly placed. It's on the outside corner
of where the bayside campground road turns and
heads back up into the woods. It's very open to the
road, but it shares the dramatic bay views filtered
through the grove of spruce.

The scent here is that potent Maine blend of the
evergreen forest and the salty tang of the ocean, topped
with a bit of wood smoke as the day draws to an end.
Take a moment after you've set up your campsite to sit
back, draw in a deep breath, and enjoy the sights,
sounds, and scents of this oceanside campground.

LILY BAY STATE PARK

IN NORTHERN MAINE, nestled on the eastern shores of Moosehead Lake, is Lily Bay State Park. There are two separate camping areas at Lily Bay and a large number of sites. On the first business day in January, when the reservation office opens for the season, the world-class lakeside sites start filling up—so make plans early if you want to secure one.

There are several secluded sites in the Dunn Point Area. Drive up a short road off to the right, and you'll find site 245 tucked off on its own. Just past the entrance to the site at the end of its "driveway," there's a trailhead for the 1.6–mile hiking trail that leads to Rowell Cove.

The sense of solitude at sites 200 and 201 is priceless. These are moderately spacious and very isolated walk-in tent sites. Each requires a short (20 to 30 feet) hike to the site. They are set on a bluff overlooking the lake, and the views are positively epic.

Farther along this same bluff, site 202 is less exposed to the views and the breeze, but still offers sliver views of the lake vista and the hills beyond, through the woods. Site 203 is the last site in this cluster on the bluff. It's very spacious, and the breezes and views filter through a wall of conifers.

There's a trail leading to the lake's beach right before you get to sites 205 and 206. Site 205 is massive. Across the campground road, site 206 is much smaller but very well secluded in dense forest. Sites 207 through 209 are moderately roomy and private.

At site 210, the forest opens up again to the lake. This site is isolated on one side by a two-level wall of young and old white pines, along with some other coniferous trees. The forest opens dramatically at the opposite side of the site, allowing for sweeping views of the lake through the loosely spaced trees that pepper the site down to the water's edge.

> *Lily Bay State Park is just one facet of the north Maine woods jewel that is Moosehead Lake.*

RATINGS

Beauty: ✿ ✿ ✿ ✿ ✿
Privacy: ✿ ✿ ✿ ✿ ✿
Spaciousness: ✿ ✿ ✿ ✿
Quiet: ✿ ✿ ✿ ✿ ✿
Security: ✿ ✿ ✿ ✿ ✿
Cleanliness: ✿ ✿ ✿ ✿ ✿

KEY INFORMATION

Set within a loose grove of conifers, sites 211 and 213 are relatively spacious and overlook the lake. Sites 213 through 215 require a short walk and are all on the lake. These sites are jewels, with a perfect mix of forest and lakeshore. It's well worth the short haul. Not that you'll be able to take your eyes off the lake for long, but these sites are also fairly isolated from each other. It's very quiet throughout the campground. All you'll hear is the soft splash of the lake and the cool rush of wind through the trees.

You might want to avoid sites 216 and 220, as they are a bit close to the restroom. Site 219 is spacious and secluded by a wall of conifers at the back, but otherwise open to the road. Site 218 is large and mildly secluded, with a view of the lake.

The next group of walk-in tent sites includes sites 221 through 224. These are completely secluded from the rest of the campground and moderately secluded from each other. They share the same clear view of the lake as the 213 through 215 group.

So, by now, you must think you have to be right on the waters of Moosehead Lake to have one of Lily Bay's primo sites, eh? Well, wait until you see site 231. It is incredibly spacious, set up on a small knoll in the middle of the forest. It's absolutely secluded from neighbors on all sides and from the campground road. Its added elevation will help you catch some of the onshore breezes. Just outside the site, there's a trail leading down to the beach.

The forest encircling the site is characteristic of the area's fantastically diverse population of mature spruce, birch, and maple. There's also a small nursery of baby white pine trees to the left of the site as you walk in. Encircled by forest, this spot feels like it's deeper in the Maine wilderness than you might expect.

A shared entryway brings you to sites 235 and 236. This would make a good pair of sites for a larger group or family needing two sites—if you can't score two magical lakeside sites. Another option for families is site 240, which has a U-shaped driveway you could pull right through. Those two openings do leave it fairly exposed to the road, though.

MAP

LILY BAY STATE PARK: DUNN POINT CAMPGROUND

MOOSEHEAD LAKE

N

HOST SITE

To BEACH

LILY BAY RD.

RESTROOM

WATER ACCESS

PARKING

BOAT RAMP

PICNIC AREA

The Rowell Cove Area also has some dramatic lakeside walk-in tent sites. Sites 33 through 38 are hike-in tent sites perched along a craggy peninsula that recalls the revered peninsula A at the eponymous campground on Mount Desert Island. Site 33 is the largest of the group.

There are ample views of the lake through loose trees from sites 20 and 21. They are also nicely secluded by dense spruce just open enough to view the lake. Site 23 is sizeable, but a bit open. Sites 25 and 28 each have a nice sense of solitude, plus a slice of the lake view through the forest.

Several massive conifers frame one side of site 26. The inside loop sites in this part of the campground are fairly well secluded from each other, while, sites 29 and 30 are both open to the campground loop road. They're also located near the parking for sites 39 through 41.

The cluster of sites that includes 39 through 46 is another majestic spot. These sites are all spacious, set right on the lake within a small cove and beneath a loosely spaced grove of spruce trees. The floor is a soft bed of pine needles over a firm, sandy surface. The sites are open to the lake, with exceptional breezes and views. Walks to the sites range from 50 to 70 feet.

GETTING THERE

Follow ME 6 north to Greenville. From Greenville, take the Lily Bay Road off to the right and follow it to the park.

LILY BAY STATE PARK: ROWELL COVE CAMPGROUND

RESTROOM
WATER ACCESS
PARKING
BOAT RAMP

N

HOST SITE

MOOSEHEAD LAKE

ROWELL COVE

Site 31 opens right to the parking area, and feels too open. Site 32 is huge and very secluded. It's surrounded by a thick wall of forest, and further isolated because it's a bit farther down the campground road.

The lower-numbered sites here aren't quite as impressive, but they aren't bad. Even though it's set right where the campground loop road rejoins itself, site 8 is spacious and isolated. Site 7 is similar, with glimpses of the lake. Site 5 feels very exposed, being open to the road, but it has a view of the lake.

It may be tiny and exposed to the road, but site 12 is set way off from any neighboring sites. Site 13 has a similar character. It's carved out of fairly dense forest. Site 14 is spacious, secluded, punctuated by three massive spruce trees, and encircled by dense, mixed forest.

There are glimpses and slivers of lake view through the forest here near the sites in the upper teens. Site 15 is open to the road and close to the restrooms. Site 16 is colossal and tucked well off the campground loop road for a deep sense of solitude. Site 17 is large and set off from its neighbors, but it's a bit open to the road. It's also very open to the sky, and the lake is visible from the site.

MOUNT BLUE
STATE PARK

MOUNT **B**LUE **S**TATE **P**ARK is actually a pair of parks. There are two sections to the park, one up on Mount Blue itself and the other down alongside Webb Lake. The trails on and around Mount Blue, Tumbledown, Little Jackson, Blueberry, and Bald mountains are suitable for hikers of all abilities. There's also a multi-use trail in the Center Hill section of the park for mountain bikers, hikers, equestrians, and ATVs.

The park's campground is located in the Webb Lake section. All of the 136 sites in the campground are within a fairly short walk of the lake. The sites are set within a dense, diverse forest with thick undergrowth. The woods are a mix of young and old deciduous and coniferous trees, with lots of spruce, birch, and maple.

While the forest varies dramatically, the sites here have a relatively standard shape and layout, though they differ in size. Surprisingly, it's not the quietest place in the world. As I set up camp at Mount Blue, the density of the forest lent me a pleasant sense of seclusion, but I found that sound traveled through the forest quite freely. After dinner, when night settles in, the campground quiets right down, but during the daytime, you'll hear noise from surrounding campsites.

As you enter the camping area, sites 1 through 10 are spread out along the main campground road. The remaining sites are grouped in two loops. The first ten sites are quite spacious, but very open to the road. A fair amount of traffic drives by, as everyone going in and out of the campground has to pass these sites. Within this cluster of sites, site 1 is actually the most secluded, thanks to the forest at the site's edge. It's still quite close to the road, however. Sites 4 and 5 have a pretty solid barrier of trees buffering them from the road, but sites 7 and 8 are exposed.

> *There's a dense, diverse forest covering the campground at Mount Blue State Park, whose lush quality recalls a rainforest.*

RATINGS

Beauty: ✪ ✪ ✪ ✪
Privacy: ✪ ✪ ✪ ✪ ✪
Spaciousness: ✪ ✪ ✪ ✪
Quiet: ✪ ✪ ✪
Security: ✪ ✪ ✪ ✪
Cleanliness: ✪ ✪ ✪ ✪ ✪

The forest enshrouding the loop with sites 11 through 78 is populated primarily by moderately tall spruce and deciduous trees. The trees aren't huge, but they are numerous and crowded with undergrowth. There is almost an almost primeval feel to the forest that translates into a wonderful sense of seclusion at most of these sites. The sites are very clean and well kept. Some have a bit more forest buffering them from their neighbors, especially sites 18, 7, and 5. Site 19 and the sites in the lower 20s are more tightly packed than the rest of this loop, but encircled by thick woods.

There's a trail leading down to the lake between sites 26 and 28. Set a good distance from site 30 at a bend in the road, site 31 is tucked into a dense stand of trees, so it offers an additional measure of privacy.

Site 34 is small, but it feels isolated within a bucolic grove where spruce tower above a dense blanket of ferns. Surrounded by dense deciduous forest with plenty of room between it and the nearest site, site 35 maintains a marvelously secluded feel.

Sites 38, 40, and 41 are set within a mature forest of tall maples and birch. The loose arrangement of trees in this part of the campground lets more sunlight filter down. Site 44 is colossal. You could land a space shuttle here, if that's how you happened to arrive at the campground.

Though they vary in size, sites 47 through 78 share a similar layout. They are also uniformly spaced. Site 54, in a loose grove of tall spruce, is large and open to the sky. A trail heads off to the beach between sites 57 and 58.

Set along the outside of the loop, sites 58 through 62 are spacious and open. Sites 69 and 71 are particularly secluded, distant from their neighbors, and carved out of a dense, deciduous forest with thick undergrowth. Size 69 is only moderately sized, but 71 is huge.

Within the loop containing sites 79 through 136, the forest is crowded with trees and underbrush. The sites are uniformly distributed along the inside and outside of the loop. The space between most sites is roughly equal to an average site, affording quite a sense of privacy. Sites 128 and up seem to have slightly more forest in between them. There are no hookups in the

MAP

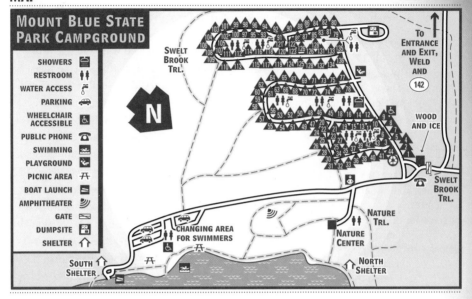

park, but even if an RV should happen to dock near you, the thick forest in this loop will obscure your view.

A trail to the lake leaves this section between sites 109 and 110. There are trails to the centrally located restrooms spread throughout both site loops. You'll never have to walk very far to find one.

Due to the dense forest at Mount Blue Campground, not many sites are open to the sky. There are a few exceptions to this, sites 44, 54, 93, and 106 among them. If you like to gaze at the night sky, check out one of these sites. Otherwise, once dusk settles, you'll feel enshrouded by the deep woods.

GETTING THERE

From the town of Weld, follow ME 142 to Weld Corner. Follow the signs for the Webb Lake section of Mount Blue State Park.

MOUNT DESERT
CAMPGROUND

> *Perched on the rugged shores at the apex of Somes Sound, Mount Desert Campground is nestled in an absolutely pristine setting.*

NESTLED NEAR THE APEX of Somes Sound on Mount Desert Island, Mount Desert Campground provides a tent-camping experience as close to perfect as any campground in this book. The entire campground is artfully carved out of the rolling woods that reach all the way down to the shoreline. The campground is also conveniently situated near the main entrance to Acadia National Park and right near the Eagle Lake and Witch Hole Pond loops.

The Mount Desert Campground doesn't have any areas set aside specifically for tent camping, but there really isn't a bad site in the place. The A-, B-, and C-area sites are the best, especially the contiguous sites on the A peninsula, A13 through A15 (which actually accounts for four sites, since site A14+ was added). To get to these sites, you have to walk about 50 feet along the peninsula. If those sites are taken, as is often the case, another piece of prime camping real estate is site A5, located on a small bluff overlooking the water.

You're in Maine. You're on an island. Do what you can to get a water site. It's well worth the effort and expense. If you set up somewhere for a night or two, and then a water site opens up, it will be worth the effort to move. Just make sure the site is truly vacant, not reserved, and let the owners know you'd like to relocate.

The waterside sites at Mount Desert follow the undulating terrain as it dives into the headwaters of Somes Sound. The terrain is beautiful, dramatic, and anything but flat. If you saw it from a distance, you'd wonder how you could ever pitch a tent here.

When you check in at the main entrance, they'll ask you if you need some nails. Excuse me, you'll think, did I somehow volunteer for campground maintenance? Say yes; you'll need them. Every site at the water's edge or on any uneven terrain has a solid wooden deck on which you can set up your tent, using

RATINGS

Beauty: ✿ ✿ ✿ ✿ ✿
Privacy: ✿ ✿ ✿ ✿
Spaciousness: ✿ ✿ ✿ ✿
Quiet: ✿ ✿ ✿ ✿
Security: ✿ ✿ ✿ ✿ ✿
Cleanliness: ✿ ✿ ✿ ✿ ✿

nails in lieu of stakes. If the campground owners
hadn't built these tent platforms, they would be lucky
to have one or two sites flat enough to pitch a tent.

Each area has its own facilities building with
sparkling clean, well-kept restrooms and coin-operated
showers. Here's another hint: Even in the summer, the
mornings will be cool. Bring more quarters than you
think you'll need. Having the water go stone cold over
a head full of shampoo may cause itchiness, headaches,
and loud cursing.

There's a charming little camp store on the road
leading into the campground that sells bundles of firewood, camping-appropriate groceries like cans of soup
and Jiffy Pop popcorn, all sorts of items you may have
forgotten like batteries and toothpaste, and guidebooks
to the hiking trails and carriage roads that take you to
some of the island's magical spots. It's also handy to
pick up a quick cup of coffee and a muffin before you
get your own breakfast fire going. You can get some
fresh-baked goodies for dessert later that night, or
make a special trip down with the kids (of any age) for
an afternoon ice cream.

Just outside the campground, there is so much to
do on Mount Desert Island and in Acadia National
Park, you could write an entire book about it. In fact,
people have! You can hike, bike, paddle, or just find a
spot to relax and enjoy the view, which alone can
restore your soul. This is classic Maine wilderness, with
gentle, rolling, forested mountains sloping right down
to the craggy coast. The Atlantic obliges and completes
the view with an endless supply of crashing surf.

Rent a canoe or kayak and launch out into Somes
Sound, the only fjord on the East Coast. Between the
rolling mountains, the rocky shoreline, and the water
that glistens like a carpet of diamonds, the paddling is
perfect. Just off the dock and boat launch at the campground, you'll paddle past a small island as you enter
the sound. This is actually a part of Acadia National
Park, and atop the tallest pine, in the center of the
island, is a bald eagle's nest.

On one brilliant August afternoon while paddling
out into Somes Sound, I was visited by several pods of
brown Atlantic dolphins swimming up the sound. I

KEY INFORMATION

ADDRESS:	Mount Desert Campground 516 Sound Drive Mount Desert, ME 04660
OPERATED BY:	Owen and Barbara Craighead
INFORMATION:	(207) 244-3710; www.mountdesert campground.com
OPEN:	May 15– September 25
SITES:	148
EACH SITE HAS:	Fire pit with grate; most have wooden tent platforms
ASSIGNMENT:	Reservations accepted for stays of 1 week or longer, otherwise first come, first served
REGISTRATION:	At camp headquar- ters at main entrance
FACILITIES:	Restrooms, hot show- ers, pay phone, camp store, fire- places, picnic tables
PARKING:	At or near individual sites
FEE:	$28–$39, depending on site
RESTRICTIONS:	**Pets:** Allowed on leash only, before July 1 and after Labor Day **Fires:** Fire pits only **Alcohol:** Sites only **Vehicles:** 1 per site **Other:** Check-in after 1 p.m., check- out by 11 a.m.; maxi- mum 2 adults per site

THE **BEST**
IN TENT
CAMPING
NEW ENGLAND

MAP

GETTING THERE

From Ellsworth, follow ME 3 onto Mount Desert Island. Follow ME 3 to ME 102/198 south. Stay on ME 198 when it turns left. The campground will be on the right, about a mile after ME 198 splits from ME 102.

first heard the quick puff of their breath as they surfaced. It didn't take long to determine the source of the noise once I saw the slender, dark shapes rising and disappearing into the water in front of me. One of the dolphins actually dove under my kayak and surfaced behind me. I almost tipped over trying to snap a picture of that bold little guy.

Both inside and outside the Mount Desert Campground, you can do as much or as little as you like, but you couldn't ask for a more peaceful setting in which to pitch your tent. One cool foggy evening, while kicking back by the campfire, I heard someone playing the flute. The song was Paul Simon's "Lincoln Duncan." If you know that tune, you know it has a hauntingly beautiful flute melody. Hearing that echoing throughout the trees, smelling the wood fire, and watching its glowing embers through increasingly sleepy eyes is a memory I will always cherish.

ORR'S ISLAND CAMPGROUND

7-07, TRAILER SITES ONLY NOW.

ORR'S ISLAND IS FAR OUT INTO CASCO BAY, so the campground is cool and breezy. From Brunswick, you drive out over Great Island before you get to Orr's Island. Just the drive out there will melt away your stress.

The letter-designated sites A through G, perched along the waterfront side of Cove Road, and sites 31 through 41, situated on the inland side of Cove Road, are the prime sites for tent camping. This row of sites overlooks Reed Cove. The lettered sites in particular are only moderately spacious, but they are extremely secluded from the other sites, as they are carved out of dense undergrowth. Most of the coveside sites also have short paths leading down to the rocky beach on Reed Cove. These sites overlook the water and are perfectly situated to catch the cool breezes blowing in off the ocean. The numbered sites are also fairly well isolated from the rest of the campground and from each other.

Site A is moderately spacious, and the site itself is open, though remarkably secluded by dense undergrowth on all sides. The side of the site facing the cove is clear, so you'll have a view of Reed Cove. Site B looks out toward the bay but is more shaded, encircled by lots of dense undergrowth and several birch trees.

There's also a secluded feel to site C, although it's smaller and narrower. Site D is fairly roomy and has a wide-open view of the water. It's set against a dense wall of deciduous trees and dense undergrowth, so it offers a solid sense of privacy.

Though it is well isolated, there's a spacious and sunny feel at site E, which boasts an open view of the water. However, it's also nicely shaded on one side by a wall of high trees. The moderately spacious site F is shaded and secluded with a clear view of the water.

Site G is the real prize of this campground. This site is incredibly well isolated and surrounded by

> *There may be a flotilla of RVs nearby, but the secluded tent sites and the views of Harpswell Bay make this campground well worth a look.*

RATINGS

Beauty: ✿ ✿ ✿ ✿ ✿
Privacy: ✿ ✿ ✿ ✿
Spaciousness: ✿ ✿ ✿ ✿
Quiet: ✿ ✿ ✿ ✿
Security: ✿ ✿ ✿ ✿ ✿
Cleanliness: ✿ ✿ ✿ ✿ ✿

ADDRESS: Orr's Island
Campground
44 Bond Point Road
Orr's Island, ME
04066

OPERATED BY: The Bond Family

INFORMATION: Orr's Island Campground, (207) 833-5595, orrsisland.com

OPEN: Memorial Day–September 15

SITES: 70

EACH SITE HAS: Fire ring, picnic table

ASSIGNMENT: First come, first served or by reservation

REGISTRATION: At office; call campground office for reservations

FACILITIES: Hot showers, dumping station, flush toilets, coin-operated laundry, boat launch

PARKING: At sites or near camp store

FEE: $24–$27 for tent sites ($28–$35 for hookup sites); $2 per person day-use fee

RESTRICTIONS: Pets: Dogs on leash only
Fires: Fire pits only
Alcohol: Sites only
Vehicles: 1 per site
Other: 2-day minimum stay for reservations (3 days for holiday weekends)

dense undergrowth. The trees and hedges that fill in the forest are of the short, hardy stock that grows along the craggy coast of Maine. The only opening in the band of undergrowth encircling site G faces the bay view. This site is open to the sky above as well, so it receives sunlight and moonlight. This is the most spacious of the letter sites on this side of Cove Road. All of the Cove Road letter sites are perfectly situated for tents and kayaks.

The number-designated sites are set along the other side of Cove Road, the side opposite the water. Cove Road is very quiet, so the general sense of openness at the numbered sites does not translate into a lack of privacy. A solid wall of trees blocks the view from Cove Road of the RV row behind the sites. There is also a grassy surface at these sites, a good, soft base upon which to pitch your tent.

Site 37 is very open. You'll get lots of breezes blowing through, and it's a good site for sunbathing, but you might crave a little shade on those hot summer afternoons. It may be a bit small, but site 39 is nicely private. The site is carved out of the dense deciduous forest and undergrowth. A craggy, sweeping beech tree guards the entrance gives the site a deep wilderness character. Site 41 and the unnumbered site just past it on the left are small sites, but very well secluded as they are set among the dense undergrowth.

The sites off Cove Road are most conducive to tent camping, but other sites are suitable. Sadly, the open sites up on North Bluff all have hookups for RVs. The view of Harpswell Sound might make you forget about the land yachts, though. It's worth checking out this part of the campground, even if you're just walking the trail that circumnavigates it. The view, the sun, and the breezes up on North Bluff are invigorating. Plus, from North and South Bluff, you'll have access to the shore for beachcombing, hanging out on the rocks, or swimming—if you're of sturdy Scandinavian stock.

Site 51, on the bluff, is quite isolated from the sites on either side, so this would be a good one to sneak into. The South Bluff sites are much more open. Skip these sites, or else you'll feel like you're stuck in a land-yacht regatta.

MAP

ORR'S ISLAND CAMPGROUND

PEBBLY BEACH

REED COVE

FLOATING DOCK

PLAYING FIELD

VISITOR PARKING

RESERVED PARKING

0.25 MILES TO 24

N

HARPSWELL SOUND

ROCKY BEACH OFF HIGH BLUFF

BATHHOUSE
WATER ACCESS
PARKING
DUMP STATION
OFFICE
TRASH

There's another secluded cluster of tent-only sites over on the other side of the campground as well. Sites 64, 66, and 68 are set aside from the RV crowd for our tent-bound brethren. These sites are tucked off to the right of Port Road (all the short roads leading through the campground have nautical names).

There is an intense sense of seclusion to site 64. There's no bay view, but it's extremely private and surrounded by the dense forest. It's smaller than site 68, but still reasonably spacious. Site 66 is also a bit smaller. It doesn't extend quite as far down from the road as site 68, but it is very secluded on the sides, as it's set among the short, dense forest. It's also very open to the sky, and there's a tantalizing slice of sound view through the trees. Site 68 is very spacious. It's long, narrow, and covered with grass. There's a beautiful but distant view of Harpswell Sound through the trees at the end of the site.

GETTING THERE

From Brunswick, follow ME 24 south onto Orr's Island. Turn right at the sign for the campground.

PEAKS-KENNY STATE PARK

> *The awe-inspiring column of conifers you'll see as you drive into Peaks-Kenny State will put you in the perfect frame of mind for your camping trip.*

DRIVING INTO Peaks-Kenny State Park will remind you why we seek out natural places. The long, winding road to the park travels through a corridor of tall, statuesque pines. Peaks-Kenny is an exceptionally quiet and remote campground, where all you'll hear is the wind rushing over the treetops. The sites here have hard, sandy surfaces that hang on to tent stakes. They're also impeccably clean. The diverse character of the dense forest and the gently rolling topography, peppered with glacial boulders, makes these woodland campsites scenic and attractive. There are 56 sites located near the shores of Sebec Lake. Most are secluded from the rest, especially on the outer side of the loops. The other sites are a curious blend of solitude and openness.

Site 1 resembles a natural cathedral or amphitheater. Its location at the start of the campground loop road is unfortunate, since it is consequently exposed to the road. Two massive white pines frame the site, and a large boulder marks the rear border. Its roadside location aside, this is a spectacular site.

There is an open feel and no neighbors to site 6, but it is also exposed to the road. Site 7 feels particularly secluded. It's a huge site set in open woods. Site 9 shares a similar character. Though sites 7 and 9 are somewhat close together, the dense forest surrounding them belies the proximity of your neighbors.

There's a long entryway leading into site 8, which is set farther off the campground road. The only drawback to this site is that it's close to the restrooms. Site 11 is a bit too open and close to the restrooms as well. Site 10, however, is spacious and surrounded by a brilliant green wall of deciduous forest.

Site 12 is small but secluded. It's also pitched at a bit of angle, so don't use one of those slippery sleeping pads here, or you'll end up in a heap at the bottom of

RATINGS

Beauty: ✿ ✿ ✿ ✿ ✿
Privacy: ✿ ✿ ✿ ✿ ✿
Spaciousness: ✿ ✿ ✿ ✿
Quiet: ✿ ✿ ✿ ✿ ✿
Security: ✿ ✿ ✿ ✿ ✿
Cleanliness: ✿ ✿ ✿ ✿ ✿

your tent by morning. Likewise, there may not be much space in site 14, but it's way off on its own. The surrounding forest is open, but its location gives it a great sense of solitude.

There's a boulder garden at the back of site 13 that provides a solid boundary and adds privacy. Sites 15 and 16 are right across the campground road from each other, but they're set off from the sites on either side. These might be a good choice for a family requiring two sites.

Site 17 is too open to the road and is fairly small. There's a trail to the lake right across from site 19, which is rather exposed and close to the restroom. Site 20 is spacious but feels very open to the road. Site 21 is well secluded but backs up against the restroom.

Site 23 is open and up off the road. It's also got a great view of the sky for stargazing. The rest of the sites in the 20s are moderately secluded, but also convenient to the trail to the lake and the restrooms. The sites on the outside of the loop provide the greatest solitude, particularly site 29 (though it's smallish).

There's a tall birch marking the entrance to site 30, and a moderately dense forest of hemlock and mixed deciduous trees surrounds the site. Located at the top of a small hill on the campground road, the site feels pleasantly isolated.

Massive hemlock trees frame site 33. It's good sized but otherwise feels a bit open, and it's perched right at the intersection of the campground loop road. Sites 31 and 32 are close to the bathrooms. Site 37 is exposed to the road, but it's otherwise well secluded, as it's on a small rise and encircled by dense coniferous forest.

There is a fantastic sense of seclusion to site 38, set back from the campground road amid a dense grove of hemlocks. You can barely see this site from the campground road, and vice versa. Site 39 is more open, but it's set way off the road in its own grove of conifers. Several birch trees frame site 40, which is open to both the campground and the sky.

There's a curiously arranged wall of boulders encircling the back of site 41. One has a white pine growing right on top of it. Site 43 has a boulder ledge

KEY INFORMATION

ADDRESS: Peaks-Kenny State Park
US 1, Box 10
Dover-Foxcroft, ME 04426

OPERATED BY: Maine Department of Conservation, Bureau of Parks and Lands

INFORMATION: Peaks-Kenny State Park, (207) 564-2003

OPEN: May–September

SITES: 56

EACH SITE HAS: Fire ring, picnic table

ASSIGNMENT: First come, first served or by reservation: (800) 332-1501, (207) 287-3824, or www.camp withme.com (extra $2 reservation fee per site, per night)

REGISTRATION: At ranger station as you enter campground, check-in after 1 p.m., check-out by 11 a.m.

FACILITIES: Hot showers, flush toilets, water spigots, canoe rentals, picnic area, bathhouse at beach

PARKING: At sites

FEE: Maine residents, $15; nonresidents, $20

RESTRICTIONS: Pets: On leash only
Fires: Fire rings only
Alcohol: Prohibited
Vehicles: Parking at sites only
Other: Quiet hours 10 p.m.–7 a.m.; 14-day maximum stay; 2-day minimum for reservations

MAP

To AMPHITHEATER AND BEACH

N

SHOWERS
RESTROOM
WATER ACCESS

GETTING THERE

Follow ME 153 north from Dover-Foxcroft for about 6 miles until you see signs for the park.

at the back of the site and rests in a stately stand of hemlocks. Site 46 is set well off the road but still lacks privacy. Site 47 is kind of small, but it's well isolated from its neighbors within a moderately dense grove of smaller trees. Sites 48 through 51—especially 49 and 51—are too exposed to the rest of the campground.

Being set off the road gives site 52 a nice sense of privacy and seclusion. There's a long entryway leading into the site with just enough of an opening to the sky to allow shafts of sunlight to filter through. There's a trail to the lake right near the site's entrance.

Site 53 is close to the restrooms. Site 55 is large and well secluded, encircled within a moderately dense, mostly deciduous forest. There's not much undergrowth in this part of the campground, so there's an open feel on the forest floor.

Several massive boulders block site 56 from view of the road. The site itself is set off the road, and it's framed on one side by a stand of hemlock and beech trees that further block the site from view of the road. The forest opens up toward the back of the site, giving it a combined sense of solitude and openness.

RANGELEY LAKE STATE PARK

THE CAMPGROUND AT Rangeley Lake State Park is exceptionally quiet. You'll occasionally hear the sound of a motorboat cruising by on the lake, but other than that, it's just you, the wind through the trees, and the birds. The sound of loons out on the lake is an essential part of the soundtrack to an evening here.

There are 50 sites spread out around a single, large loop. Sites 3, 6, 10, 14, 17, 21, 27, 33, 42, and 48 are first come, first served. The rest can be reserved. The campsites here are set beneath a dense, truly mixed forest of young and old deciduous and coniferous trees. A nice amount of forest and space between sites provides a solid sense of seclusion just about everywhere. This is a very remote campground with relatively few sites.

There is a delightfully secluded atmosphere at site 9, which is surrounded by a dense forest of birch and spruce trees. Just beyond, there's a footpath leading down to the beach on Rangeley Lake. Past the footpath is a small, open field with a playground area and a volleyball net. The playground is scenic, overlooking the lake through the trees.

Site 11 is also extraordinarily secluded. This moderately spacious site is carved out of a dense grove of conifers. All the sites numbered in the teens are well screened from each other. Site 13 is a bit more open, but you can catch glimpses of the lake through the woods. Site 17 is very secluded and set in the coniferous forest.

A thick wall of woods encircles site 19, but privacy isn't this site's best aspect. There's a 50-foot path leading to your own little slice of the lake. This artfully composed lakeside cove has several birch trees growing out over the lake and a short rock jetty leading out from shore. (I suspect some of the other sites on the lake side of the loop also have these little escape routes

> *Rangeley Lake is the perfect spot to seek out if you just want to unplug for a while in the arboreal solitude of northwestern Maine.*

RATINGS

Beauty: ✩ ✩ ✩ ✩
Privacy: ✩ ✩ ✩ ✩
Spaciousness: ✩ ✩ ✩ ✩
Quiet: ✩ ✩ ✩ ✩ ✩
Security: ✩ ✩ ✩ ✩ ✩
Cleanliness: ✩ ✩ ✩ ✩ ✩

KEY INFORMATION

ADDRESS:	Rangeley Lake State Park HC 32, Box 5000 Rangeley, ME 04970
OPERATED BY:	Maine Department of Conservation, Bureau of Parks and Lands
INFORMATION:	Rangeley Lake State Park, (207) 864-3858
OPEN:	May–September
SITES:	50
EACH SITE HAS:	Fire ring, picnic table
ASSIGNMENT:	First come, first served or by reservation: (800) 332-1501, (207) 287-3824, www.campwithme.com (additional $2 reservation fee per site, per night)
REGISTRATION:	At ranger station as you enter campground, check-in after 1 p.m., checkout by 11 a.m.
FACILITIES:	Hot showers, flush toilets, playground, boat launch, swimming
PARKING:	At sites
FEE:	Maine residents, $15; nonresidents, $20
RESTRICTIONS:	**Pets:** On leash only **Fires:** Fire rings only **Alcohol:** Prohibited **Vehicles:** Parking at sites only **Other:** Quiet hours 10 p.m.–7 a.m.; 14-day maximum stay

to the water, but I couldn't intrude on my neighbors' sites to find out.)

There is also a path leading to the lake from site 23, which has an airy feel. It's open to the sky and set within a loose grove of young trees. As you come to site 25, the campground road starts to head slightly uphill. Site 26 is open and sunny, and it's encircled by a grove of mostly young deciduous trees that form a solid green wall. Site 30 is similarly bright and green. Sites 27 and 29 are close to the restrooms, so I'd stay away from these.

Sites 30 and up seem to have a bit more forest between them. Though site 33 is small, it's tucked into dense forest and relatively distant from its neighbors, even site 34 across the road. Site 34 itself is at an angle from the road and screened by a dense stand of trees. It has a dark, cool feel.

There's a sense of seclusion to site 35, but it's also open to the sky, so sunlight makes its way to the site floor. Site 36, like site 34, is nestled in the trees. There's a large hemlock growing to the right of the site as you enter. Site 38 is secluded, but very spacious and open to the sky.

The sites on the outside of the loop, including sites 40 and up, have plenty of forest between them for privacy. Most of these sites are also open to the sky, so stargazers take note. Site 42 has a long entryway, which adds to the considerable sense of seclusion.

Site 44 is open to the road, and thus has less privacy than most of the other sites at Rangeley Lake. Site 47 is right across from the restroom, but it's set back and up from the road in thick, mixed forest. Sites 49 and 50 are spacious, but they're situated right where the campground road splits off and consequently receive more traffic noise.

Rangeley Lake is pristine. Its remote location in northwestern Maine means it receives a lot less traffic than Sebago Lake farther south in Maine or Lake Winnipesaukee in New Hampshire. The lake is perfect for whatever draws you to water: canoeing, kayaking, swimming, or fishing (for information on fishing licenses, see Appendix C, page 224). If you're of the latter persuasion, you'll appreciate that Rangeley is

MAP

renowned among anglers for its population of land-locked trout and salmon.

There's plenty to do on land here as well. There are hiking trails for all abilities around the park. Try the nearby 3–mile trail up Bald Mountain, a 2,443-foot peak with commanding views of the lake and the surrounding forests and hills. Within the park, the Moose Country Corridor Trail is a good choice for a short hike with the little ones. As always, when in this remote, densely forested part of Maine, the bird-watching and wildlife-viewing are unparalleled. When passing any wet, marshy spots in your travels, keep an eye out for moose.

GETTING THERE

Follow ME 4 north from Farmington to Rangeley, and follow the signs to the state park.

Southwest Harbor

SEAWALL CAMPGROUND

> *Seawall's setting on Mount Desert Island and near all of Acadia National Park makes it that much better.*

THE **PARK SERVICE** manages two campgrounds within Acadia National Park: Seawall and Blackwoods. The latter is more popular, and more often crowded, by virtue of its location along the oceanside Park Loop Road. In fact, I've often camped there for that reason. It is extremely convenient to the Park Loop Road's prime attractions—Sand Beach, Thunder Hole (a hole in the rocks carved out by the surf in which the waves cause a thunderous boom), Otter Cliffs, and some great hiking trails up and over the short, steep cliff known as the Beehive.

So I was pleasantly surprised, if not completely converted, the first time I pulled into Seawall Campground. There are three areas to check out at Seawall: the drive-in tent sites in areas A and B and the walk-in tent sites in area D. There are no tents allowed in area C, the RV section.

The A loop is set beneath a dense coniferous forest. The character of the forest and the fact that most of the sites are set well off the road gives them complete solitude. The campground road runs along two sides and rejoins itself after making a large loop right at site 1, which is a bit open but quite spacious. Site 2 is also spacious, and it's set farther from the road in a dense grove of mixed conifers. Site 3 is tucked into a grove of slender, young conifers and is open to the sky. Site 6 is way back from the road and has a calming sense of isolation. Sites 7 and 8 share an entryway. Site 8 is completely secluded from the road, and site 7 is partially secluded. Site 10 is buffered on the sides, but it's a bit close to the road.

Dense undergrowth surrounds sites 11 and 13, providing an air of deep-woods seclusion. Sites 14 and 15 are open and abut a clearing. They are open to each other too, which may appeal to groups and large families, but fairly secluded from the campground road.

RATINGS

Beauty: ✿ ✿ ✿ ✿
Privacy: ✿ ✿ ✿ ✿
Spaciousness: ✿ ✿ ✿ ✿ ✿
Quiet: ✿ ✿ ✿ ✿
Security: ✿ ✿ ✿ ✿
Cleanliness: ✿ ✿ ✿ ✿ ✿

Site 16 is set far back in this clearing, farther from the road but open to the field shared by 14 and 15. A wall of foliage borders the field.

Perched at a campground road intersection as it is, site 20 feels too open to that road. Sites 19 and 22 are set within the woods way off the road for an absolute sense of solitude. Sites 23 through 25 also have moderately long entryways. They are screened by greenery but open to the sky. Site 27 is designed for easy access. There's a long entryway into site 31, which is well secluded but a bit close to the restrooms. Site 33 also has a fairly long "driveway."

Even the sites that feel open here are thoughtfully spaced within the ample, thick forest. The ingenuity of the layout joins the beauty of the setting to complete your experience of wooded solitude.

Site 35 is a prime example of the smart layout at Seawall, placed so as to be unseen from the road. This site is fantastically secluded and set within dense hemlocks. Sites 36 and 38, however, are a bit open to the road in comparison.

A more loosely spaced forest is predominant along the B loop, at least at the forest floor level. There's much less undergrowth, and the forest is populated with older spruce and hemlock that are bare halfway up the trunks, so there's an airy feeling on the ground and a soothing, evergreen canopy overhead. The predominantly coniferous forest here imparts a heady perfume—a lingering, spicy, tangy scent.

Site 3 is tucked into the trees off the road. Site 5 is a bit small and open, and sites 6 and 7 are very exposed to the road. Sites 8 through 11 are moderately secluded from each other. These sites are all quite spacious and set within a stately hemlock grove.

Sites 12 and 13 are very open to each other and somewhat open to the road. They're huge, so they're perfect for a group needing two contiguous sites. Sites 15 and 16 are another (slightly smaller) pair of sites. Another pair of large sites, 21 and 22, shares an entryway; these are also fairly open to each other.

There's a nice sense of solitude to site 19, as it is set well off the road. Site 26 is a very spacious site also fairly distant from the campground road. Note, how-

KEY INFORMATION

ADDRESS: Seawall Campground ME 102A Southwest Harbor, ME 04679

OPERATED BY: National Park Service

INFORMATION: Acadia National Park P.O. Box 177 Bar Harbor, ME 04609 (207) 288-3338

OPEN: Late June– September

SITES: 170 tent sites (plus 5 group sites and 43 RV-only sites)

EACH SITE HAS: Fire ring, picnic table

ASSIGNMENT: First come, first served (get there early in summer)

REGISTRATION: At ranger station as you enter the campground

FACILITIES: Flush toilets, water spigots, dump station; no hookups

PARKING: At sites and central area within D loop

FEE: $14–$20 (depending on site location)

RESTRICTIONS: Pets: On leash only
Fires: Fire rings only
Alcohol: Sites only
Vehicles: Parking at sites only, or parking areas near D sites
Other: Quiet hours 10 p.m.–7 a.m.; maximum 6 people per site

MAP

SEAWALL CAMPGROUND

RESTROOM
WATER ACCESS
PARKING
WHEELCHAIR ACCESSIBLE
PUBLIC PHONE
RANGER STATION
AMPHITHEATER

CAMP SITE DESIGNATION Ⓐ
GROUP SITE ⚠

To ROUTE 102 AND ROUTE 102A →

SERVICE ROAD ONLY – NO THROUGH TRAFFIC

TRAIL

GETTING THERE

Follow ME 3 onto Mount Desert Island. Bear right onto ME 102/198 toward Southwest Harbor. Stay on ME 102. Follow ME 102 to ME 102A. Stay on ME 102A and follow the signs to the campground

ever, that sites 23 and 24 are very open to the road and to the dumpster, of all things. I don't know of anyone who would want one of these positioned just outside their campsite. Also, site 27 is susceptible to noise from passing traffic.

Generally, the spaciousness of the forest in the B loop doesn't mean a lack of privacy, though you will see your neighbors. It's more like you're nestled within the deep woods. There's a comforting openness to the forest floor, with moss and fern ground cover that lends a rain forest–feel to the woods. The dense, deep, rich greens of the trees contrast dramatically with the lighter greens of the ferns. It's also very quiet here, except for the sounds of the woodland birds and critters. The cries of seagulls remind you that you're not only in the forest, but also right near the ocean.

The D area has the walk-in tent sites. This is the stuff. This "village" of tent sites scattered throughout the forest is sublime. You park along a central loop, then walk into your site. The sites are anywhere from 20 feet to more than 100 feet from the parking area. There are signs along the parking loop that tell you which sites you're parking near.

These tent sites are all relatively uniform in size and character, are moderately spacious, and are liberally sprinkled throughout the fairly thick forest of slender coniferous trees. There's an airy quality to the subcanopy here similar to that of the B loop. At night, the forest seems to close in around you and your campsite—it gets very quiet. All you'll hear are muffled conversations punctuated by the occasional snap of a campfire.

This community of tent sites is unlike anything I've seen at any other campground. The sense of solitude here is deep and complete. There's a network of walking paths just inside the woods that lead to all the sites. There are little signposts at the intersections that guide you to specific sites. It could get a bit confusing, so you'll definitely want to make sure you have one of the campground site maps handy.

The whole D area is phenomenal. There are a few sites spread farther out than the others, but overall the character of the forest, the site spaciousness, and sense of solitude are relatively similar throughout the sites. Anywhere within the D area is a great place to spend a few nights in a tent.

You can tell the veteran D-area campers (like the veteran campers at Grout Pond in Vermont)—they arrive with some sort of wheeled cart or wagon to haul in their gear. Whether or not you have wheels, it is well worth the extra effort to get yourself to one of these sites within the D-area tent village in the woods. You will be rewarded with a feeling of intense wilderness solitude.

SEBAGO LAKE STATE PARK

> *Sebago Lake is a popular destination and a large campground, but every site is just a short walk from the beach.*

EVERY SITE AT THE Sebago Lake Campground is just a short walk from either Witch Cove or Naples Beach, both on Sebago Lake. Sebago Lake State Park is a big campground, and the lake is an extremely popular recreation destination. This means you're not exactly going to get the completely secluded, deep-wilderness experience you'll find in other Maine state parks, but it's still a welcome retreat.

The tent-only area at the Sebago campground should be the first place you check out. Sites 105 through 119 are set up on a small knoll overlooking the lake. The small cluster of tent-only sites that includes sites 111 through 119 is a short walk from the nearest parking area. These sites are closely grouped, but they overlook the lake, so the view and the breezes are well worth it. The sites are moderately spacious and set beneath a loose forest of mostly deciduous trees. The only drawback to these sites is that there isn't much in the way of privacy due to the loose forest and their proximity to each other.

There's another group of sites perched on the same knoll, set back a bit farther from the lake. Sites 105 through 110 feel a bit more secluded than the 111 through 119 group, but they're still in fairly thin forest. Site 105 is the most secluded of the group.

Considering they are set right along the campground road, sites 120 and 121 are surprisingly secluded. There's a separate parking spot for these sites, then a 20- to 30-foot walk to the sites. The forest is a bit denser here, which helps isolate the sites from the road and the parking area.

The Witch Cove area includes sites 122 through 249. The sites within this area are set beneath a loose forest of tall spruce trees with virtually no undergrowth, so there's a very open, cathedral-like atmosphere. This cuts down on the privacy a bit, but it

RATINGS

Beauty: ✪ ✪ ✪ ✪
Privacy: ✪ ✪ ✪
Spaciousness: ✪ ✪ ✪ ✪
Quiet: ✪ ✪ ✪
Security: ✪ ✪ ✪
Cleanliness: ✪ ✪ ✪ ✪

allows for breezes and views of the lake—even at campsites set farther from the water. The sites here vary in size from compact to absolutely enormous.

The sites are all quite close to Witch Cove beach, so it can be a bit noisy during the day, but you can't beat the easy access to the beach. The configuration and layout of the Witch Cove sites are similar to that at Blackwoods Campground in Acadia National Park. There is a large, outer loop intersected by shorter roads cutting across the loop, with sites spread along either side of both the intersecting roads and loop.

The sites on the outer side of the far end of the loop, numbered 206 and up, provide a bit more seclusion than most of the centrally located sites, if for no other reason than because you'll have fewer neighbors. Generally speaking, the sites located on the outside of the main loop tend to be a bit larger and a bit more private. Site 213 is right next to a short trail leading to another little cove around the corner from Witch Cove. This looks like it would be a great spot to drop a hook in the water.

Site 231 is a bit farther off the campground loop road. The site bends around to the left beneath a loose grove of spruce trees. It has a more secluded feel than the others along this stretch of the road.

Over on the other side of the campground is the loop near Naples Beach containing sites 1 through 102. This side of the campground has a similar layout, with a large loop with shorter roads intersecting, but the inside roads are a bit more helter-skelter than the uniform arrangement at Witch Cove. Also, the forest is more dense, and there's a lot more undergrowth on this side of the campground—so most of the sites provide a deeper sense of seclusion. Sites 9 through 13 are set within a mixed forest right on Naples Beach, very close to the lake.

Their location at the end of a short loop and backed up against a large rock pile gives the small group of sites 29, 42, and 31 a remote and interesting character. The dead-end feel of this part of the campground road—and the rocks—add to the sense of seclusion. This cluster of sites is well worth investigating.

ADDRESS:	Sebago Lake State Park
	11 Park Access Road
	Casco, ME 04015
OPERATED BY:	Maine Department of Conservation, Bureau of Parks and Lands
INFORMATION:	Sebago Lake State Park, (207) 693-6231
OPEN:	Mid-May– mid-September
SITES:	250
EACH SITE HAS:	Fire ring, picnic table
ASSIGNMENT:	First come, first served or by reservation: (800) 332-1501, (207) 287-3824, www.campwithme. com (additional $2 reservation fee per site, per night)
REGISTRATION:	At ranger station as you enter campground, check-in after 1 p.m., check-out by 11 a.m.
FACILITIES:	Hot showers, flush toilets, water spigots, boat ramp, sand beach with lifeguard, grills
PARKING:	At sites or at several general-access areas (for walk-in sites)
FEE:	Maine residents, $15; nonresidents, $20
RESTRICTIONS:	**Pets:** Prohibited **Fires:** Fire rings only **Alcohol:** Prohibited **Vehicles:** Maximum 2 per site **Other:** Quiet hours 10 p.m.–7 a.m.; 14-day maximum stay

MAP

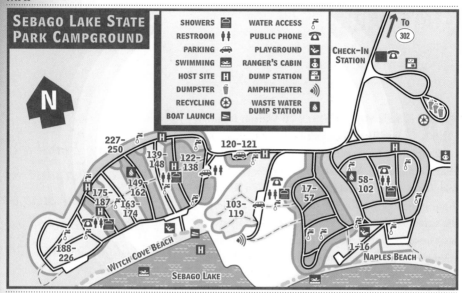

GETTING THERE

Follow ME 302 east from Naples. Turn left at the sign for Sebago Lake State Park. Follow this road for several miles and follow signs to campground.

Farther back from the lake, both the forest and the undergrowth grows denser, so the inland sites generally provide a better sense of solitude and privacy. There's still a fairly open feel, but not wide open like the other side.

When camping at Sebago, it's all about the lake. All the campsites are close to the lake, one whole side of the campground is mostly lakefront beach, and most (if not all) of the activities to choose from are based on the lake. This is the place if you want your summer camping days to be filled with swimming, water-skiing, sailing, canoeing, kayaking, and even scuba diving.

Sebago Lake is the also primary attraction in southwestern Maine, so it does get a little crazy during the day. If you're camping here, though, once all the boaters and skiers and day crowds have packed up and gone home, you'll still be there by the side of the lake, enjoying the sublime transition from day into night.

WARREN ISLAND STATE PARK

WHEN YOU JOURNEY TO Warren Island, you'll see the truth in the statement "half the fun is getting there." After all, Warren Island is an island. You can't drive there, you can't hike there, and you certainly can't park an RV there. You can get there by kayak or canoe, one placid paddle stroke at a time. You can also get there by motorboat or sailboat, but most of the people you'll see camped out on Warren Island arrive by sea kayak.

While most of the island's ten campsites (and arguably the nicest sites) are spread along the shore, the rest are located toward the center of the island. There are eight primitive tent sites and two Appalachian Mountain Club–style lean-tos. The day-use picnic sites and the overnight camping sites are available by reservation or, otherwise, on a first come, first served basis. The only sites you can't reserve are 4, 5, and 6.

The island is covered in a verdant, dense spruce forest. Island camping in general, and certainly a night spent on Warren Island, is an olfactory sensation. At any moment, you can smell the crisp aroma of the spruce forest and the rich scents of the sea.

It's funny to look down as you're walking along the Island Trail and see bits of shell mixed in with the pine needles and fallen leaves on the forest floor. The Island Trail is a walking trail that essentially circumnavigates the 70-acre island and brings you past most of the sites.

As you start to set up your camping gear, you'll notice a five-gallon white bucket next to every fireplace and grill. It should be full of water. If it's not, be a good citizen and fill it up at the shore. This is Warren Island's volunteer fire department—and you're the firefighter. If your fire gets out of control, there's no calling 911. There's no truck on the island waiting to come douse the flames. An out-of-control campfire could be lethal, and that scenario is a major concern for island

> *Warren Island is a slice of paradise—enjoy the pristine view and the magnificent scents of both sea and forest.*

RATINGS

Beauty: ✫ ✫ ✫ ✫ ✫
Privacy: ✫ ✫ ✫ ✫ ✫
Spaciousness: ✫ ✫ ✫ ✫ ✫
Quiet: ✫ ✫ ✫ ✫ ✫
Security:✫ ✫ ✫ ✫ ✫
Cleanliness: ✫ ✫ ✫ ✫ ✫

ADDRESS: Warren Island State Park
P.O. Box 105
Lincolnville, ME 04849

OPERATED BY: Maine Department of Conservation, Bureau of Parks and Lands

INFORMATION: Contact Camden Hills State Park, (207) 236-3109 or (207) 941-4014

OPEN: May–September

SITES: 8 tent sites, 2 lean-tos

EACH SITE HAS: Picnic table, stone hearth, fire bucket

ASSIGNMENT: First come, first served or by reservation: (800) 332-1501, (207) 287-3824, www.campwithme.com (extra $2 reservation fee per site, per night)

REGISTRATION: At ranger station, check-in after 1 p.m., check-out by 11 a.m.

FACILITIES: Pit toilets, water spigots, pier, moorings

PARKING: Pull your kayak up onto the beach!

FEE: Maine residents, $14; nonresidents, $19; day-use fee, $1

RESTRICTIONS: Pets: Prohibited
Fires: Fire rings only
Alcohol: Prohibited
Vehicles: No vehicles on the island
Other: Damaging trees prohibited; must carry out all trash; no dish washing at water spigots; quiet hours 10 p.m.–7 a.m.; 14-day maximum stay

dwellers and Warren Island State Park's ranger. Be extra cautious with your fire, and make sure that bucket is full and next to the hearth.

There's no camp store on Warren Island, and it is strictly forbidden to cut down or otherwise damage any trees. The rangers leave small caches of firewood here and there for campers. Be frugal and conserve wood. Only build a fire as large as you need to cook, stay warm, and keep the fireside ambiance in your site. You'll save wood, minimize the risk to Warren Island, and still have a fantastically peaceful evening.

After reaching the island from whichever direction you approach, you can access it via the pier on the east side, facing the Islesboro ferry terminal. Just off the end of the pier is the ranger station and the day-use area with grills and picnic tables. If you're just pulling in for the day, the fee is $1, which you pay at the Iron Ranger posted at the head of the pier.

Head out on the Island Trail to the north (or to the right as you look onto the island from the end of the pier), and you'll find the campsites. Site 1 is situated on a grassy area, close to the restrooms and the pier, on the island's eastern shore. This site is on the inland side of the Island Trail.

Site 2 is the first of the sites situated right on the water. This site is marvelously spacious and secluded. You can see the narrow bay that separates Warren Island and Islesboro through the loosely spaced trees that define the site. This site has two picnic tables, as well as a stone hearth.

Deep in the woods on the forest side of the trail, site 3 is very secluded and private. The inland sites at Warren Island are indeed lovely campsites. But this is an island, so you'll probably be tempted to try and secure a waterfront site. It's well worth a little extra effort or wait.

The next oceanfront site is 3A. This site is very spacious and open, with cool breezes blowing off the ocean through the site. It has dramatic views of the bay. You can pull your kayaks right up to the edge of the site. If you arrive by a larger boat, or don't paddle right up to the campsite, there are wheeled carts available for hauling your gear from the pier.

MAP

WARREN ISLAND STATE PARK

GRINDLE PT. · GRINDLE POINT · LIGHTHOUSE

To LINCOLNVILLE
FERRY (TOLL)

BROAD COVE

ISLEBORO ISLAND

N

NORTH SHELTER

WEST PENOBSCOT BAY

WARREN ISLAND

GILKEY HARBOR

SPRUCE ISLAND

GROUP PICNIC AREA

WEST SHELTER

THE GUT

SEVEN HUNDRED ACRE ISLAND

TIDAL FLAT

BIRCH POINT

LAURA'S ROCK

RESTROOM
WATER ACCESS
PICNIC AREA
PICNIC PAVILLION
RANGER'S CABIN
ADIRONDACK SHELTER
SMALL PIER
MOORINGS

Keep heading up the trail past sites 3 and 3A, and you'll come to the North Shelter, one of the island's lean-tos. The North Shelter is set in an open grove of birch and spruce trees, and it looks out over Penobscot Bay to the north. Its location perfectly blends a woodland setting and proximity to the island's shoreline.

The remaining inland sites are 4, 5, and 6. These sites are set in a grassy field and a loose grove of mixed forest in the center of the island. To reach them, take the short hiking trail that leads straight from the pier (heading west), past the ranger station on the left. There are remnants from the foundation of a historic mansion out here. There's a water pump located between sites 4 and 5, within the stone piles that belie the fact that a mansion stood here more than 80 years ago.

This mansion must have been quite a sight. It was once the property of William Folwell, a woolen manufacturer from Philadelphia who purchased the land in 1899. When it was built at a price of $75,000 (in turn-of-the-century dollars), it was believed to be one of the most expensive log cabins ever built in New England. The elegantly appointed cabin had 22 rooms, including a massive living room, dining room, and kitchen.

GETTING THERE

Drop your kayak in the water in Camden Harbor, Lincolnville Beach, or Duck-trap Harbor, and paddle east toward Islesboro. Warren Island is just southwest of the Islesboro ferry terminal.

Sadly, the cabin burned to the ground in 1919.

Beyond sites 4 and 5 and the remnants of the Folwell mansion, site 6 is set off in its own little field. The trio of inland sites is quite open and extraordinarily spacious. They offer less privacy than the shoreline sites and lack ocean views, but they are still beautiful. The breezes, the scent of the ocean, and the melancholy cry of the seagulls will remind you that you're on an island.

The West Shelter is set way down on the Penobscot Bay (west) side of the island. Follow a short hiking trail from the open area near sites 4 and 5, and you'll find the shelter, which faces an absolutely priceless view of the bay.

Site 7 sits toward the southern end of the island. You can pull up to the pier on the east side and cart down your gear, or spot the site from the water and paddle right up to it. I prefer the second option.

This site has the most complete and deep sense of seclusion of any campsite in New England. You're at least 100 feet from the nearest site, and all you can see are the woods and the bay. There are two picnic tables at site 7 and makeshift log benches by the fireplace. The site is set within a moderately spaced grove of spruce and other deciduous trees,; it's open from above, so plenty of sunlight and moonlight filter down.

More often than not, there's a breeze blowing through the island, but on those still days, or during the morning and evening lull, the bugs can be ferocious. There is simply no escape. Think ahead, and be prepared. Bring a head net and some of your favorite bug repellent.

Penobscot Bay is big water. Don't paddle to Warren Island on your first (or second) kayak camping trip. Plan your trip carefully with respect to the winds, the tides, and the weather. If you're at all hesitant, either wait for better weather or hire one of the area's registered guides. If you get in a jam where you don't feel comfortable paddling back, paddle over to the ferry terminal on nearby Islesboro and see if you can hop on the ferry, which leaves Islesboro every hour on the half hour. A one-way adult ticket runs $3.25. Bikes are $2, and vehicles less than 20 feet are $10.50. A kayak should be somewhere in between.

NEW HAMPSHIRE

BEAR BROOK STATE PARK

BEAR BROOK STATE PARK is enormous—it's the largest state park in New Hampshire. Its size (the entire park spans 8,008 acres) and the myriad outdoor activities available here make this as much a destination as a place to set up camp. On the long road leading through the park and to the campground, I was convinced I had missed it. If you get this sensation, keep cruising because you're almost there. You'll come to another Bear Brook State Park sign that points the way into the campground. The last stretch is a beautiful ride through a stately forest of pine and spruce trees that are at least 100 feet tall.

Bear Brook State Park has a massive network of trails, some of which pass right through the campground. You'll see trailheads for the Broken Boulder Trail and the Pitch Pine Trail on the last section of the campground road. Both of these trails eventually lead to Smith Pond.

The first loop within the campground with sites 1 and up is set beneath an open forest with very little undergrowth. These sites don't offer a lot of privacy, but they are spacious and centrally located within the campground. They're also covered by a blanket of pine needles. This loop is near an open field with a baseball diamond. There is even a small playground with a slide and swings—nice if you're camping with kids. If you want to be near these parts of the campground, check out sites 35 and 36, which are close to the baseball field.

Past the field, there are sites tucked into the woods on the stretch of the campground road leading down to the small beach area on Beaver Pond. Sites 22 through 24 are nicely secluded and close to the pond. Of the other sites near the pond, site 31A is nice, as it's set on the end of a short road jutting off the main campground road.

> *Bear Brook State Park has some great spots to camp while you explore the rest of the park on foot, on a bike, or in a canoe.*

RATINGS

Beauty: ✪ ✪ ✪ ✪
Privacy: ✪ ✪ ✪ ✪
Spaciousness: ✪ ✪ ✪ ✪
Quiet: ✪ ✪ ✪ ✪ ✪
Security: ✪ ✪ ✪ ✪
Cleanliness: ✪ ✪ ✪ ✪ ✪

ADDRESS:	Bear Brook State Park 157 Deerfield Road Allenstown, NH 03275
OPERATED BY:	New Hampshire Division of Parks and Recreation
INFORMATION:	Bear Brook State Park, (603) 485-9869 (campground office) or (603) 485-9874 (park office)
OPEN:	Early May– mid-October
SITES:	96
EACH SITE HAS:	Fire ring, picnic table
ASSIGNMENT:	First come, first served or by reservation: (603) 271-3628, www.nhstateparks.org
REGISTRATION:	At campground headquarters
FACILITIES:	Flush toilets, showers, laundry, camp store, boat and canoe rentals
PARKING:	At sites
FEE:	$15
RESTRICTIONS:	Pets: Dogs on leash only Fires: Fire rings only Alcohol: Sites only Vehicles: Parking at campsites only, maximum 2 vehicles per site Other: Reservations require 2-night minimum stay; check-in 1–8 p.m., check-out by noon; quiet hours 10 p.m.–7 a.m.

The beach at Beaver Pond is a great spot to spend an afternoon. You can paddle, fish, or just sit in the sand. Being out in the deep woods and far from the ocean, there are no seashells on this beach—only pine cones! You don't have to worry about finding anything else in the sand either, as there are no glass bottles, pets, or horses allowed on the beach. The Beaver Pond trailhead is at the far end of the beach. This trail circumnavigates the pond, coming back in through the campground. There's also a small dock toward the end of the beach to launch kayak or canoe adventures.

Heading back toward the main part of the campground, sites 40 and 41 are quite spacious, although they're close to the headquarters and set within the open forest that covers most of the central campground loop. Like the lower-numbered sites, these are also blanketed with pine needles.

Site 55 is excellent; it's one of the more secluded at Bear Brook. It's set off by a short perimeter of pines, standing around the border as if guarding the site. Its neighbor site 56 is also nicely isolated.

If you set up camp at site 64, you'll be able to pick up the Beaver Pond trail right next to your campsite. Site 65 is off on its own near the restroom, with a view of the pond through the loosely spaced forest that divides the campsites from the shores of the pond in this section of the campground.

Farther back on the campground loop road and away from the campground headquarters, you'll find site 94, another of Bear Brook's better choices. It is a spacious site set off on a small loop heading away from the pond. There is open forest on the far side, as well as overhead, so a lot of sunlight reaches down—you'll have a nice view of the night sky. There's also a self-guided nature trail just adjacent.

Site 95 is truly secluded, set at the end of a short spur leading off the main campground road. It has its own little cul-de-sac right in front of the site, so it's extremely spacious. It's set up against a small embankment and nestled within a grove of mixed hardwoods and conifers. Just outside the site to the left, there's a break in the forest that gives you access to the pond. There's no beach, but there's plenty of room to launch

MAP

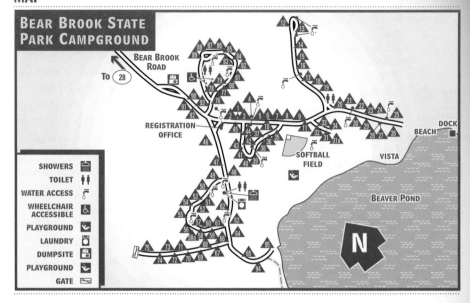

BEAR BROOK STATE PARK CAMPGROUND

BEAR BROOK ROAD

To 28

REGISTRATION OFFICE

SHOWERS

TOILET

WATER ACCESS

WHEELCHAIR ACCESSIBLE

PLAYGROUND

LAUNDRY

DUMPSITE

PLAYGROUND

GATE

SOFTBALL FIELD

VISTA

BEACH

DOCK

BEAVER POND

N

---

a canoe or kayak. This site is also near a trailhead that leads out of the campground.

Site 75 is another secluded spot, set at another end of the campground loop road and right on a dirt road leading out of the campground proper. Overall, sites 46 through 75 are more secluded than the rest of the campground. Some are much more spacious, and a few are positively perfect. The shower and laundry facilities are also located within this group.

There's a special pond just for fly-fishermen near the beginning of the road winding in toward the campground. The season runs from the fourth Saturday in April through October 15, and there's a limit of two brook trout per day. There are also two archery ranges within the park (apparently the only ones within the New Hampshire state park system). For information on fishing licenses, see Appendix C, page 224.

If hiking, mountain biking, and paddling are more your speed, there's plenty of room for those as well. Many trails wind through Bear Brook State Park—more than 40 miles' worth—so you will have to spend a lot of time here before you cross over the same trail twice.

GETTING THERE

Take Interstate 93 north through Manchester to the exit for NH 28 and NH 3 north. In Suncook, take NH 28 toward Allenstown. Turn right on Bear Brook Road toward the park.

BIG ROCK CAMPGROUND

> *You'll know how this campground got its name as soon as you pull in.*

THE MOMENT YOU pull into Big Rock Campground, you'll see the unique geological feature for which the campground was named—a huge rock. Besides being a namesake and a curiosity, this massive chunk of granite (a phrase that proved far too cumbersome for a campground name) gives climbers a good spot for a little spontaneous bouldering. It's a nice way to warm up for or cool down from a day spent climbing the massive walls of Cathedral Ledge in nearby North Conway.

Big Rock is actually quite a small campground, which makes it an excellent place to set up camp. There are only 28 sites, many of which have a decent amount of space and a feeling of moderate solitude. If you've come camping with a group or need several sites, try to secure something in the range of sites 24 through 29. There's a small parking area that's central to these sites, so you'll have to haul in your gear, but not too far. These sites sit atop the small hill around which the campground is situated, so they provide a sense of isolation from the rest of the campground, if not from each other. There's also a restroom right down the access road for this group of sites.

Other prime tent spots within Big Rock are sites 7 through 10 and 13 through 18. All are on the same loop (the main loop of the campground). The forest here is a bit thicker than the open woods of nearby Hancock Campground (see page 84). It's a mixed forest of coniferous and deciduous trees, so at the height of summer, the dense woods give each site a sense of being off on its own.

I especially like the fact that this is such a small campground. Yes, it fills up quickly as a result, but if you get here early enough and secure a spot, you can rest assured that you'll have peaceful, quiet nights in the woods. Big Rock is only the second campground

RATINGS

Beauty: ✿ ✿ ✿ ✿
Privacy: ✿ ✿ ✿ ✿
Spaciousness: ✿ ✿ ✿ ✿
Quiet: ✿ ✿ ✿ ✿ ✿
Security: ✿ ✿ ✿ ✿
Cleanliness: ✿ ✿ ✿ ✿

you'll come across as you travel east on the the Kanca-magus Highway (or the "Kanc" as this delightful stretch of road is known to the locals and regulars), so it's still fairly close to Lincoln.

Big Rock is a great spot from which to launch your outdoor adventures. It's within a short drive or walk from some prime hikes and sights along the Kanc. Right across the road runs the Hancock Branch of the Pemigewasset. Stroll over there with a fishing rod or a towel, depending on your preference (for information on fishing licenses, see Appendix C, page 224).

Several hiking trails are just a stone's throw down the Kanc. Turn left out of the campground heading toward Conway, and you'll soon come to trailheads for the East Pond Trail and the Hancock Notch Trail. This trail follows the North Fork of the Pemigewasset for a while, then bears east toward Mount Huntington, Hancock Notch, and the Sawyer Pond Scenic Area. It would be a fairly sturdy hike from the Hancock Notch trailhead all the way to Sawyer Pond, so bring plenty of food and water if you're coming this way.

Across the Kanc from these trailheads is the Greeley Ponds trail that leads to the Greeley Ponds Scenic Area. If you hike in this far and still want to explore, the Mount Osceola Trail leads you up to East Peak, West Peak, and Mount Osceola. You'll also be able to sneak occasional views of Mount Kancamagus to the east.

It can sometimes be a challenge to secure one of the prime tent spots at Big Rock. It is one of the first campgrounds to fill during the busy summer weekends. Even if you've come to the Kanc at the height of the season, it's well worth your time to take a swing through Big Rock just in case there's an open spot.

Who knows what the campground might have been called had a careless glacier not casually dropped that massive boulder near the entrance several million years ago? On the other hand, who cares? Big Rock is small and cozy, and that makes it a perfect-sized campground and a great spot to pitch a tent.

KEY INFORMATION

ADDRESS:	Big Rock Campground Kancamagus Highway Lincoln, NH 03818
OPERATED BY:	United States Forest Service
INFORMATION:	Saco Ranger Station 33 Kancamagus Highway RFD 1, Box 94 Conway, NH 03818 (603) 447-5448
OPEN:	Mid-May– mid-October
SITES:	28
EACH SITE HAS:	Fire ring, picnic table
ASSIGNMENT:	First come, first served
REGISTRATION:	Select site, then pay at self-service fee station
FACILITIES:	Vault toilets
PARKING:	At sites
FEE:	$16
RESTRICTIONS:	Pets: Dogs on leash only Fires: Fire rings only Alcohol: Sites only Vehicles: Maximum 2 per site Other: Maximum 8 people per site; 14-day maximum stay

MAP

GETTING THERE

From Lincoln, follow Kancamagus Highway to Big Rock campground on the left.
From Conway, follow Kancamagus Highway to Big Rock campground on the right.

BLACKBERRY CROSSING CAMPGROUND

Albany

THERE MAY BE JUST SIX SITES set aside for tent camping at Blackberry Crossing Campground, but its character, history, and location on the Kancamagus Highway make a trip here time well spent. It's another of the area's fairly small campgrounds, about the same size as Big Rock.

The six tent sites are set off in a small field on the eastern edge of the campground. They are tent-only sites by virtue of the fact that you have to lug your gear in a short distance from the parking area for this loop. Sites 21 through 26 are at the woods' edge around a central clearing about one-quarter the size of a football field. The open space between these tent sites adds a community flavor to this part of the campground. On those crystal-clear, jet-black New England nights, you'll be thankful that you're far from any light pollution that might interfere with stargazing. The break in the trees over the field affords magnificent views of the skies. Keep an eye to the sky if you're there in mid-August, and you could catch the Perseid meteor showers.

During the daylight hours, the field is a great spot for a quick game of Frisbee or a group picnic. It's also a great space to let the kids run around in and blow off steam while you kick back in the sun—or in the shade of the birch, pine, and mixed deciduous forest. Either way, you'll still have a full view of your gang. It's also just 6 miles west of Conway if you need anything, from groceries to a hot pizza.

If you've come to pitch your tent at Blackberry Crossing during the winter, the clearing in the middle of the tent loop is especially nice because you'll get the full benefit of the sun (when it's out). The campground isn't plowed in the winter, so you'll have to ski or snowshoe in with your gear, but the campsites are half price. Of course, during the winter, you might not need to hike your gear over to the tent loop. Hancock

> *Blackberry Crossing is rich in history, with tall, stone hearths remaining from its days as a Civilian Conservation Corps camp.*

RATINGS

Beauty: ✩ ✩ ✩ ✩
Privacy: ✩ ✩ ✩
Spaciousness: ✩ ✩ ✩ ✩
Quiet: ✩ ✩ ✩
Security: ✩ ✩ ✩ ✩
Cleanliness: ✩ ✩ ✩ ✩

ADDRESS: Blackberry Crossing Campground Kancamagus Highway Albany, NH 03818

OPERATED BY: White Mountain National Forest

INFORMATION: Saco Ranger Station 33 Kancamagus Highway RFD 1, Box 94 Conway, NH 03818 (603) 447-5448

OPEN: Year-round

SITES: 26

EACH SITE HAS: Fire ring, picnic table

ASSIGNMENT: First come, first served

REGISTRATION: Select site, then pay at self-service fee station

FACILITIES: Vault toilets, hand pump for water

PARKING: At sites; separate parking area for tent loop

FEE: $16, $8 during winter as the campground is not plowed

RESTRICTIONS: Pets: Dogs on leash only
Fires: Fire rings only
Alcohol: Sites only
Vehicles: Maximum 2 per site
Other: Maximum 8 people per site; 14-day maximum stay

tends to get most of the winter campers, so you might have Blackberry Crossing all to yourself.

Blackberry Crossing looks quite different than it did 60 years ago. Nearly 200 men lived and worked here between 1935 and 1941 as part of President Roosevelt's "Tree Army." Blackberry Crossing was home to Company 1177 of the Civilian Conservation Corps, which cut most of the trails in and around the White Mountains that we still enjoy today.

Besides preserving and providing access to wilderness, the CCC employed men during the depths of the Great Depression. There are still a few remnants from Blackberry Crossing's days as a CCC encampment, most notably two large stone hearths—one right by site 20 and the other between sites 8 and 9. These are all that remain of the camp's original headquarters and recreation hall.

The sites in the tent loop are obviously the best for tent camping, but if you've come with a large group or several families and that loop is already occupied, you could also look into sites 7 through 10. These are located around the central loop, off to the left as you enter the campground. You'll be close to one of the beautiful old stone hearths and a historic marker with photos of the camp as it appeared in its heyday. These sites are wide open, but they're set amid a lovely grove of birch trees. Sites 14 and 15, roughly between the central loop and the tent-only loop, are also set off on their own.

Whether you've come to Blackberry Crossing to camp for one night or for a whole week, don't miss Rocky Gorge. Visit the gorge by heading out of the campground and taking a left. This series of natural pools and rock baths leads to a fairly steep and wild waterfall. The Swift River gets narrow and speeds through Rocky Gorge. There's a footbridge right over the waterfall, so you can get a spectacular view of the show beneath.

Follow the footbridge to the trail on the opposite side of the river, and a short hike will lead you to Falls Pond, a placid, quiet pond in direct contrast to the thundering water just a few feet away. There's a hiking trail that leads all the way around the pond as well.

MAP

BLACKBERRY CROSSING CAMPGROUND

To ← LINCOLN

To CONWAY →

KANCAMAGUS HWY.

RESTROOM
WATER ACCESS
PARKING

N

Blackberry Crossing campground is directly across the street from Covered Bridge Campground (page 71), which is kind of amusing. It's your choice. If you're camping with a large group or have a particular affinity for historic sites, Blackberry Crossing is definitely worth a look. If it's just you and a friend or a couple of friends, check across the street at Covered Bridge—another spot rich in character.

GETTING THERE

From Lincoln, follow the Kancamagus Highway to Blackberry Crossing Campground on your right. From Conway, follow Kancamagus Highway to Blackberry Crossing Campground on your left, right across the street from Covered Bridge Campground.

COVERED BRIDGE CAMPGROUND

> *The campground's proximity to massive rock gardens and two trailheads make Covered Bridge a great spot for hikers.*

WHAT DO BIG ROCK and Covered Bridge campgrounds have in common (besides the fact that they're both located on the Kancamagus Highway)? As soon as you pull in to either, you'll see the campground's namesake. In the case of Covered Bridge Campground, it's a classic New England covered bridge that spans the Swift River. The original bridge was built in the late 1800s by the townsfolk of Albany; it was rebuilt in the 1970s.

On either side of the road leading to the bridge, there are huge timbers spanning the road at an eight-foot height to ensure that "adventurous" RV or camper owners don't try to drive through the bridge. While effective and admirable as a means of preserving this historic covered bridge, the timbers also help keep the larger RVs out of Covered Bridge Campground. (You can get into the campground from the Dugway Road, 6 miles west of Conway, but don't tell anyone in an RV!)

Coming into the campground from the Kancamagus, you'll pass under the RV trap with ease, traverse the covered bridge (keep an eye out for pedestrians, as covered bridges throughout New England always draw camera-toting crowds), and bear right on Dugway Road. The campground is on the left about half a mile down the road. As soon as you cross the bridge and bear right, you'll see the parking area and trailhead for the Boulder Loop Trail on the right. Make a mental note to walk back later for a quick hike.

Covered Bridge Campground is moderately sized, with 49 sites. There aren't any sites designated as tent-only, but there are some practical landscape considerations that make this a great campground for a night in the nylon. As soon as you pull into the campground, keep bearing left. This will bring you to the small, dead-end loop with sites 25 through 27. These are great sites, set off on their own amid the fairly dense, mostly

RATINGS

Beauty: ✿ ✿ ✿ ✿ ✿
Privacy: ✿ ✿ ✿ ✿
Spaciousness: ✿ ✿ ✿ ✿
Quiet: ✿ ✿ ✿ ✿ ✿
Security: ✿ ✿ ✿ ✿
Cleanliness: ✿ ✿ ✿ ✿ ✿

coniferous forest. Just outside this loop is site 24, which is set against a garden of massive boulders—no doubt spilled over from the Boulder Loop Trail.

Generally speaking, the outer-loop sites are the best. If you're fortunate enough, you'll be able to score one of the northernmost sites set off on their own platforms, which means you have to lug your tent and other gear up a short incline. If you're on the southern end of the loop, you might be somewhere near an RV, but the sites are spacious and distant enough to provide solitude.

The northern-loop sites that make up the prime tent spots at Covered Bridge are 17, 19, 41, 43, 45, 47, and 49. These sites back up to a massive cliff that rises just behind the campground. During the summer, the forest may be too dense for you to fully appreciate this grand formation, which is part of the granite pile left by the glaciers that scraped through here thousands of years ago.

One other way to appreciate the geologic uniqueness of this area is to head down Dugway Road back toward the covered bridge and take a spin around the Boulder Loop Trail. The trail will take you up and around the side of this cliff and through a delightful garden of huge boulders. The beginning of this trail resembles a massive stone staircase. You almost expect it to lead to a giant's castle. The glaciers inadvertently created a hiker's playground here, but watch your step: It's quite easy to twist an ankle when hiking and bounding through the boulders.

Another nice trailhead right near the campground is the Lower Nanamocomuck Ski Trail, which is just past the covered bridge coming from the campground. This makes a fairly level hike during the spring, summer, and fall, and a dramatic backcountry ski or snowshoe trek in the winter. While Covered Bridge Campground isn't open during the winter, Blackberry Crossing, which is literally right across the street, is open for camping at half the regular rates since it isn't plowed out like Hancock, the other Kancamagus campground that is open year-round.

There's one historical aspect to Covered Bridge that can add a bit of spice to your ghost stories around

KEY INFORMATION

ADDRESS:	Covered Bridge Campground Kancamagus Highway Albany, NH 03818
OPERATED BY:	White Mountain National Forest
INFORMATION:	Saco Ranger Station 33 Kancamagus Highway RFD 1, Box 94 Conway, NH 03818 (603) 447-5448
OPEN:	Mid-May– mid-October
SITES:	49
EACH SITE HAS:	Fire ring, picnic table
ASSIGNMENT:	First come, first served, or sites 29–49 by reservation: (877) 444-6777, www.reserveusa.com
REGISTRATION:	Select a site, then pay at self-service fee station
FACILITIES:	Vault toilets, near fishing pier on Swift River
PARKING:	At sites
FEE:	$16 per site, per night
RESTRICTIONS:	**Pets:** Dogs on leash only **Fires:** Fire rings only **Alcohol:** Sites only **Vehicles:** Maximum 2 per site **Other:** Maximum 8 people per site; 14-day maximum stay

MAP

COVERED BRIDGE CAMPGROUND

RESTROOM
WATER ACCESS

To LINCOLN

To CONWAY

SWIFT RIVER

DUGWAY RD.

KANCAMAGUS HWY.

GETTING THERE

From Lincoln, follow Kancamagus Highway to Covered Bridge Campground on your left. From Conway, follow Kancamagus Highway to Covered Bridge Campground on your right, right across the street from Blackberry Crossing Campground.

the campfire. As soon as you enter the campground, there's a small, fenced-off burial plot. After dinner, take a stroll down to the burial site, make sure no one from the Lane family (the name on the headstone) is up and about, then go whip up a couple of ghoulish ghost stories with a local connection!

CRAWFORD NOTCH CAMPGROUND

NESTLED WITHIN the wilderness of Crawford Notch, the campground of the same name is a perfectly peaceful spot to pitch your tent—whether you've come to Crawford Notch for the climbing, hiking, fishing, or just sitting and watching the Saco River (for information on fishing licenses, see Appendix C, page 224).

The Crawford Notch Campground is meticulously maintained, with a clean, sandy surface on the roads leading throughout the campground and at the individual sites. A dense forest of mostly young maples and beech covers the campground. The deciduous forest imparts a brilliant, shimmering green character to the forest, especially when all the leaves are backlit by the sun. The dense forest also gives most of the sites a marvelous sense of seclusion. There are many sites here located on or near the shores of the Saco River, and these are by far the most spectacular.

Close to the entrance into the campground is the S loop. These sites are all encircled with short stone walls built within the forest of young birch trees. This makes for a peaceful and scenic setting. The sites are all moderately sized and fairly well secluded by the birch forest. There's a bright, open character to the forest here, as it is populated primarily by deciduous trees and fewer conifers. Sites 5 through 9 are set back a bit farther from the road and closer to the river, making them preferable.

The rest of the first sites as you drive into the campground are the RV sites with hookups. These sites are also close to the road and are fairly open to each other. Considering the magical quality of some of the riverside hike-in spots here, keep driving to find the primo sites.

A bit deeper into the campground, sites 38 and 39 are hike-in sites carved out of the beech forest. As

> *Deep in the wilderness of Crawford Notch, campsites here are carved out of dense forest, and many are perched on the banks of the Saco River.*

RATINGS

Beauty: ✿ ✿ ✿ ✿ ✿
Privacy: ✿ ✿ ✿ ✿
Spaciousness: ✿ ✿ ✿ ✿
Quiet: ✿ ✿ ✿ ✿
Security:✿ ✿ ✿ ✿
Cleanliness: ✿ ✿ ✿ ✿ ✿

KEY INFORMATION

ADDRESS: Crawford Notch
Campground
US 302
Harts Location, NH
03812

OPERATED BY: Crawford Notch
General Store and
Campground

INFORMATION: Crawford Notch
Campground, (603)
374-2779

OPEN: Mid-May–
mid-October

SITES: 74

EACH SITE HAS: Fire ring or stone
hearth, picnic table

ASSIGNMENT: First come, first
served, or by reser-
vation (recom-
mended in July and
August or during
foliage season, late
September–early
October)

REGISTRATION: At campground
office and store
located on US 302

FACILITIES: Portable toilets,
shower building,
water spigots

PARKING: At campsites or
shared parking areas

FEE: $21

RESTRICTIONS: Pets: Dogs on leash
only
Fires: Fire rings only
Alcohol: At sites
Vehicles: Maximum
1 vehicle per site
Other: Check-in
after 2 p.m., check-
out by noon

such, they are very well secluded. Site 42 has about a 50-foot hike into the site. It's nicely secluded on all sides and not far from the portable toilets. It's also close to the river. Site 43 is also secluded by a hike. Continuing on the path the leads to this site will bring you to site 45—more on that in a minute.

Site 43 is near a cul-de-sac with parking for sites 44, 45, 46, and 46A. All of these sites are set near the Saco, and all share open views into Crawford Notch, and breezes sweeping through—site 46A a bit less so, as it's open to the cul-de-sac, but set deeper in the woods.

Sites 47 and 48 are hike-in sites with shared parking. This area also includes sites 47A, which is located at the end of a 30-foot hike to a modest-sized and delightfully secluded site. Sites 47 and 48 are set a bit deeper into the woods, but still near the riverbanks. These two sites are carved out of a grove of older beech trees and their saplings. These sites are perfectly secluded and absolutely beautiful.

The trail that leads you to these two sites continues on to sites 45 and 44. Site 45 is *the* site at Crawford Notch Campground. It is absolutely perfect, pristine, intensely secluded, very spacious, has a stone hearth, is set on the shore of the Saco River at a picturesque bend, and it's open to the sky for stargazing and a command-ing view up into the cliffs of Crawford Notch. Need I say more? There are some dramatically beautiful hike-in sites along the Saco River here at the Crawford Notch Campground. Site 45 is the granddaddy of them all.

The drive-in sites are easier to get into and unload your gear, but the hike-in sites provide a sense of wilderness and seclusion that astounds me. I always prefer these types of sites, even if it means a little extra effort hauling gear.

Located near the intersection of the campground road, sites 49 and 50 are open to that road. Still, at night when everyone is snug in their sites, sitting around the campfires cooking dinner and telling sto-ries, this won't be a big deal. Even when the moon is full overhead, once night falls at the Crawford Notch Campground, the dense forest ensures a dark night.

These hike-in sites in the lower 50s—53, 54, 55, 55A, 55B, and 55C—are the crown jewels of the

Crawford Notch Campground. These incredibly remote-feeling, yet easily accessible sites are all perched along or near the shores of the Saco River, so you'll fall asleep to the soft rushing of water. Of these, site 53 is very well secluded, set at the end of a 75-foot hike. Sites 54 and 55 are closest to the river, so they are off the charts in seclusion and beauty.

The last end of the campground road has sites 56 through 64. Site 56 also has a short hike in. It's a secluded but somewhat smaller site. There's also a short hike into site 62, but it's huge and very private. This would be an excellent site for larger group. There's also a short hike into site 61, although this site is much smaller. It's isolated from the road and from neighboring sites.

Site 63 is very spacious. It also has its own tent platform, so you're guaranteed a level, dry space upon which to pitch your tent. Sites 63A and 64 are both secluded, and set against the stream leading off the Saco River.

Sites 65 through 71 are all drive-in sites situated on a short spur off the primary campground road. Sites

GETTING THERE

From North Conway, follow US 302 north into Crawford Notch and the White Mountain National Forest. The campground will be on your right, 13.5 miles past the intersection where NH 16 splits from US 302.

65 and 66 are both moderately sized, and they are very secluded from each other and from the other sites on this part of the loop. The site locations are staggered on either side of the road, so your site here won't be open to the neighboring site across the street. Plus, these sites are all carved from a dense forest.

Site 68 is a large site, and it's peppered with slightly older beech and birch trees that provide a beautiful canopy of leaves overhead. Site 69 is set well off the road, so it carries a decent sense of seclusion, even though it is also close to the toilets. Sites 70 and 71 share a parking area, but there is enough forest separating the two sites that they also share a deep-woods sense of seclusion. Site 70 is also framed by a bed of ferns that give it an almost primeval feeling. This site is a bit smaller than the others in this loop, but the scenic sense of seclusion is well worth it. Site 71 is much larger.

The rest of the sites in this loop, 72 through 75, are located along a cul-de-sac at the end of the road. Sites 74 and 75 are especially close to the water, which makes these sites preferable.

Crawford Notch is home to renowned climbing routes at Frankenstein Cliffs, hiking trails that wind past numerous waterfalls, and of course the Saco River. Whatever brings you to the area, the Crawford Notch Campground is a scenic and secluded spot to set up base camp.

DOLLY COPP
CAMPGROUND

THE **WHITE MOUNTAIN** National Forest is a paradise for camping, hiking, biking, fly-fishing, canoeing, and nearly every other outdoor pursuit: it's "The Land of Many Uses," as the Forest Service signs proclaim. All those sound like pretty good uses to me, and I'm certainly not alone. During all four seasons, a steady flow of fun-hogs pours into the Mount Washington Valley. Don't be too dismayed if it seems like everyone else in the free world is heading north with you. Many also come for the indoor activities, like outlet shopping in North Conway.

You can escape some of the crowds that may not head any farther north than the outlets by heading farther north yourself to Dolly Copp Campground. The campground is just north of Mount Washington and right off NH 16. Don't make the mistake of pulling into the Dolly Copp picnic area. The campground is another mile up the road.

Dolly Copp is a good-sized campground, and it's not crowded with sites. There are 176 sites in four separate areas within the campground, and there is plenty of room between those areas. There aren't any tent-specific areas within Dolly Copp, but there are a few areas where trailers aren't allowed. These loops are more secluded, densely forested, and perfect for pitching a tent. The only area that you would definitely want to avoid is the Big Meadow area, which includes sites 1 through 50. This area has most of the open sites where the land yachts come to drop their anchors.

A respectful distance farther up the campground access road is where you'll find the prime tent sites. Brook Loop is a great spot for tent campers. No trailers are allowed here. This loop includes sites 75 through 91. Within Brook Loop, sites 80 through 84 are in their own little miniloop that is perfect if you're camping with a large group. Even if some other folks are

> *Dolly Copp is like several small campgrounds rolled into one, with lots of cozy spots tucked into the dense forest.*

RATINGS

Beauty: ✩ ✩ ✩ ✩
Privacy: ✩ ✩ ✩ ✩
Spaciousness: ✩ ✩ ✩
Quiet: ✩ ✩ ✩ ✩
Security: ✩ ✩ ✩ ✩
Cleanliness: ✩ ✩ ✩ ✩

KEY INFORMATION

ADDRESS: Dolly Copp Campground
NH 16
Gorham, NH 03581

OPERATED BY: White Mountain National Forest

INFORMATION: Androscoggin Ranger Station
300 Glen Road
Gorham, NH 03581
(603) 466-2713

OPEN: Mid-May–mid-October

SITES: 176

EACH SITE HAS: Fire pit

ASSIGNMENT: First come, first served, or sites 29–49 by reservation: (877) 444-6777, www.reserveusa.com

REGISTRATION: At campground headquarters

FACILITIES: Flush toilets, water

PARKING: At sites

FEE: $18

RESTRICTIONS: Pets: Dogs on leash only
Fires: Fire pits only; no unattended fires
Alcohol: Sites only
Vehicles: Max 1 per site; trailers prohibited in Spruce Woods or Brook Loop

already camped out in the 80 through 84 loop, you'll still be able to experience a sense of solitude. From where you park your vehicle, you have to walk up to tent platforms for two of the sites within the loop, and down to a platform for another, so they are a bit more set off and secluded.

Spruce Woods is another great spot for tents. No trailers are allowed here, and the road is narrow and winding, so you're not likely to see any large, self-contained campers. The Spruce Woods Loop includes sites 51 through 72. As soon as you turn off into this loop, you'll feel as if you're driving deeper into the forest. The whole area is densely wooded with fir, pine, and spruce trees, so there's a nice sylvan atmosphere. The forest floor remains cool even on the sultriest summer day, and the sunlight filters down through the trees in fractured columns, adding a mystical air to the woods. Even if you have neighbors on both sides of your site, you may not be able to see them. This is my favorite section of Dolly Copp.

The only drawback to the dense forest is that you won't have a very good view of the night sky for stargazing. On a clear night, you can always take a short walk to an open area or even down to the banks of the Peabody River, which flows by just outside the campground.

There are several campground hosts who stay at the same well-marked sites throughout the season. The hosts are a good source of friendly information on campground regulations, what to do in the area, and a bit of Rockwellian local lore, if you have a moment to chat. The rangers at Dolly Copp also run various visitor programs and interpretive walks during the season. If you've come to the White Mountains for some fly-fishing, you'll be able to find quite a few secluded fishing spots on either the Peabody River or the Moose River, which is just a bit farther north (for information on fishing licenses, see Appendix C, page 224).

Then, there's the hiking. It's everywhere. Dolly Copp is a great place to set up your base camp if you have come to the White Mountains to hike Mount Washington, the rest of the Presidential Range, or anywhere within the White Mountain National Forest.

MAP

To GORHAM
To NORTH CONWAY
16
PEABODY RIVER

BIG MEADOW
19-28, 41-50

BIG MEADOW
1-18, 29-40

M. LANE
116-123
H. FIELD
125-136

BROOK
75-91
LITTLE MEADOW
92-96A

RIVERSIDE
137-160

BIRCH LANE
162-168

END LOOP

N

SPRUCE WOODS
51-74

H WOODS, H FIELD
97-109, 110-115

TOILET

Driving along the Kancamagus Highway or up NH 16, there are numerous trailheads. You can find a hike that is long, short, steep, gradual—whatever suits your mood, energy level, or the amount of time you have before heading back to the real world.

As someone who skis Tuckerman Ravine every spring, I always find myself questioning my sanity when I get a good view of the Left Gully and the rest of the ravine without snow. It's almost unthinkable that people hike up there, much less ski down.

If you come to the Mount Washington area for winter activities like mountaineering or ice climbing and you want to camp, you won't be able to camp in Dolly Copp, as it closes in mid-October. However, Barnes Field, which is right off the same access road leading into Dolly Copp, is open year-round for winter camping or for group camping in season by reservation only.

GETTING THERE

From North Conway, follow NH 16 North past the AMC Pinkham Notch Base Camp and the Mount Washington Auto Road. The campground will be on the left. From Gorham, follow NH 16 south to the campground on your right. If you come to the Mount Washington Auto Road traveling south, you've gone too far.

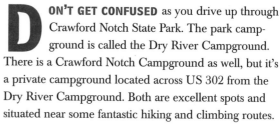

Twin Mountain

DRY RIVER CAMPGROUND

> *Dry River Campground is quiet and intimate. It's one of those campgrounds where there's really not a bad site in the whole place.*

DON'T GET CONFUSED as you drive up through Crawford Notch State Park. The park campground is called the Dry River Campground. There is a Crawford Notch Campground as well, but it's a private campground located across US 302 from the Dry River Campground. Both are excellent spots and situated near some fantastic hiking and climbing routes.

Dry River is one of those campgrounds where there's not a bad site in the place. It's a small campground set within a moderately dense forest of mixed deciduous trees. There are lots of maple, birch, and ash trees in the forest. All of the campsites are very clean and spacious. The setting in Crawford Notch doesn't hurt one bit either. From your campsite, you are minutes from dramatically beautiful and challenging trails, world-class rock climbing at Frankenstein Cliffs, and towering waterfalls. You won't run out of things to do or places to explore when staying here.

Most of the campsites are spread out along a short loop that shoots off to the left as you enter the campground. There are several sites down a short road running straight off to the right, but we'll get to those later. Sites 2 and 3 are close to each other and would make a good pair of sites for a larger group. Site 4 is set well off the campground road and is isolated, although it's close to the restroom and shower building.

No matter which site you land on here, you'll experience a sense of seclusion in a deep wilderness atmosphere. The trees open above most of the sites, which allows lots of light to filter down. Overall, Dry River's sites are laid out thoughtfully, both individually and in relation to one another. The sites aren't too densely packed together, and they fit in well with the forest character.

The campsites situated on the outside of the campground loop road provide the greatest sense of

RATINGS

Beauty: ✿ ✿ ✿ ✿ ✿
Privacy: ✿ ✿ ✿ ✿
Spaciousness: ✿ ✿ ✿ ✿
Quiet: ✿ ✿ ✿ ✿
Security: ✿ ✿ ✿ ✿ ✿
Cleanliness: ✿ ✿ ✿ ✿

seclusion. They are also a bit larger. In fact, site 12 is huge! This would be a great site if you have the five-adult maximum in your camping group. You'll have plenty of room to spread out your tents and the rest of your gear, and still have room to let the kids run around and tire themselves out.

There is simply more room to spread out on the outer side of campground loops, and there's typically more forestation between sites, which deepens the feeling of solitude. Sites 9, 11, and 16 through 21 are located on the outside of the campground loop road, and all provide a pleasant sense of isolation and spaciousness. Just past site 9, there's a trailhead for a short path down to Dry River.

One of the prettiest sites here is site 16. It's set off the campground loop road, with lots of room between it and neighboring sites. It's also the site closest to the Dry River. Between sites 18 and 19, there are trails to the Dry River Connection. From the campground, it's 0.2 miles to the Dry River, 2 miles to the Webster Cliff Trail, and 3 miles to the historic Willey House site.

Set way off on its own, site 20 is another epic spot. It's incredibly spacious and surrounded by colossal deciduous trees with a few conifers mixed in, which gives the forest a diverse and interesting character.

There is still a decent sense of solitude to site 8, even though it's probably the most open site at Dry River. It's situated right where the campground loop reconnects with itself. Sites 4 through 7 and 22 through 24 are set up along the campground road leading to the loop, but they are all well off the road for a decent sense of seclusion.

Sites 27 through 31 are closer to US 302, but they are among the nicest sites I've seen. Situated along a short spur off the road, just off to the right as you enter the campground (even before the ranger station), these sites are very spacious and very spread out.

The only site to which I wouldn't immediately gravitate is site 31, which is set at the very end of this short road. The site opens directly to the road, so anyone driving down the road would look like they're going to just drive right into your site. Still, it's very

KEY INFORMATION

ADDRESS: Dry River Campground Crawford Notch State Park P.O Box 177 US 302 Twin Mountain, NH 03595

OPERATED BY: New Hampshire Division of Parks and Recreation

INFORMATION: Crawford Notch State Park, (603) 374-2272

OPEN: Mid-May–mid-December

SITES: 36

EACH SITE HAS: Fire ring, picnic table

ASSIGNMENT: First come, first served or by reservation: (603) 271-3628, www.nhstateparks.org

REGISTRATION: At campground headquarters

FACILITIES: Hot showers, pit toilets

PARKING: At sites

FEE: $15

RESTRICTIONS: Pets: On leash only
Fires: Fire rings only
Alcohol: Sites only
Vehicles: Parking at campsites only
Other: Reservations require 2-night minimum stay; check-in 1–8 p.m., check-out by noon; quiet hours 10 p.m.–7 a.m.

MAP

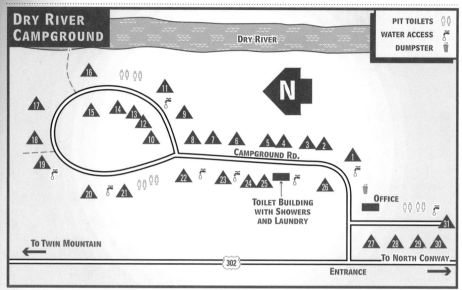

DRY RIVER CAMPGROUND

DRY RIVER

PIT TOILETS
WATER ACCESS
DUMPSTER

N

CAMPGROUND RD.

TOILET BUILDING
WITH SHOWERS
AND LAUNDRY

OFFICE

TO TWIN MOUNTAIN

TO NORTH CONWAY

302

ENTRANCE

GETTING THERE

From North Conway and Bartlett, continue north on US 302 and look for signs for the campground on the right as you head north.

spacious and otherwise isolated, so it's not that bad. The only other drawback—and this is very minor—is that these sites are closer to US 302. This can make for a bit of daytime road noise, but at night, it's as silent as the rest of the White Mountains.

The character of Dry River Campground mirrors that of its setting within Crawford Notch. There's a pleasant, diverse feel to the forest and the campground, and no matter where you end up, you'll be in an excellent spot.

HANCOCK CAMPGROUND

Lincoln

IF YOU START TRAVELING along New Hampshire's fabled Kancamagus Highway heading east, or from the Lincoln side to the Conway side, Hancock Campground is the first of the six Kancamagus campgrounds you'll encounter.

It's also one of two campgrounds along the Kancamagus that is open year-round. The other is Blackberry Crossing, at the other end of the "Kanc," as the locals call it. If you come to the Kanc for cross-country skiing or snowshoeing, or if you come to ski at nearby Loon Mountain and you want to do it on the cheap and with a dash of added adventure, pitching your tent at Hancock is the way to go.

Sites 1 through 21 are Hancock's tent-only sites. Within this tent zone, the sites that seem the most off on their own are 1, 2, 10, 12, 14, and 15. Check out these sites first to see if they're available and if they fulfill your need for solitude.

There's a central parking area situated near the two loosely spaced loops along which all the tent sites are located. You don't park right at the site as is the case with many campgrounds, so be prepared to lug in your gear a short distance. There are several areas within the Kancamagus campgrounds that have these types of sites, which are perfect for tent camping.

The tent-only sites at Hancock are moderately sized and reasonably spaced. This area also has its own restroom, located right across from the sites in the parking area, so you don't have far to walk for those times when nature calls in the middle of the night.

The rest of the campground's 56 sites are located a respectable distance from the tent-only area. You shouldn't discount these sites (22 through 56), even though you might find an RV or two. The sites are fairly spacious, and since the forest is pretty dense here, they're nicely buffered from each other, espe-

> *Hancock is open year-round for winter camping, and it's close to Lincoln—so it's a good spot to camp with kids.*

RATINGS

Beauty: ✪ ✪ ✪ ✪
Privacy: ✪ ✪ ✪
Spaciousness: ✪ ✪ ✪
Quiet: ✪ ✪ ✪ ✪
Security: ✪ ✪ ✪ ✪
Cleanliness: ✪ ✪ ✪ ✪

KEY INFORMATION

ADDRESS:	Hancock Campground Kancamagus Highway Lincoln, NH 03251
OPERATED BY:	White Mountain National Forest
INFORMATION:	Saco Ranger Station 33 Kancamagus Highway RFD 1, Box 94 Conway, NH 03818 (603) 447-5448
OPEN:	Year-round
SITES:	56
EACH SITE HAS:	Fire ring, picnic table
ASSIGNMENT:	First come, first served
REGISTRATION:	Select site, then pay at self-service fee station
FACILITIES:	Flush and vault toilets, fully plowed in winter
PARKING:	At sites or within the parking area for tent sites
FEE:	$18
RESTRICTIONS:	**Pets:** Dogs on leash only **Fires:** Fire rings only **Alcohol:** Sites only **Vehicles:** Maximum 2 per site **Other:** Maximum 8 people per site; 14-day maximum stay

cially those on the outer end of the loop (sites 35 through 40).

These sites are also set within a beautiful birch grove. The first time I visited Hancock campground was on a classic New England fall day. There wasn't a cloud in the sky, and the air was cool and dry. The sky took on a crystalline azure color. With the combination of the brilliance of the sun and the reflection of the light off the green and yellow leaves of the birch trees, the forest seemed to sparkle.

Also within this loop is where you'll find the trail-head for the short path to the East Branch of the Pemigewasset River, which is a perfect spot to drop a hook in the water (the trail departs between sites 43 and 45 on the outer side of the loop). There are also a few spots where you can drop yourself in the water, but be careful. Even late in the summer, that water can be mighty chilly. When you're looking for the path, just look beyond the trees for the looming presence of Black Mountain to the south of Hancock Campground, and you'll know you're heading in the right direction.

All of the Kancamagus campgrounds are a stone's throw from a pristine river or any number of fabulous hiking trails. It would take you most of the summer to hike them all. Hancock is certainly no different. Right across the street, there's a trail that takes you up and over Potash Knob and Big Coolidge Mountain (and all the way to Mount Flume and Mount Liberty, if you're so inclined). For a mellower hike, you can walk along the course of the Pemigewasset River.

Hancock is also the campground on the Kancamagus that is closest to civilization. At 5 miles east of Lincoln, it's close enough to run over and pick up bread, milk, batteries or anything else you may have forgotten or run out of. You could also have dinner or see a movie if you've been sleeping in a tent for several nights on end and need a little diversion.

The proximity to Lincoln makes Hancock one of the better Kancamagus campgrounds for families with small children. Kids love camping, but sometimes their tastes for dinner might include a pizza or hamburger, and if the weather hasn't been cooperative, an afternoon matinee can be just the antidote for a case of crankiness.

MAP

HANCOCK CAMPGROUND

To Lincoln ←

Kancamagus Highway   To Conway →

TOILET 👥
WATER ACCESS 🚰

PATH TO RIVER

GETTING THERE

From Lincoln, follow Kancamagus Highway to Hancock Campground on your right. It's the first campground you'll come to. From Conway, follow Kancamagus Highway to Hancock campground on your left. From this side, it will be the last campground you come to.

JIGGER **J**OHNSON is the largest campground on the Kancamagus, but with its well-spaced loops, there's plenty of room for some quality tent camping beneath the statuesque conifers of the forest. There's one tent-only loop, which has nine sites reserved for our nylon-bound brethren, but the rest of the campground has plenty of sites where you can experience an air of woodland solitude.

The tent loop is the first loop on the left, containing sites 1 through 9. These are all spacious sites set amidst the rolling contours of the forest floor. There is also a water spigot and a restroom just for this loop, so you won't have to go far for those essentials. Sites 6, 7, and 8, located at the far end of the loop, are the most spread out within the tent-only area. Whether you're only occupying one site or have come with several sites' worth of campers, head to the end of the loop first to see what's available.

If the tent loop is full, don't despair. There are plenty of other great sites throughout Jigger Johnson. Most of the sites along the northeastern end of the campground near the banks of the Swift River are spacious and set amid fairly dense forest. I especially like sites 47, 48, 50, 51, 53, 54, and 57. These have the most insular feel to them, plus they're close to the water spigots and the Swift River.

The sites on the loop to the right as you enter the campground, while a bit more out in the open, are also excellent spots. True, you run the risk of an RV lumbering up next to you, but if there are already a number of tents in the area and on either side, which is often the case, you know you'll be in for a nice night. Most of the RVs seem to gravitate toward the sites on the main road heading through the campground.

Over on the right-side loop, the shorter trees and lower brush are somewhat sparse. This does open up

RATINGS

Beauty: ✪ ✪ ✪ ✪
Privacy: ✪ ✪ ✪ ✪
Spaciousness: ✪ ✪ ✪ ✪
Quiet: ✪ ✪ ✪ ✪
Security: ✪ ✪ ✪
Cleanliness: ✪ ✪ ✪ ✪

the whole area at the ground level, but that effect combined with the towering pines that form the tall forest canopy engenders a surreal, almost mystical quality to the forest. This is particularly noticeable as dusk draws near. The sky overhead is still light, and the smoke from the campfires wafts through the trees and up to the forest canopy as darkness sneaks in beneath the pines. There's a cathedral-like atmosphere in this part of the campground in the quiet hours after dinner. The stillness is broken only by the occasional crack of a campfire.

Jigger Johnson, like the other campgrounds along the Kancamagus, is a self-serve kind of place. Enter the campground and find your perfect spot, then return to that odd-looking green cylinder, the "Iron Ranger" in Forest Service vernacular. Here's where you fill in your registration envelope, pay your fee, and slip it through the Iron Ranger's drop slot. If you need to speak with a real ranger or buy some firewood, you'll find the rangers down the road that leads off to the right just past the Iron Ranger.

This is also where you'll find the showers. Jigger Johnson is the only campground along the Kanc that has coin-operated hot showers, so don't be surprised if there are a few people waiting to clean up. There's even a little parking loop off to the left as you enter the campground for shower-seekers from the other Kanc campgrounds.

There is a series of interpretive programs on Saturday evenings throughout the summer. They focus on a particular aspect of the local flora and fauna and can be quite informative and entertaining. The rangers who present these programs truly know their stuff, and they love to share their knowledge. The programs are usually held in the small, open area off to the left as you're heading down the short road to the showers.

Jigger Johnson is located near the intersection of Bear Notch Road and the Kanc, so you could get here easily from Bartlett or from either side of the Kanc. If you run out of something, it's 9 miles to Bartlett and 13 miles to Conway.

The campground is also very close to some classic White Mountain hiking. Turn left out of the camp-

KEY INFORMATION

ADDRESS: Jigger Johnson Campground 33 Kancamagus Highway Albany, NH 03818

OPERATED BY: White Mountain National Forest

INFORMATION: Saco Ranger Station 33 Kancamagus Highway RFD 1, Box 94 Conway, NH 03818 (603) 447-5448

OPEN: Mid May– mid-October

SITES: 75

EACH SITE HAS: Fire ring, picnic table

ASSIGNMENT: First come, first served

REGISTRATION: Select site, then pay at self-service fee station

FACILITIES: Pay showers, flush toilets, water spigots

PARKING: At sites

FEE: $18

RESTRICTIONS: Pets: Dogs on leash only
Fires: Fire rings only
Alcohol: Sites only
Vehicles: Maximum 2 per site
Other: Maximum 8 people per site; 14 - day maximum stay

MAP

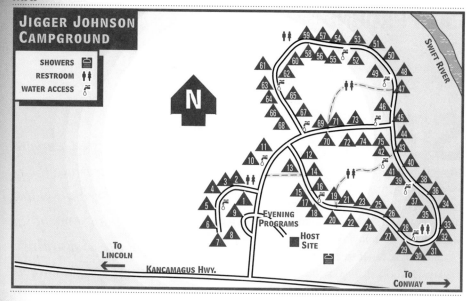

JIGGER JOHNSON CAMPGROUND

SHOWERS
RESTROOM
WATER ACCESS

N

SWIFT RIVER

To
LINCOLN ←

To
CONWAY →

KANCAMAGUS HWY.

EVENING PROGRAMS

HOST SITE

GETTING THERE

From Lincoln, follow the Kancamagus Highway to Jigger Johnson Campground on your left. From Conway, follow the Kancamagus Highway to Jigger Johnson Campground on your right, shortly after Bear Notch Road, also on the right.

ground to get to trailheads for the Champney Falls Trail (which leads to the Three Sisters and the Middle Sister trail) or the Bolles Trail. Turn right on the Kanc out of Jigger Johnson to get to the Oliverian Brook, Downes Brook, Sabbaday Brook, or Sawyer Pond trails. Pack a few extra energy bars and plenty of water if you embark on a hike up the Champney Falls or Middle Sister trails. These lead to Mount Chocourua and the Three Sisters, a beautiful but intense hike.

You can enjoy some great hikes leaving right out of the campground as well—no driving required! The trail that leads down to the banks of the Swift River intersects with a trail that runs along the backside of the campground. This mellow path follows the Swift both upstream and downstream for a distance, passing by some beautiful bends in the river and through delightfully aromatic groves of birch and pine. It's a great hike to take with kids, because it's relatively flat and there are all sorts of wonderful things to see and experience. Kids can spend hours poking around the banks of the Swift River, and despite its name, this segment of the river is usually fairly tame.

LAFAYETTE CAMPGROUND

SIMPLY BY VIRTUE of its location, Lafayette Campground is worth inclusion in this guidebook. The fact that it's a super campground makes it that much better. Lafayette is nestled in the base of the Franconia Valley. As you drive up the Franconia Notch Parkway toward the campground, your view is framed by Cannon Mountain to the left and Mount Lafayette to the right.

Franconia Notch is a veritable sculpture garden displaying works shaped by the forces of nature. From the glaciers that carved the landscape millions of years ago to the tenacious and incessant wind and water, the lay of the land here is as dramatic as anywhere else in New Hampshire. From the waterfalls of the Flume Gorge and the swirling pools of the Basin to the Old Man of the Mountain and Indian Head formations presiding over the eastern flanks of the Presidential range, you could spend weeks here before retracing your steps.

The notch is also headquarters for just about any outdoor activity. There's fly-fishing at nearby Echo Lake (for information on fishing licenses, see Appendix C, page 224); a bike path that winds along the base of the notch; and some fantastic treks for hikers of any ability. Right from the campground, the Lonesome Lake Trail takes you 1,000 feet above the floor of the notch to Lonesome Lake. The trailhead for the 1.5-mile hike is near the entrance to the campground.

There's also a trailhead over between sites 67 and 68 that leads to the Basin. From the Basin, you could hike up to Kinsman Falls on Cascade Brook. Follow the half-mile Basin Cascades Trail from the Basin to reach this beautiful and secluded spot.

Lafayette Campground is set beneath a fairly dense forest of conifers and hardwoods. Sites 1 through 51 are available only by reservation, so if you haven't

> *Lafayette Campground is tucked into the valley of Franconia Notch, home to some of the White Mountains' most spectacular hiking and mountain vistas.*

RATINGS

Beauty: ✩ ✩ ✩ ✩
Privacy: ✩ ✩ ✩
Spaciousness: ✩ ✩ ✩ ✩
Quiet: ✩ ✩ ✩
Security: ✩ ✩ ✩
Cleanliness: ✩ ✩ ✩ ✩

KEY INFORMATION

ADDRESS: Lafayette
Campground
Franconia Notch
State Park
Franconia Notch
Parkway
Franconia, NH 03580

OPERATED BY: New Hampshire
Division of Parks
and Recreation

INFORMATION: Lafayette Campground, (603) 823-
9513

OPEN: Mid-May–
Columbus Day

SITES: 98 sites

EACH SITE HAS: Fire ring, picnic
table

ASSIGNMENT: First come, first
served or by reser-
vation for sites 1–51:
(603) 271-3628, www.
nhstateparks.org

REGISTRATION: At campground
headquarters

FACILITIES: Hot showers, flush
toilets, water

PARKING: At sites

FEE: $16

RESTRICTIONS: Pets: Prohibited
Fires: Fire rings only
Alcohol: Sites only
Vehicles: Parking at
sites only
Other: Reservations
require 2-night mini-
mum stay; check-in
1–8 p.m., check-out
by noon; quiet hours
10 p.m.–7 a.m.

made one, start your search at site 52 and work your way up.

The sites numbered in the upper 40s are very spacious. The forest overhead is open to the sky, which lets a lot of sunlight filter down through to the floor of the campsites. Sites 47 and 49 are too open. These sites are also situated right along the campground road. Site 50 is open and set right on the road, but it also has the Pemigewasset River running along behind it. Site 51, across the campground road from 50, is also very exposed to the road.

Farther down the campground road on this side, site 52 is a secluded site. It's set off the road and also has the Pemigewasset running along behind it. The platform where you'd set up your tent and a picnic table are set down a bit lower than the road, which adds a degree of seclusion.

The Lonesome Lake Trail runs between sites 53 and 54. Sites 54, 56, and 57 are open and have little privacy from each other or the neighboring sites. Sites 56 and 58 would be good pair of sites for a larger group needing two contiguous sites. There is a bit of road noise in the background in this part of the campground from the Franconia Notch Parkway. This decreases as you get farther back from the road and deeper into the woods.

There's a nice sense of seclusion between sites 61 and 63 and the neighboring sites. These two sites are also quite spacious. Sites 64 and 66 make another good pair of sites well suited for a large group. They are also situated right along the banks of the Pemigewasset, which defines the eastern border of the campground.

Both the ground cover and the forest canopy are less dense in this corner of the campground, so there's a spacious and sunlit character to sites 58 through 70. Lots of breeze flows through here.

A huge maple tree grows up through the center of site 88. This spacious site is set up on the outside of the campground loop. It's fairly well isolated from the sites on either side, but it's a bit open to the road.

Set off the campground road on a small rise and surrounded by a fairly dense grove of young deciduous trees, site 97 provides a nice sense of

LAFAYETTE CAMPGROUND

SHOWERS
RESTROOM
WATER ACCESS
PARKING
WHEELCHAIR ACCESSIBLE
PUBLIC PHONE
PICNIC AREA

LONESOME LAKE TRAIL

PEMIGEWASSET RIVER

RECREATIONAL TRAIL

N

FRANCONIA NOTCH PARKWAY

To 93

LAFAYETTE LODGE (STORE)

TO PROFILE LAKE

VISITOR CENTER

RECREATIONAL TRAIL

WALKING TUNNEL UNDER ROAD

seclusion. However, it's right across the road from the restrooms. Sites 92 and 94 are too open, and 94 is also next to the restroom building on the same side of the road. The Lonesome Lake Trail runs through the campground between sites 93 and 95 on one side of the road and sites 92 and 94 on the other, so these would be good sites to choose if you wanted to be right on the trail; but expect passers-by.

The area with sites 73 through 78 is pleasant. These sites feel a bit more set off than some of the sites on the outside of the campground loop. Site 73 is very spacious, open, and sunny. Site 76 is a bit more shaded. Site 75 is also bright, airy, and framed by a wall of maple trees. Alas, site 79 is too close to the restrooms.

Now, back to the reservation-only sites. Perched at an odd little intersection of the campground loop roads, site 43 has lots of woods surrounding it with no neighbors on either side. By virtue of its location, this site provides seclusion. Sites 40 and 29 are also at odd angles in this three-way intersection, but consequently they provide decent privacy. Site 29 is very open and

GETTING THERE

Follow Interstate 93 north to the Franconia Notch Parkway. This is a divided highway, so you'll actually drive past the campground and take the next exit off the parkway, then head south. From there, follow the signs for the campground on the right as you head south.

sunny, with large granite boulders framing the back border of the site.

Sites 36 and 37 are set up for wheelchair access. These are large sites set within a grove of fairly dense, mixed forest. Site 27 is very spacious, but it's a bit too open and is set right on the campground loop road.

Set in the woods around a small grassy field, there's a nice, open, pastoral sense to sites 22 through 26. They are a bit open and not quite as private as the more densely wooded sites, but scenic nonetheless. Sites 20 and 21 are also on the outside edge of this open field. Site 21 is a tiny site wedged in between sites 20 and 22, almost as if it were an afterthought.

There's an open, yet secluded sense to site 17, set on a small rise overlooking the field through a loosely spaced grove of young deciduous trees. Sites 15 and 16 are group sites. Right on the grassy field, these are wide-open prairie camping. There's no privacy, but you'd have plenty of room for a group, and a clear shot at the sky for stargazing. Sites 18 and 19 are close to the restrooms, but tucked into the woods a bit deeper for a decent sense of seclusion. Within this group, sites 11 and 12 are also a bit too close to the restrooms.

The small loop with sites 1 through 10 also surrounds a small grassy field. These areas make great spots to let kids run around, throw a Frisbee, or otherwise burn off some steam while you're relaxing. Sites 7 through 10 are quite nice. They are spacious, open, and fairly well isolated from neighbors. Sites 5 and 6 and sites 1 and 3 would make good pairs of sites for larger groups, as they are open to each other. If you didn't know your neighbors before setting up camp here, you would shortly thereafter.

There's a small amphitheater and rows of benches at the entrance to the 1 through 10 loop where the rangers run nature programs. Check with them as you register to find out what's on the schedule.

MOUNT MONADNOCK STATE PARK

Jaffrey

MOUNT MONADNOCK is renowned as the most frequently climbed mountain in the world, a distinction that used to belong to Mt. Fuji in Japan. On warm, summer weekend days, there is often a veritable conga line of hikers making their way up the fabulous White Dot Trail or any of the other classic routes to the bald, treeless summit. Its popularity, however, does nothing to detract from its allure and magnificence.

Why do so many people flock to Monadnock? For one thing, perched as it is in the southwestern corner of New Hampshire, it's fairly accessible from most of southern New Hampshire, northern Massachusetts, and eastern Vermont. It's a moderate hike, certainly when compared to some of the longer or steeper hikes you'll find farther north in the New Hampshire's White Mountains or Vermont's Green Mountains. But the most predominant attraction has to be the view from Monadnock's summit. It is absolutely huge. It's expansive. It's a sweeping, panoramic view that extends in every direction as far as you can see, which is pretty far when the air is clear and sun is brilliant.

You see nearby Dublin Lake and the gently rolling and densely forested topography of southern New England. Small towns here and there punctuate the undulating coniferous carpet. The unfettered views from Monadnock's summit are a product of Monadnock's history. It appears to poke above the tree line, but at 3,165 feet, it's really not quite tall enough. The mountain owes its treeless summit to settlers in the early 1900s who burned off the forest at the peak in an effort to control the local wolf population. Such maneuvers to direct the forces of nature rarely work, but it has resulted in Mount Monadnock going prematurely bald.

While the day crowds at the mountain may seem a bit overwhelming, once they've returned home for

> *Mount Monadnock State Park is the perfect launch pad for your southern New Hampshire hiking adventures.*

RATINGS

Beauty: ✩ ✩ ✩ ✩
Privacy: ✩ ✩ ✩
Spaciousness: ✩ ✩ ✩ ✩
Quiet: ✩ ✩ ✩ ✩
Security: ✩ ✩ ✩ ✩
Cleanliness: ✩ ✩ ✩ ✩ ✩

ADDRESS: Mount Monadnock
State Park
P.O. Box 181
NH 124
Jaffrey, NH
03452-0181

OPERATED BY: New Hampshire
Division of Parks
and Recreation

INFORMATION: Mount Monadnock
State Park, (603) 532-
8862

OPEN: Year-round; campground not plowed
in winter; reserva-
tions taken mid-
May–Columbus Day

SITES: 21 individual sites, 7
group sites

EACH SITE HAS: Fire ring, picnic
table

ASSIGNMENT: First come, first
served or by reserva-
tion: (603) 271-3628,
www.nhstateparks.
org

REGISTRATION: At campground
headquarters

FACILITIES: Coin-operated showers, flush toilets,
vault toilets, camp
store, water spigots

PARKING: At sites; additional
parking available

FEE: $15

RESTRICTIONS: Pets: Prohibited
Fires: Fire rings only
Alcohol: Sites only
Vehicles: Sites only
Other: Reservations
require 2-night mini-
mum stay; check-in
1–8 p.m., check-out
by noon; quiet hours
10 p.m.–7 a.m.

the night, you and a small group of campers will have the park and the campground at the mountain's base to yourselves. The campground is fairly small, with 21 individual and 7 group sites. As you enter the park, you pass the ranger's toll station. Here, you instantly discover the park's primary restriction if you happen to have a four-legged member of the family in your car. There are no dogs allowed at the campground or any-where within Mount Monadnock State Park. Assuming you're not breaking that most sacred of rules, continue into the park. The campground is just up the road off to the right.

Most of the sites within this campground are avail-able by reservation only. The letter-designated sites, A through G, are the group sites. These are available exclusively by reservation. This poses an interesting predicament, as some of the nicer sites, in my view, are the nonreservable sites. You could wing it and try your luck getting one of these sites. If fortune smiles, you'll have a grand camping experience. However, you could also find the campground full to capacity, which is a very real possibility considering the traffic this state park gets during the summer.

Even though the campground is right off the road leading into the park (near the day parking for hikers, the camp store, and the primary trailhead for getting onto the mountain), you'll still feel as if you've left all that behind when you turn into the campground. Heading right on the campground loop road brings you to sites 6 through 8. These are tucked off on their own and provide a sense of isolation. The forest of mixed conifers, birch, and other hardwoods is fairly dense here, so you still feel as if the woods are sur-rounding you and your campsite. Site 14 is another of the nonreservable sites that's tucked into its own grove of trees. All of these sites on the outer side of the campground have a bit more space in between.

Mount Monadnock State Park is a great spot to come with a group for some weekend hiking. The sites designated for group camping are quite lovely, and I'd be thrilled to spend a few nights in one with a band of hiking compadres. Site C is one of the better group sites. It's set against a gently sloping hill within a grove

MONADNOCK STATE PARK CAMPGROUND

RESERVOIR

CABIN

HIKERS CABIN

VISITOR CENTER

N

OPEN SHELTER
STORE

TOLL HOUSE

1
2
3
5
4
6
9
10
7
8
11
12
13
14
15
16
18
17
19
21
20
F
G
A
B
C
D
E

SHOWERS
FLUSH TOILET
PIT TOILET
WATER ACCESS
PARKING
GROUP SITE

To
DUBLIN

of loosely spaced, homogenous pine trees. Site D is another beautiful site that also sits within its own pine grove. There's a stand of young white pines lining the perimeter like a vigilant group of sentries. All of the group sites have two picnic tables (the individual sites have one), which is a thoughtful setup since in these sites, you'll certainly have more people needing a place to sit.

There are numerous vault toilets spread throughout the campground, so you'll never have to amble too far when nature calls. If you prefer, there are also flush toilets located just outside the campground. There are several water fountains, but when you need to fill your drinking-water bottles, there's a spring up on the mountain not too far from the campground. Assemble the troops and take a short hike up the White Dot Trail to the spring, just below the junction where the Spruce Link trail veers off to the left. Treat yourself to some cold, crystal-clear, mountain spring water.

Ah yes, the hiking. There is a plethora of hiking trails winding their way through Monadnock State Park, all leading up, over, and around the mountain.

GETTING THERE

Follow NH 101 to Dublin. If heading west on 101, take the Jaffrey Center Road on the left after going through town. There's a sign for Mount Monadnock State Park. Heading east on 101, take the Jaffrey Center Road on the right, after Dublin Lake and before downtown Dublin. Follow this road for several miles to the campground on the right.

The White Dot Trail is the most popular route up to the summit—an easy-to-moderate hike of about 90 minutes to the peak. The White Cross Trail, which forks off the White Dot Trail just past the Spruce Link Trail, is another good option. Both have a few spots where you're doing a little hand-over-hand scrambling up and over the rocks. Both also pass across a couple of open ledges on the way up, where you'll get your first taste of the sweeping vistas.

From the summit, and from several other trails leading off the mountain in all directions, you could hike as far as Mount Sunapee if you're so inclined. That brings up a point about directions. If you're coming into the park from Dublin on the Dublin road, you'll see two places marked as Mount Monadnock State Park. The first is the trailhead for the Birchtoft Trail. Don't turn in here—keep going another half mile or so to the main part of the park and the campground. Keep the location of that trailhead in mind, though. If you want to try a longer route to the summit of Monadnock, the Birchtoft Trail is a fantastic hike.

Mount Monadnock does get a lot of hikers, but there's always a bit of the mountain with a good view that you can have all to yourself, just for the moment.

PASSACONAWAY CAMPGROUND

THE SITES WITHIN Passaconaway Campground are all quite spacious. This can be both a blessing and a curse. Of all the campgrounds along the Kancamagus, Passaconaway is probably most conducive to RVs. They are neither catered to (no hookups) nor excluded, but many of the smaller campsites at the other Kancamagus campgrounds naturally keep out the land yachts just by virtue of their size or shape.

On the other hand, the spaciousness of the Passaconaway sites makes them well suited to larger groups or families that need a little extra breathing room. The relatively central location along the Kancamagus Highway also puts you in a convenient spot if you're not sure what part of the Kanc you want to explore. You'll be close to Rocky Gorge, Sabbaday Falls, the Swift River picnic area, and the myriad trailheads spread along the length of this superlative stretch of road.

The forest separating the individual sites at Passaconaway is fairly dense, so even if an RV or a larger group plunks down next to you, you won't see all that much of them. There is lots of undergrowth, which provides seclusion and adds to the silence of the woods. Besides spacious sites, quiet is a prevailing attribute of Passaconaway. All you'll hear is an occasional vehicle zipping past on the Kanc and the soft rush of the wind in the evergreens, punctuated by the chatter of the forest birds and animals.

There are two loops in which the sites are situated. Sites 1 through 11 are in the loop off to the right as you enter the campground. Sites 12 through 33 are in the loop off to the left. The campsites are carved out of a dense forest of mostly coniferous trees, casting a cool, dark, shade over the campground.

At the beginning of the 1 through 11 loop, sites 2, 3, and 11 are too open and close to the restrooms. Sites 5 through 11 are set along the outer edge of the loop

> *Passaconaway is a relatively small campground with spacious sites carved out of a dense evergreen forest.*

RATINGS

Beauty: ✿ ✿ ✿ ✿
Privacy: ✿ ✿ ✿ ✿
Spaciousness: ✿ ✿ ✿ ✿ ✿
Quiet: ✿ ✿ ✿ ✿ ✿
Security: ✿ ✿ ✿ ✿
Cleanliness: ✿ ✿ ✿ ✿

ADDRESS: Passaconaway
Campground
Kancamagus
Highway
Bartlett, NH 03818

OPERATED BY: White Mountain
National Forest

INFORMATION: Saco Ranger Station
33 Kancamagus
Highway
RFD 1, Box 94
Conway, NH 03818
(603) 447-5448

OPEN: Mid-May–
mid-October

SITES: 33

EACH SITE HAS: Fire ring, picnic
table

ASSIGNMENT: First come, first
served

REGISTRATION: Select site, then pay
at self-service fee
station

FACILITIES: Vault toilets, hand
pumps for water

PARKING: At sites

FEE: $16

RESTRICTIONS: **Pets:** Dogs on leash
only
Fires: Fire rings only
Alcohol: Sites only
Vehicles: Maximum
2 per site
Other: Maximum 8
people per site; 14 -
day maximum stay

off to the right. These sites, mostly by virtue of their location on the outside of the loop, provide the greatest sense of solitude. There's simply more room between the sites.

My favorite site on this loop, and one of the best in the campground, is site 10. This site is set off on its own, with plenty of space between the neighboring sites on either side. It's also farther off the campground loop road for an enhanced sense of isolation.

In the 12 through 33 loop, the forest is even more dense than in the 1 through 11 loop. This side of the campground is comprised primarily of pines and maples, many towering around 80 feet. A moderately dense understory fills in the forest picture and adds to the seclusion between individual campsites. In this loop, sites 13, 14, and 15 are close to the restroom.

The sites on this loop are located both along the inside and outside of the campground road. There's a small picnic area near site 13. There are pros and cons to this. It's a nice place to have the kids running around close to the campsite, but it could also tend to be a bit noisy during the day. Like many of life's decisions, whether or not you choose this site will probably be dictated by the presence of little ones.

There's a trailhead right next to site 18. From Passaconaway Campground, you are near several hiking trails suitable for all ability levels. There is the long but not too steep Sawyer Pond Trail, plus the shorter but steeper Downes Brook, Sabbaday Brook, and Oliverian Brook trails across the Kanc.

The campground host is located at site 19. This is a good place to stop if you need a suggestion on daytime activities, or just to catch a bit of local lore.

The sites numbered in the lower 20s are generally a bit smaller than the rest of Passaconaway's spacious sites and are packed in more tightly. In this group, you're closer to your neighbors and sacrifice a modicum of privacy and quiet, but you're also less likely to have an RV land nearby. Still, there is a decent amount of forest buffering these sites.

Huge maples frame sites 22 and 23. There are also massive maples growing up within the sites themselves. You are camping among magnificent trees.

MAP

PASSACONAWAY
CAMPGROUND

N

RESTROOM
WATER ACCESS
PICNIC AREA

To
LINCOLN

KANCAMAGUS HWY.

To
CONWAY

There's a short hike in to site 24 from where you park. Site 24 is the key site here at Passaconaway. The distance from the campground loop road lends it a deep sense of seclusion.

Site 29 is way too close to the restroom. Sites 31 and 33 are very open to the road.

Considering Passaconaway's central location on the Kanc, it's a fine spot to set up camp, especially if you are able to secure site 10 or site 24.

GETTING THERE

Passaconaway Campground is almost in the center of the Kancamagus Highway. From Lincoln, follow the Kancamagus Highway for 16 miles to Passaconaway Campground on the left. From Conway, follow Kancamagus Highway for 15 miles to Passaconaway Campground on the right.

Nottingham

PAWTUCKAWAY
STATE PARK

> " *The campground at Pawtuckaway State Park has a lot of sites— many right on the shores of Lake Pawtuckaway.* "

RATINGS

Beauty: ✿ ✿ ✿ ✿
Privacy: ✿ ✿ ✿ ✿
Spaciousness: ✿ ✿ ✿ ✿
Quiet: ✿ ✿ ✿
Security: ✿ ✿ ✿ ✿
Cleanliness: ✿ ✿ ✿ ✿

THERE ARE CAMPSITES at Pawtuckaway State Park that give you the atmosphere of island camping with the ease of car camping. It's a big place, with 195 sites, but the three separate camping areas feel like individual campgrounds.

Horse Island has many of the best sites within the campground—that is to say, the most sites right on the shores of Pawtuckaway Lake. Big Island has some pristine waterview sites, but most of the sites in this area are located inland. Neal's Cove is located near the store, the beach, and the group camping area. These sites, because of their proximity to the beach and playground, are great for families with kids.

Horse Island is home to sites 1 through 80. The island is covered in a fairly dense forest, which lends a woodland feel and sense of privacy to most of these sites. The forest is composed of mixed hardwoods and, predominantly, conifers, which fill in the forest and provide a cool, dark stillness and seclusion. The sites themselves are clean and spacious, and most have a firm, sandy surface on which to pitch your tent.

The top-notch Horse Island waterfront sites include 38 and 42 through 47. Swimming is not permitted from campsites because there is a considerable amount of boat traffic in the lake, especially on the weekends. But you could easily launch a canoe or kayak right from your site. Swimming is allowed in the beach and boat-launch areas.

While site 48 is situated near an intersection of the campground road, its lakeside setting more than compensates for any traffic that may pass by. Sites 74, 75, and 77 also have nice lakeside settings.

The cluster of sites 65 through 70 is grouped at one end of Horse Island. These sites also have dramatic, lakeside settings. Sites 67 through 69 are perched on their own peninsula jutting out from the southeastern end of the island. If your group is large enough to need three sites and you secure these, you will be set.

There is a boat launch and lake access right near sites 58, 60, 62, and 63. These are perfect sites if you like to begin or end your day with a blissful paddle on the still waters of the sleepy lake. Sites 53, 54, and 55 are also primo lakeside spots. These sites are set within loosely spaced forest right on the shore, which allows for dramatic views, cool breezes, and shafts of sunlight. I have no real evidence to support this, but these lakeside sites seemed less buggy than the inland sites.

Sites 1, 2, and 25 are right off the campground road leading onto Horse Island, but they have a decent sense of seclusion, as they are all tucked down off the road amidst a dense grove of spruce. Sites 4 and 7 are nicely isolated and set down off the campground loop road facing a small cove. These sites are in a dense spruce grove, where the forest floor gently rolls down to the lakeside. The main body of the lake is around the corner, so it's quieter here as you're removed from the primary thoroughfare through Pawtuckaway Lake. The lake can get pretty heavily populated with ski boats, Jet Skis, and other vessels making more noise than the rhythmic splash of a kayak or canoe paddle.

The sites numbered in the teens are set beneath a loose forest and within view of a small cove. The water is often peaceful and quiet here, but does get stirred up during the day. Site 21 is on the water and has a perfectly flat, easy access for launching a canoe or kayak. This site is a paddler's dream. Sites 26 and 27 are isolated from both the road and from other sites, but they are close to each other. They would make a good pair of sites for a larger family or group.

The Big Island (like Hawaii) section of Pawtuckaway State Park is home to sites 81 through 169. Sites 96 through 169 are available by reservation only. The first-come, first-served sites are spacious and set within fairly dense forest. A couple of the sites on the left as you enter the Big Island area have steep driveways.

Overall, Big Island is hillier than the rest of the campground. There are many sites with steep entries up

KEY INFORMATION

ADDRESS:	Pawtuckaway State Park 128 Mountain Road Nottingham, NH 03290
OPERATED BY:	New Hampshire Division of Parks and Recreation
INFORMATION:	Pawtuckaway State Park, (603) 895-3031
OPEN:	Mid-May–Columbus Day (Neals Cove and Big Island close after Labor Day weekend)
SITES:	195
EACH SITE HAS:	Fire ring, picnic table
ASSIGNMENT:	First come, first served or by reservation: (603) 271-3628, www.nhstateparks.org
REGISTRATION:	At campground headquarters
FACILITIES:	Flush toilets, coin-operated hot showers, water spigots, boat launch, canoe and paddle boat rentals
PARKING:	At sites
FEE:	$16–$22 for premium water sites
RESTRICTIONS:	Pets: On leash only Fires: Fire rings only Alcohol: Sites only Vehicles: Parking at campsites only, maximum 2 vehicles per site Other: Reservations require 2-night minimum stay; check-in 1–8 p.m., check-out by noon; quiet hours 10 p.m.–7 a.m.

MAP

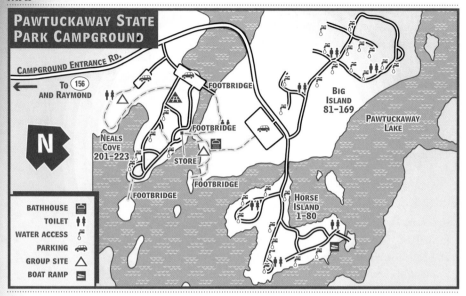

PAWTUCKAWAY STATE PARK CAMPGROUND

CAMPGROUND ENTRANCE RD.

← To 156 AND RAYMOND

N

FOOTBRIDGE

FOOTBRIDGE

NEALS COVE 201–223

STORE

FOOTBRIDGE

FOOTBRIDGE

BIG ISLAND 81–169

PAWTUCKAWAY LAKE

HORSE ISLAND 1–80

BATHHOUSE
TOILET
WATER ACCESS
PARKING
GROUP SITE
BOAT RAMP

GETTING THERE

Follow NH 101 to NH 156 in Raymond. Follow NH 156 to Mountain Road, and then follow the signs for the park.

or down from the road. Keep that in mind as you select a site, as this is especially true of sites 164 through 169.

RVs and trailers are not prohibited from the sites on Horse Island or Big Island, but those steep, twisty, or narrow entries leading into the sites would preclude one of these behemoths plunking down next to you. Some sites are more open than others, but for the most part, access (or lack thereof) is your best friend.

The Big Island sites are also fairly well isolated from each other, especially sites 162 and 163. These two are situated at the end of a short spur off the campground road, and set within a dense forest of mixed hardwoods and evergreens.

Sites 90 through 93 sit within a deep, dark spruce forest. After site 93, the forest shifts to more deciduous trees. Walking through the campground road past these sites, it can feel like someone just turned on the lights. You move from the dense, dark spruce forest to the more open and brilliant green deciduous forest.

Big Island doesn't have as many waterview sites, but it does have some. Site 108 gets you back on the water. Sites 113 through 118, in their own little loop, all

**PAWTUCKAWAY STATE PARK:
BIG ISLAND CAMPGROUND**

TOILET
WATER

N

PAWTUCKAWAY
LAKE

have an unfettered view of the lake and access to launch a canoe or kayak.

The most desirable site within this section is site 122. Feel free to request this site, unless, of course, I happen to be traveling to Pawtuckaway that day. Or in that case, you can still request it. We'll just have to share the site, which shouldn't be a problem since it's absolutely huge.

Site 122 already booked? Not to worry. There are plenty of other great sites in this part of the campground and the 123 through 133 loop. Sites 130 and 133 are well isolated at the end of this loop. Site 131, on the other hand, is too open. It looks like you could drive right through the site if you didn't know it was there. The sites in this corner of the campground are set beneath an open deciduous forest, so there's a light and open feel.

At the end of the 134 through 146 loop, sites 141 through 143 are secluded in their own little cluster. Sites 141 and 142 are actually quite close together, but well situated for a group needing two contiguous sites. Sites 150 through 152 are set off the road and secluded. Site 96 is perched off an intersection of the road to

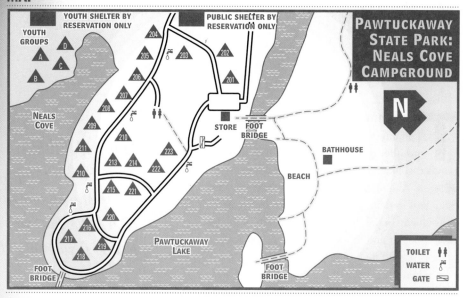

sites 150 through 154, but the site is isolated by the dense forest and is quite large.

Neals Cove is actually the first camping area you come to on the 2-mile access road leading into Pawtuckaway State Park. Most of these sites are smaller, but they're carved out of dense forest—so what they lack in spaciousness, they make up for in seclusion. There's an inland feel as you enter this part of the campground, even though you're still close to the lake. The beach, camp store, picnic area, reservation-only group-camping areas, playground, and baseball field are also near Neals Cove.

Within this part of the campground, sites 206 and up are set along the water within a loosely spaced forest for dramatic water views and some nice breezes cooling your campsite. Site 221 is somewhat open to the road but is set beneath a thick, statuesque spruce grove. The towering spruce trees populating the forest at Neals Cove give the woods a majestic feel. There's a footbridge right next to site 218 leading onto another small island. This island doesn't have any campsites, but it's a perfect spot to hike out with a lunch, or to just sit and watch the lake at dawn or dusk.

PILLSBURY STATE PARK

Washington

THE WOODS AND THE WATER make a powerful combination. Pillsbury State Park has both in just the right proportions—a series of crystalline ponds cast like scattered jewels against a dense blanket of forest. Although it's part of the New Hampshire State Park system, Pillsbury is a little-known gem. It rests quietly in the deep forest just south of the far more popular and more frequently visited Sunapee State Park, and that's just fine.

When I first entered this campground, I was immediately struck with a moral dilemma. "Do I really want to tell anyone else about this place?" I didn't ruminate on this thought for long, though. After considering the proclivities and desires of a reader would naturally seek out magical spots like this, I had to include Pillsbury State Park. There is not a bad site in the whole place, and many of the sites are elevated to paradise status—especially those at the water's edge.

As soon as you pull into the lengthy access road, which winds first along the shores of Butterfield Pond and then May Pond, you'll know you've found someplace special. If you've come to fully immerse yourself in the solitude of the deep wilderness, you have most definitely come to the right place. The campsites are spread out along this road, either alone or in clusters. Most are right on or very close to the shores of May Pond. Several are inland, tucked into the dense forest that surrounds the ponds and marshy areas in the park.

The first sites you'll come to are 1 and 1A, off the main access road to the left at the end of a short drive. You can park at site 1, but 1A is a walk-in site. These are the only two sites on the shores of Vickery Pond, one of the smaller ponds in the park. Want to be off by yourself? Bring a small group, even just two couples, you'll have this pond to yourself.

> *Many of Pillsbury State Park's campsites are so spread out from each other that you'll feel as if you have the campground to yourself.*

RATINGS

Beauty: ✿ ✿ ✿ ✿ ✿
Privacy: ✿ ✿ ✿ ✿ ✿
Spaciousness: ✿ ✿ ✿ ✿ ✿
Quiet: ✿ ✿ ✿ ✿ ✿
Security: ✿ ✿ ✿ ✿ ✿
Cleanliness: ✿ ✿ ✿ ✿ ✿

KEY INFORMATION

ADDRESS: Pillsbury State Park
NH 31
Washington, NH
03280

OPERATED BY: New Hampshire
Division of Parks
and Recreation

INFORMATION: Pillsbury State Park
(603) 863-2810

OPEN: Early May–
Columbus Day

SITES: 41 sites, including 2
canoe sites

EACH SITE HAS: Fire ring

ASSIGNMENT: First come, first
served or by reser-
vation: (603) 271-
3628, www.nhstate
parks.org; all but 11
sites reservable

REGISTRATION: At campground
headquarters

FACILITIES: Pit toilet, water spigots, playground,
canoe rentals

PARKING: At sites, or small
parking areas for
lug-in or canoe sites

FEE: $13

RESTRICTIONS: Pets: Dogs on leash
only
Fires: Fire rings only
Alcohol: Sites only
Vehicles: Parking at
or near campsites;
maximum 2 vehicles
per site
Other: Reservations
require 2-night mini-
mum stay; check-in
1–8 p.m., check-out
by noon; quiet hours
10 p.m.–7 a.m.

Next along the main road is site 2. Although this site is right off the access road, it is also completely on its own. This is another great site to choose if you want to enjoy waterfront camping in relative solitude. Site 2 is perched on the shore of Butterfield Pond. The only other site on this pond is site 39, which is on the other side of the pond and is accessible only by canoe or kayak.

Sites 3 through 7 are grouped together in a small cluster farther up the road on the right. These are set on a small peninsula that helps define the border between Butterfield Pond and May Pond. There is also a pair of pit toilets here. Farther along the road, also waterside, is the small loop with sites 9 through 19. These sites are within the largest and most densely packed cluster of sites in the park, but even these are quite nice. Within this loop, go for sites 11, 12, and 14, as they are right on the shores of May Pond. Site 15 is pretty darn close to the pond as well.

Toward the end of the campground road are sites 23, 24, 26, and 40. At site 40, you park across from a footbridge over a small stream. Cross the bridge and turn right on the footpath that leads down to site 40, nestled on the shoreline of the pond. It is worth every trip to the car. You'll have your own slice of forest right on your own corner of the pond.

If you're a paddler, do what you can to reserve either site 38 or 39. These are the canoe- or kayak-accessible sites. It's just a short paddle across May Pond to site 38 or Butterfield Pond to site 39. Then you'll feel as if you're camping on an island, and you'll have your canoe or kayak right there to explore both of the interconnected ponds. Some of the same consid-erations of island camping apply here, besides the pack-in, pack-out ethic. Be sure you have brought everything you need. A trip back to your vehicle will take some effort.

Besides the paddling, wildlife viewing, and relax-ing, there is a massive network of hiking trails winding through Pillsbury State Park. The park and its trails are part of the Monadnock-Sunapee Greenway, a 51-mile route that connects the two peaks. It's sort of like a mini–Appalachian Trail.

The Monadnock-Sunapee Trail is the main thoroughfare here. You could get quite far along the trail, so set a predetermined turnaround time to leave yourself enough light to make it back to camp. The peaks of Kittredge Lovewell Mountains, both within Pillsbury State Park, are fun day hikes from the campground on this trail. The Ayers Pond Trail is a long route that ultimately (and unsurprisingly) leads out to Ayers Pond.

Back at camp, the mirror-like surface of a pond will reflect the last light of the day. You may be treated to the sight of a great blue heron swooping down for a final landing, or you might spot a moose wandering about the wetlands. Pillsbury State Park is a true wilderness getaway.

GETTING THERE

Follow NH 31 from Hillsborough and Washington. The park is on the right, about 15 miles past the center of Washington.

WHITE LEDGE CAMPGROUND

White Ledge is certainly convenient, and it's a great spot to make camp to launch your White Mountain hiking adventures.

WHITE LEDGE CAMPGROUND is a small campground located right off NH 16 in Albany, just south of North Conway. This place is a perfect base camp from which to launch your adventures hiking the White Ledge or Carter Ledge trails, or any of the trailheads located off the Kancamagus Highway to the immediate north, or Mount Chocorua to the south. It's also close to both the Swift and Saco rivers for fly-fishing (for information on fishing licenses, see Appendix C, page 224).

This is a fairly small, cozy campground. As you enter, you'll pass the day-use area and the campground host at site 2, on your right. Sites 1 through 5 are very open to the road and the central grassy area in the middle of the campground loop road. Moving farther up the road, you'll pass sites 3, 4, and 5, all of which are open to the road and to each other. They're situated just across the campground road from the restrooms. These wouldn't be my favorite sites in the campground, but they are convenient.

Deeper into the campground, sites 6 and 7 are set off the road a bit on a grassy platform. The ground here is firm and flat, which makes a solid surface for your tent. Also, you won't have to worry too much about plunging your tent stakes into a root or rock, although there are always errant chunks of the Granite State lurking in the ground. There's a hiking trail leading off into the woods just past site 7 on the outside of the campground loop road. Site 8 is where the camping at White Ledge starts to get good. This site is set off the road in a dense spruce grove. The woods open up behind the site, and a small embankment leads down to a streambed. The open forest makes this a perfect place for the kids in your group to explore. There's a delightful sense of solitude to this site.

RATINGS

Beauty: ☆ ☆ ☆ ☆
Privacy: ☆ ☆ ☆ ☆
Spaciousness: ☆ ☆ ☆ ☆
Quiet: ☆ ☆ ☆
Security: ☆ ☆ ☆
Cleanliness: ☆ ☆ ☆ ☆

As you round the campground road as it passes by site 8, you'll notice there's a beautiful pine grove at the center of the campground loop. This is a great spot for a picnic or to take some pictures. There's no camping here, but that doesn't mean you shouldn't spend some time in this scenic area.

On the outside of this part of the campground loop is site 9. It's fairly close to the open, grassy area where some of the day hikers park, but it's set off from the road. The stream that runs behind site 8 separates this site from the road, so a short footbridge leads you into the site, adding to the sense that this is your own home in the forest—at least for a little while.

Sites 10 and 11 sit deep within a wooded grove, but they're also open to the central green—a bit too open for my tastes. These would be two good sites for a larger group or family needing a bit of elbow room.

Sites 12 and 13 have a sense of solitude as they are set well off the road. Site 13 is set particularly far back, with a short hike in from the parking spot.

Moving over to the left loop that is home to sites 14 through 28, site 14 is huge and clean. It's framed by a large boulder and a grove of mixed conifers. However, its location at the intersection of White Ledge's two loops and its relative proximity to NH 16 make it a bit less private and more noisy.

Sites 15 and 16 are set across from each other. Site 15 is spacious, site 16 a bit less so. Site 15 also has an embankment enshrouded in pine needles behind it. Site 16 is smaller, but it gets hit with the sun for most of the day. Site 17 is open to the road but encircled by a forest of mixed conifers and deciduous trees.

Deeper into the loop on this side of the campground, the sites get more secluded. Sites 18 and 19 share a parking area and are set off the road, making them more private. Site 18 is off to the right, 19 to the left. Both are sufficiently secluded, yet they would also make for a nice pair of sites for a larger group.

If you're here solely for the hiking, check out site 20. This site is off the road, a bit open, and somewhat smaller, but it's right next to the trailhead for the Carter Ledge Trail. How cool would it be to do a hike like that, and have it end right at your campsite?

KEY INFORMATION

ADDRESS:	White Ledge Campground NH 16 Albany, NH 03818
OPERATED BY:	National Forest Service
INFORMATION:	Saco Ranger Station (603) 447-5448
OPEN:	Mid-May– mid-October
SITES:	28
EACH SITE HAS:	Fire ring, picnic table
ASSIGNMENT:	First come, first served, or by reservation
REGISTRATION:	With campground host in site 2, or by reservation: (877) 444-6777, www. reserveusa.com
FACILITIES:	Vault toilets, water pumps
PARKING:	At campsites or shared parking areas
FEE:	$16
RESTRICTIONS:	**Pets:** Dogs on leash only **Fires:** Fire rings only **Alcohol:** At sites **Vehicles:** Maximum 2 vehicles per site **Other:** Maximum 8 people per site; 14-day maximum stay

MAP

WHITE LEDGE CAMPGROUND

To CONWAY

TOILET 👫
WATER ACCESS 🚰
PICNIC SHELTER ⛺

GETTING THERE

From Conway, head south for 5 miles on NH 16 to Albany. The campground will be on the right.

Sites 21 and 22 are on the small side, and you're getting closer to NH 16 here on the loop, so there's more road noise from NH 16. Site 24 is cut between the campground road and the campground loop road.

Sites 23 and 25 are generous-sized sites set against a small hill in the middle of this side of the campground loop road, but again, there will be road noise during the day here. The hill behind them gives these sites a sheltered feel. Site 26 is open to the campground road and NH 16. However, site 27 is secluded, set deep within a mixed grove of spruce and beech. Site 28 is surrounded by beech trees and maples, which gives it a shimmering green look when the sun is shining through the forest canopy. The only bummer here is that you're still close to NH 16.

You know what the say about real estate and location. There are some very nice sites at White Ledge. While you may hear some road noise from NH 16, you won't be far from the exquisite trails and mountains that draw people to the White Mountain National Forest.

VERMONT

ALLIS STATE PARK

Randolph

If silence and solitude are what you seek, Allis State Park is a fantastic choice.

ALLIS STATE PARK is one place you won't find by accident, but it's definitely worth the trip. It's not too far from Interstate 89, which cuts through the middle of Vermont, but it's a circuitous route to the park from the highway. You'll turn down a state road that starts out looking like someone's driveway and then promptly turns into a dirt road. At that point, you're almost there! When you do arrive, you'll be glad you found it, as it is a phenomenally peaceful campground. Its isolation is part of its charm.

While there are a few sites along the edge of an open field in the center of the campground, most are fantastically nestled into the dense forest. Allis State Park has 18 tent sites. Sites 15 through 18 are set along the border of the forest and the field. This pleasant pastoral setting, is not quite as privacy. You'll also get some delightful breezes blowing across the field and through your site, and you will be in a perfect spot to relax in the sun or spend time stargazing at night.

There's a combined sense of isolation and pastoral openness to site 13. It's carved out of the dense forest and set down from the edge of the field. Although sites 17 and 18 are visible across the field, site 13 is still quite isolated from the rest of the campground.

The next site along the campground loop road is one of the most profoundly secluded sites in Vermont. Site 14 is set along a road leading off the main campground loop to the right. This road eventually rejoins the main road leading into Allis State Park, but site 14 is the only campsite on this road—it's completely on its own. You couldn't ask for a deeper sense of solitude and wilderness isolation. The moderately spacious site is set within a fairly dense forest, and the undergrowth is thick with lush ferns. The road leading up to and past the site becomes increasingly less maintained, and it would make a perfect short hike or mountain-bike

RATINGS

Beauty: ✩ ✩ ✩ ✩ ✩
Privacy: ✩ ✩ ✩ ✩ ✩
Spaciousness: ✩ ✩ ✩ ✩ ✩ ✩
Quiet: ✩ ✩ ✩ ✩ ✩
Security: ✩ ✩ ✩
Cleanliness: ✩ ✩ ✩ ✩

ADDRESS: Allis State Park
RD 2 Box 192
Randolph, VT 05060

OPERATED BY: Vermont Agency of
Natural Resources,
Department of
Forests, Parks, and
Recreation

INFORMATION: Allis State Park,
(802) 276-3175 (sum-
mer), (888) 409-7579
(October–May)

OPEN: Mid-May–Labor Day

SITES: 18 tent sites, 8 lean-
to sites

EACH SITE HAS: Stone hearth, picnic
table

ASSIGNMENT: First come, first
served or by reser-
vation: (888) 409-
7579

REGISTRATION: At ranger station at
entrance to park

FACILITIES: Coin-operated hot
showers, flush toi-
lets, water spigots

PARKING: At sites

FEE: $14 for tent sites, $21
for lean-tos

RESTRICTIONS: Pets: On leash only
Fires: Fireplaces
only
Alcohol: Sites only
Vehicles: Parking at
sites only
Other: Reservations
require 2-night mini-
mum stay; check-in
after 2 p.m., check-
out by 11 a.m.; quiet
hours 10 p.m.–7
a.m.; maximum 8
people per site

ride, as its connection with the entrance road allows
for a loop route. The beautiful, diverse character of the
surrounding forest and its absolute isolation make site
14 at Allis State Park one of the top sites you'll find
anywhere in New England.

There's a solid sense of seclusion to site 12 as well,
even when compared to the magical solitude of site 14.
For site 12, park right on the campground loop road
and hike in about 50 feet. You can see through the forest to neighboring site 13, but it's still very quiet and
secluded, set beneath a moderately dense grove of
mixed spruce and maple trees.

Site 11 bears off to the left, which adds to the privacy from the road. There's also a lot of woodland
between this site and its neighbors. The site is open to
the sky, moderately spacious, and set within a grove of
mixed birch and maple trees.

The juxtaposition of sites 9 and 10, and the fact
that they are mirror images of each other, makes for an
unusual situation. Site 10 is set off the road at an angle
to the left within a dense grove of spruce. Site 9 mirrors its shape and character to the right. Despite their
proximity, each site provides decent privacy, but this
would also make a good pair of sites for a larger group
needing two sites.

Site 8 is long and narrow. It's a very open and spacious site. It is quite exposed to the road, which makes
it a bit less appealing than some of Allis State Park's
other sites; but if you need or want a lot of room, this is
a great spot. Set beneath a dense grove of spruce,
maple, and birch trees, the spacious site 7 bends back
to the left, so the trees surrounding it provide further
isolation from the road. The only other site you'll probably be able to see from here is the Elm lean-to (more
on the lean-tos momentarily).

There's a charmingly diverse character to site 6.
This one is set off the road on a hill with separate levels for parking your car and setting up your tent. It's
mostly covered with grass punctuated by baby and
adult spruce and maple trees. An extraordinarily varied forest of young and old deciduous and coniferous
trees frames the site. It faces the road, but it's otherwise
very secluded.

MAP

ALLIS STATE PARK CAMPGROUND

LEAN-TOS
1. BIRCH
2. OAK
3. ELM
4. HEMLOCK
5. APPLE
6. SPRUCE
7. PINE
8. POPLAR

TURNAROUND

SERVICE ROAD ONLY

TO PARK ENTRANCE AND 65

GROUP CAMPING SITE

FIRE TOWER

TOILET	♦♦	SHELTER	⇧⬆
WATER ACCESS	🚰	FIREWOOD	🪵
PARKING	🚗	DUMP STATION	🗑
WHEELCHAIR ACCESSIBLE	♿	RANGERS QUARTERS	🏠
DUMPSTER	🗑	PICNIC AREA	🏕
RECYCLING CENTER	♻	GATE	▱

The drive into site 5 is actually a short loop. This spacious and secluded site is set beneath a varied forest of young and old birch and spruce trees. From site 5, you can see site 4, but no others. Site 4 is moderately spacious and set in a spruce grove. It has a moss- and grass-covered surface. Between sites 4 and 5 is a trail-head for the Tower Trail. These two sites would be great for a large group.

To get to site 3, you have to drive down off the campground loop road. Once you're down in the site, you can't even see the road. The towering spruce as you enter the short driveway separates the site from view of the road, but the back of the site opens to the grassy field in the center of the park, so it feels both open and secluded. The site itself is also dotted with several birch trees.

Even though it's tucked back off the road, site 2 is still very exposed. It is spacious, narrow, long, and grass covered, so it would make a comfortable surface for your tent. Site 1 is huge and grassy, but it's wide open to the road. The water spigot is also located near site 1, so you'll have thirsty campers tramping by.

GETTING THERE

From Interstate 89, take Exit 4. Head west on VT 66 to the intersection with VT 12. Turn right on VT 12 north. Follow this for 12 miles to VT 65. Turn right here and follow the road to the park entrance on the right.

The lean-tos at Allis State Park are grouped together in a small neighborhood at the far end of the campground loop road. They look like true wilderness cabins with their own yards and lawns.

The Elm, Oak, Hemlock, and Spruce lean-tos are all set on grassy lawns buffered from one another by dense forest. The Apple lean-to is set up for wheelchair access, so it's also close to the restroom. The Pine lean-to is on the outside of the campground loop road.

The Poplar lean-to is set way off on its own, mixed in with a grove of spruce and birch. This is the one to go for if you want a secluded lean-to.

The Bear Hill Nature Trail, the nearest and most prominent hiking attraction within Allis State Park, is a self-guided nature trail that highlights the varied stages of forest growth; it features a stand of red spruce, butternut trees, and a view to North and South ponds that just opened following the great ice storm of 1998. Eventually though, this view will be reclaimed by the steady and undeniable persistence of the forest.

BRANBURY STATE PARK

THERE ARE TWO SEPARATE camping areas at Branbury State Park. One of the camping areas is pretty nice, but the other one is positively spectacular. Branbury State Park is located on the eastern shore of Lake Dunmore, and there's plenty to do on this beautiful central Vermont lake: paddling, fishing, sailing, swimming, or just sitting on a beach chair burrowing your feet into the sand (for information on fishing licenses, see Appendix C, page 224).

The camping area near the lake is set on an open field back from the beach. For the Lake Dunmore side of the campground, the privacy rating is one star, since it's an open field. There are a few trees spread out within the field, but for the most part, the only thing between you and the neighboring sites is air. The campsites across the street rate a four on the privacy scale, and some a solid five.

Sites 1 through 17 are the open sites near the lake. These are pleasant, as they're close to the lake and you'll get some cool breezes, but they are all quite similar and all very open. If you prefer seclusion, the campsites across the street (sites 18 through 41) are where you want to be. This portion of the campground is set within a beautiful mixed forest of old and young trees. This loop has some scenic and secluded sites, as well as a few lean-tos. In Vermont State Park style, the lean-tos are all named for tree varieties: Elm, Spruce, Oak, and so on. These are unobtrusively mixed in with the tent sites.

Site 25 isn't bad. It's slightly elevated from the road, but it's right at the entrance to this side of the campground where campers drive in, so it lacks privacy and quiet. Sites 27 and 28 are probably the least private of the sites on this side, as they have the main road (VT 53) on one side and the campground loop road on the other. Travel just a bit farther up this loop, though, and the sites become increasingly gorgeous.

> *Here you can choose between campsites on a grassy field near the lake or nestled deep in the woods.*

RATINGS

Beauty: ✿ ✿ ✿ ✿
Privacy (West): ✿
Privacy (East): ✿ ✿ ✿ ✿ ✿
Spaciousness: ✿ ✿ ✿ ✿
Quiet: ✿ ✿ ✿ ✿
Security: ✿ ✿ ✿ ✿
Cleanliness: ✿ ✿ ✿ ✿

KEY INFORMATION

ADDRESS: Branbury State Park
3570 Lake Dunmore
Road, VT 53
Salisbury, VT 05733

OPERATED BY: Vermont Agency of
Natural Resources,
Department of
Forests, Parks, and
Recreation

INFORMATION: Branbury State Park,
(802) 247-5925 (summer), (888) 409-7579
(October–May)

OPEN: Mid-May–
Columbus Day

SITES: 41 tent sites, 6 lean-to sites

EACH SITE HAS: Fire ring, picnic
table

ASSIGNMENT: First come, first
served or by reservation: (888) 409-7579

REGISTRATION: At ranger station

FACILITIES: Flush toilets, water,
coin-operated hot
showers, sandy
beach on Lake Dunmore, boat rentals

PARKING: At sites

FEE: $16 for tent sites, $23
for lean-tos

RESTRICTIONS: Pets: Dogs on leash
only
Fires: Fire rings only
Alcohol: Sites only
Vehicles: Sites only
Other: Reservations
require 4-night minimum stay; check-in
after 2 p.m., checkout by 11 a.m.; quiet
hours 10 p.m.–7
a.m.; maximum 8
people per site

Site 32 is nicely isolated, situated on the inside of the campground loop near the Birch lean-to. Sites 29 and 31 are even farther up on the spectacular scale. These well-isolated sites are set up on a small rise from the campground road and are surrounded by thick forest. Site 30 sits in the middle of these two sites, so it's more open, but it's still a fine site. Sites 29 and 31 on either side are set back enough in the woods that you won't be too close to your neighbors.

Farther up the loop, there are several sites against small, granite cliff walls. Sites 36 and 37 are tucked right against these ledges. The whole side of the loop here is quite dramatic in its scenery, thanks to the cliffs, forest, and gently rolling terrain.

There are three sites on this side of the Branbury State Park campground that are set at the end of cul-de-sacs within the campground: sites 34, 41, and 21. Site 34 is perfectly situated for deep wilderness isolation. It's nestled in a dense grove of conifers, so it feels like a campsite from some deep mystical woods out of Tolkien's Middle Earth.

Site 41 might as well be the companion to site 34, set off on its own in a pine grove up against the cliffs. This site is next to the Spruce lean-to. Sites 39 through 41 are interspersed with the shelters against and among the cliffs. Site 39 is an isolated site, even though it sits right next to the Oak Shelter.

Then, we come to site 21 (elated cinematic music should be sounding in your head right now). Site 21 couldn't possibly be a more perfect place to spend a few days camping. There's a short distance to lug in your gear. Make sure to drop your stuff and just look around as you walk into the site. You'll feel as if you've entered a cathedral. The site is majestically framed by statuesque spruce trees and set against a steep cliff wall. As if that's not enough, the Sucker Brook softly splashes by right behind the site. You'll fall asleep to the sounds of the stream as it runs down from the Falls of Lana toward Lake Dunmore.

When I was chatting with the Vermont Youth Conservation Corps members working in the ranger station in early spring, the coveted site 21 was already reserved for most of the summer. Plan years in advance, do a

MAP

BRANBURY STATE PARK CAMPGROUND

SUCKER BROOK

CHAIN-LINK FENCES

NATURE CENTER

BASKETBALL COURT

OVERFLOW PARKING

RESTRICTED AREA FOR SWIMMERS

POST BARRIER

To MIDDLEBURY AND 7

SHOWERS	
RESTROOM	
WATER ACCESS	
PARKING	
WHEELCHAIR ACCESSIBLE	
PARKING GARAGE	
DUMPSITE	
PLAYGROUND	
PICNIC AREA	
RANGER QUARTERS	
CONCESSION	
BOAT LAUNCH	
FIREWOOD	

ASST. RANGER QUARTERS

RANGER QUARTERS

CONTACT STATIONS

To FOREST DALE

PARK ENTRANCE

NATURE TRAIL

MOOSALOAMOO RANGER CABIN

LEAN-TOS	4. BIRCH
1. PINE	5. MAPLE
2. ELM	6. OAK
3. ASPEN	7. SPRUCE

---

sun dance, and try to get yourself some time in site 21. You'll be glad you did!

While most Vermont State Parks have a two-night minimum for reservations, there's a four-night minimum at Branbury State Park. That should be fine though, especially if you get yourself into site 21. Otherwise, consider sites 20, 22, 29, 31, 34, and 41 for the most secluded wilderness experience. Once you land there, you won't want to leave for at least four nights!

Besides being able to fish, paddle, and lay in the sun on the shores of Lake Dunmore, the hiking in and around Branbury State Park is as dramatically beautiful as site 21. There's a nature trail that loops up and over the small cliffs at the back of the wooded side of the campground. There are two hikes in particular that you won't want to miss if you're spending at least a couple of days here: the 1.5-mile, occasionally strenuous hike up to Rattlesnake Point, a rock promontory overlooking the forest and Lake Dunmore; and the relatively easy, 1-mile hike up to the Falls of Lana, over which Sucker Brook flows on its way toward site 21 and Lake Dunmore.

GETTING THERE

From Middlebury, Vermont, travel south on US 7, then south on VT 53 until you see signs for the park.

CHITTENDEN BROOK RECREATION AREA

> *This is a spectacularly scenic and isolated campground set deep within the woods of the Green Mountain National Forest.*

THE **CHITTENDEN BROOK** Recreation Area, like many campgrounds perched along the spine of the Green Mountains in Vermont, offers a deep-woods atmosphere and easy access to some of the world-class hiking trails that wind through the state.

The 2.5-mile access road (Fire Road 45) into the Chittenden Brook campground is quite a trip in and of itself. It leads up and over a ridge with Chittenden Brook running on either side along the way. Farther up, as you near the campground, the road falls off steeply to the right. Even though the forest is dramatically beautiful here, keep your eyes on the road.

Chittenden Brook is one of those campgrounds (and there are certainly plenty in New England) where there isn't a bad site in the place. It's an intimate campground with only 17 sites, which means it can fill up quickly. Once you're there, it's calm and quiet, and it has a delightful sense of solitude.

The whole campground is situated near the ridgeline of the Green Mountains, the course followed by the nearby Long and Appalachian trails. You are at a moderate elevation in the Green Mountains, so the forest isn't quite as towering here. Consequently, lots of light filters down into the sites. There's also the ever-present rush of Chittenden Brook, punctuated by the staccato chirping of the forest birds. It's a profoundly peaceful combination.

Site 1 is down off the road, near the restrooms but set off on its own enough to be fairly well isolated. It's also close to the hand water-pump. Continuing along the campground loop road, sites 2 through 5 are fairly close together, but each has plenty of room. These sites have an open feel, and are probably the least-isolated sites in the campground. Still, even these offer a reasonable sense of seclusion.

RATINGS

Beauty: ✿ ✿ ✿ ✿ ✿
Privacy: ✿ ✿ ✿ ✿ ✿
Spaciousness: ✿ ✿ ✿ ✿ ✿
Quiet: ✿ ✿ ✿ ✿ ✿
Security: ✿ ✿ ✿ ✿
Cleanliness: ✿ ✿ ✿ ✿

While it doesn't have a lot of dense forest surrounding it, site 6 is nicely isolated, as it is set off from the other campsites. It's also situated right next to a trailhead between sites 6 and 7 that leads to the Chittenden Brook Trail, the Beaver Pond Trail, and the Campground Loop Trail. You can hike right out of your campsite. Site 7 is larger, so it would be perfect for a slightly larger group or large family. It's also next to the restroom.

The tent platform for site 8 is set off the campground loop and back in the woods, so this site scores higher on the solitude and isolation scale. Between its location and the trees around the site, you probably won't even be able to see your neighbors. Sites 9 and 10 are right across the campground loop road from each other. Both are pretty, spacious sites surrounded by trees that lend a sense of isolation on either side, although not directly in front of the campsites.

Sites 11 and 12 are right next to each other and have a loosely spaced, fairly open forest in between, so these would be good sites if you're with a group large enough to need or want two sites. There's another hand pump for water located across from site 13 and next to site 14.

Sites 13 and 15 are set off from the campground loop road, with a short path leading to the tent platform. These sites not only provide a sense of wilderness and isolation, but are also extra scenic since they are set within groves of young deciduous trees, loaded with brilliant green leaves bouncing around in the sunlight.

Sites 16 and 17 are my favorites at Chittenden Brook Recreation Area. In site 16, the tent platform is set off the road, and then from there, the space with the picnic table and fire ring is set down farther still, so both your sleeping spot and hanging-out spot are off on their own. There's also a buffer of woods between sites 16 and 17, as well as the sites on either side. Site 17 is a bit more level, but still marvelously isolated, quite spacious, and surrounded by a cloak of young trees. It's located near the end of the campground loop road, and close to the recycling station. These recycling stations are very much in evidence within the

KEY INFORMATION

ADDRESS: Chittenden Brook Recreation Area Fire Road 45 VT 73 Chittenden, VTt 05737

OPERATED BY: Green Mountain National Forest

INFORMATION: Green Mountain National Forest Rochester Ranger District 99 Ranger Road Rochester, VT 05767-9431 (802) 767-4261

OPEN: Memorial Day– Labor Day

SITES: 17

EACH SITE HAS: Fire ring with grill, picnic table

ASSIGNMENT: First come, first served

REGISTRATION: Pay at self-serve fee station

FACILITIES: Pit toilets, hand water-pumps

PARKING: At sites

FEE: $5

RESTRICTIONS: Pets: On leash only
Fires: Fire rings only
Alcohol: Sites only
Vehicles: Maximum 2 per site; national forest closed to ATVs
Other: Quiet hours 10 p.m.–6 a.m.; check-out by 2 p.m.; 14-day maximum stay; pack out all trash

MAP

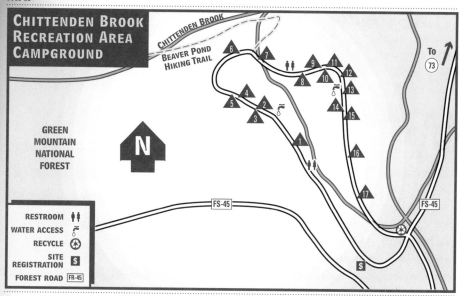

CHITTENDEN BROOK RECREATION AREA CAMPGROUND

CHITTENDEN BROOK

BEAVER POND HIKING TRAIL

GREEN MOUNTAIN NATIONAL FOREST

To 73

N

FS-45

FS-45

RESTROOM	👫
WATER ACCESS	🚰
RECYCLE	⊕
SITE REGISTRATION	🅂
FOREST ROAD	FR-45

GETTING THERE

Follow VT 73 to Road 45 and the sign for Chittenden Brook Recreation Area, which will be on the left if you're heading west on VT 73, or on the right if you're heading east. Follow Road 45 about 2.5 miles to the campground.

Green Mountain National Forest campgrounds and recreation areas. Bravo to that!

This is the place to make base camp if you're planning on exploring portions of the Long Trail or Appalachian Trail. There are trailheads leading right out of the campground. As you drive in on the access road, you'll pass other trailheads also leading off toward the Long Trail.

COOLIDGE STATE PARK

WHEN YOU'RE HIKING through the gentle trails of Coolidge State Park (so named for the nearby birthplace of Calvin Coolidge, 30th president of the United States), you'll come across lots of old stone walls and what's left of foundations. Close your eyes for a moment and imagine what this area was like when the homes of farmers stood here. The land upon which you're hiking and camping looked a lot different just 100 years ago. What was once agricultural land has been thoroughly reclaimed by the forest's persistent growth.

The campground at Coolidge State Park is set within a dense, mixed forest of mostly deciduous trees. There's a stately character to the forest, as most of the trees tower 75 to 100 feet overhead. The trees are mostly maples, birch, and pine. The tent sites are generally very spacious, with lots of space and trees between most of the sites, so the sense of seclusion is supreme. The campground is very quiet. The only sounds you'll hear are the woodland birds and the breezes rustling through the trees.

Unlike most other Vermont state parks, there are two distinct areas for most of the lean-tos and the tent sites. The White Birch, Alder, and Poplar lean-tos are the only three mixed in with the tent sites. The White Birch lean-to is located at the head of the tent loop, the Alder across from site 4, and the Poplar off the main campground road.

While it's smaller than the other low-numbered sites, site 1 is well isolated. The main campground road runs behind the site, but you won't notice it once the sun sinks beneath the trees. It's also directly across the campground loop road from site 2, which is framed by a grove of spruce and young deciduous trees. A huge, grand old pine tree guards the entrance to site 2, with branches hanging down redolent of a weeping willow.

> *The character of the forest and the views of the surrounding hillside make this park a gem.*

RATINGS

Beauty: ✪ ✪ ✪ ✪
Privacy: ✪ ✪ ✪ ✪ ✪
Spaciousness: ✪ ✪ ✪ ✪
Quiet: ✪ ✪ ✪ ✪ ✪
Security: ✪ ✪ ✪ ✪ ✪
Cleanliness: ✪ ✪ ✪ ✪

ADDRESS: Coolidge State Park
855 Coolidge State
Park Road
Plymouth, VT 05056

OPERATED BY: Vermont Agency of
Natural Resources,
Department of
Forests, Parks, and
Recreation

INFORMATION: Coolidge State Park,
(802) 672-3612 (sum-
mer), (888) 409-7579
(October–May)

OPEN: Mid-May–
mid-October

SITES: 25 tent sites, 35 lean-
to sites

EACH SITE HAS: Fire ring, picnic
table

ASSIGNMENT: First come, first
served or by reser-
vation: (888) 409-
7579

REGISTRATION: At ranger station

FACILITIES: Coin-operated hot
showers, flush toi-
lets, playground, pic-
nic area, dump
station for RVs

PARKING: At sites

FEE: $14 for tent sites, $21
for lean-tos

RESTRICTIONS: Pets: On leash only
Fires: Fire rings only
Alcohol: Sites only
Vehicles: Parking at
sites only
Other: Reservations
require 4-night mini-
mum stay; check-in
after 2 p.m., check-
out by 11 a.m.; quiet
hours 10 p.m.–7
a.m.; maximum 8
people per site

There's a fairly well-isolated air about site 3, although it's close to site 2. A decent amount of forest separates the two, and both are very spacious. Site 4 is also very spacious, and it's right across the road from the Alder lean-to. The site is framed by a grove of young deciduous trees and a few older spruce. Site 5 is another well-isolated site. It's at least 100 feet from neighboring sites on either side, but it is open to the back, and you can see the restrooms behind the site. Site 6 is set off the campground road. It's spacious and pretty well isolated. There aren't any sites close to you on either side, but it is right across the road from another footpath to the restrooms.

The trailhead for the CCC Trail (Civilian Conservation Corps) is right across from site 7. This is a convenient site for easy access to the hiking trails that wind throughout the park, but expect passing foot traffic. Sites 7 and 8 are somewhat close together and set up off the campground loop road. Site 9 is very open and has a small grassy area within. It's right next to site 10, so unlike most of the campground, there isn't much privacy between these two sites. These two pairs of sites would suit large groups or families needing more than one site.

Site 11 is another open and spacious spot. Site 12 is smaller and more secluded. It's surrounded by a dense grove of young deciduous trees. Site 13 is tucked far off the campground road, so it provides a feeling of isolation, even though it's right next to a short footpath that leads up to the restrooms.

There's a shared entranceway to sites 14 and 15, but there's enough space and forest between the two to afford sufficient privacy. Both sites are very spacious and set far off the road. Site 15 offers a fabulous sense of solitude, boasting a grassy area, plus a brook flowing by.

There isn't much privacy between sites 16 and 17. However, there's plenty of room on either side of both sites, so they're well isolated from the rest of the campground, if not from each other—another possibility for groups. Site 17 is set off the road a bit, and has a grassy surface in its center. There are also several maples growing up through the site, and it's framed by shorter deciduous trees—mostly maple and birch—and by ferns

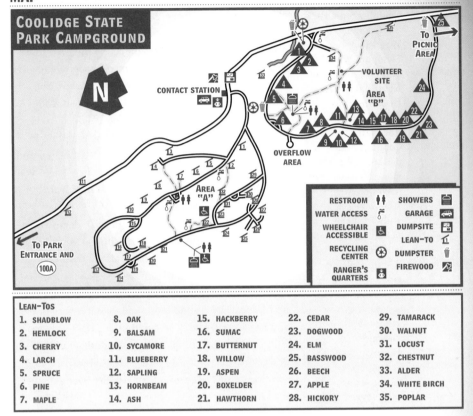

COOLIDGE STATE PARK CAMPGROUND

To PICNIC AREA

VOLUNTEER SITE

AREA "B"

CONTACT STATION

OVERFLOW AREA

AREA "A"

To Park Entrance and 100A

RESTROOM		SHOWERS	
WATER ACCESS		GARAGE	
WHEELCHAIR ACCESSIBLE		DUMPSITE	
RECYCLING CENTER		LEAN-TO	
		DUMPSTER	
RANGER'S QUARTERS		FIREWOOD	

LEAN-TOS

1. SHADBLOW	8. OAK	15. HACKBERRY	22. CEDAR	29. TAMARACK
2. HEMLOCK	9. BALSAM	16. SUMAC	23. DOGWOOD	30. WALNUT
3. CHERRY	10. SYCAMORE	17. BUTTERNUT	24. ELM	31. LOCUST
4. LARCH	11. BLUEBERRY	18. WILLOW	25. BASSWOOD	32. CHESTNUT
5. SPRUCE	12. SAPLING	19. ASPEN	26. BEECH	33. ALDER
6. PINE	13. HORNBEAM	20. BOXELDER	27. APPLE	34. WHITE BIRCH
7. MAPLE	14. ASH	21. HAWTHORN	28. HICKORY	35. POPLAR

at the ground level for an added sense of seclusion. The ferns give the site a primeval feel and fill in the forest with their brilliant green leaves. When the sunlight filters down on a clear day, the forest looks as if it's glowing green.

Site 18 is a bit smaller than 17, but also has a grassy surface within it. Site 19 is very spacious and there's plenty of forest on either side of the site, but not too much privacy from the road. I'm always willing to sacrifice a bit of site spaciousness for more forest and a deeper sense of seclusion.

There's a similar character to sites 20 through 23. Site 20 is up off the road. This is a moderately spacious site, also with a grassy surface. Sites 22 and 23 are across the road from each other. Site 23A is a lug-in site set up off the road. It's almost a part of site 23, so if you don't know your neighbors in site 23 before your trip, you will

GETTING THERE

Follow VT 100 (the skier's highway) to VT 100A in Plymouth. Follow VT 100A for about 2 miles to the sign for the park on the right.

before long. Site 23A isn't huge, but it's set way off from the road and the rest of the campground. It is surrounded by a dense, low wall of ferns and a grove of slender, young spruce trees. It has a deep sense of seclusion on all sides, save where it abuts site 23.

One of the last sites on this part of the campground loop road is site 24. This is by far the most isolated site within the loop. It's perfectly situated for wilderness isolation, as it's surrounded by dense forest and is a good distance from its neighbors. It's not the most spacious site, but it's marvelously well isolated.

There's a dichotomy to site 25. It sits way off on its own, but it's located near the point where the campground loop road rejoins the main state park road. It's moderately spacious and very well isolated from the other sites, but it is right at that intersection.

Between the tent loop and the lean-to loop, there's a little playground near the ranger station as you enter the park—a good thing to keep in mind if you're camping with little ones. The lean-to loop has very dense forest coverage as well. Most of the lean-tos are quite well isolated from each other, although some are positioned in pairs, like Cherry and Larch, or groups, like Beech, Basswood, and Apple. Between the dense forest and the loose spacing, the individual lean-to sites have a sense of isolation, especially the Sumac, Willow, and Butternut lean-tos. It also bears mentioning that the Cedar lean-to is wheelchair accessible.

The Ash lean-to has an outrageously scenic view of the opposing hillsides and valley. This alone makes it worth keeping the tent packed and hopping in one of these lean-tos. The Aspen, Box elder, Beech, Basswood, Elm, and Hawthorn lean-tos also share this dramatic view. All these lean-tos face out toward the hills, which would be the first thing you see in the morning. I couldn't imagine a nicer way to greet the day.

Once you're up and about, whether you've spent the night in your tent or in a lean-to, there's plenty of great hiking right within the park. Try the 0.75-mile CCC Trail that connects the tent area and the lean-to area for a mellow morning hike. Then try the 1.5-mile trail to the summit of the 2,174-foot Slack Hill and treat yourself to lunch with a commanding view of the surrounding hills.

EMERALD LAKE STATE PARK

YOU CAN'T HELP but notice the steep embankment leading up from one side of the road and down from the other as you drive into the Emerald Lake State Park campground. This place was essentially carved out of the hillside. It makes for a dramatic setting, but consequently, a steep bank encircles many of the camping areas here, so keep an eye on any little ones you may have running around. You'll hear a little road noise from nearby US 7, but hardly any at night.

The first area you'll come to, Area A, has a pleasing mix of tent and lean-to sites, much like the rest of the campground. In the 1 through 12 section of the loop, most of the tent sites are set toward the center of the loop, with the lean-tos on the outside. For the most part, the lean-tos are secluded on the sides, with the open side of the lean-to facing out from the A-loop road.

The Willow lean-to and site 1 are small and adjacent sites. Site 1 is secluded on the sides, but open to the road. Willow is set a bit farther back, making it secluded. Cherry is fairly spacious and secluded, as it is set off the road in a dense grove of young maple and beech trees. Both the Pine and Hickory lean-tos are on smaller sites, but feel moderately private.

Like the other tent sites in this part of the loop, site 5 is of moderate size, but doesn't offer much privacy from the other sites. Site 6 is spacious and open to the road, but is a bit more secluded than the other tent sites nearby. The Elm and Alder lean-tos are small and face the main campground road leading to the B and C areas, but they still feel secluded. Site 7 is open to the road, but it does have several large spruce trees growing up through it.

Poplar is on a good-sized site that is fairly well secluded on the sides, but it's a bit open to the road. Site 8 is set up off the road, but still has an open feel. It's encircled by slender beech trees and several large

> *Emerald Lake State Park is artfully carved out of the densely forested side of Dorset Mountain.*

RATINGS

Beauty: ☆ ☆ ☆ ☆ ☆
Privacy: ☆ ☆ ☆ ☆
Spaciousness: ☆ ☆ ☆ ☆
Quiet: ☆ ☆ ☆ ☆
Security: ☆ ☆ ☆
Cleanliness: ☆ ☆ ☆ ☆ ☆

ADDRESS: Emerald Lake State Park
65 Emerald Lake Lane
East Dorset, VT 05253

OPERATED BY: Vermont Agency of Natural Resources, Department of Forests, Parks, and Recreation

INFORMATION: Emerald Lake State Park, (802) 362-1655

OPEN: Mid-May– mid-October

SITES: 69 tent sites, 37 lean-to sites

EACH SITE HAS: Fire ring, picnic table

ASSIGNMENT: First come, first served or by reservation: (888) 409-7579

REGISTRATION: At ranger station at entrance to park

FACILITIES: Day-use area, flush toilets, hot showers, water spigots

PARKING: At sites

FEE: $16 for tent sites, $23 for lean-tos

RESTRICTIONS: **Pets:** On leash only
Fires: Fireplaces only
Alcohol: Sites only
Vehicles: Parking at sites only
Other: Reservations require 2-night minimum stay; check-in after 2 p.m., check-out by 11 a.m.; quiet hours 10 p.m.–7 a.m.; maximum 8 people per site

maples and spruce. The Spruce lean-to, as you may imagine, is set within a fairly dense spruce grove, although the lean-to itself is close to the road.

Locust is very spacious and offers an excellent sense of seclusion, set amidst a loosely spaced grove of spruce. Larch is also spacious and secluded. It's set way off the campground road within a shimmering, green grove of young beech trees. Birch is on a good-sized site and moderately secluded by a grove of spruce, although it's right on the corner of the campground road. It's also right next to the trail that leads to the lake. Beech is a smaller site. It's close to the road but has a decent sense of seclusion with the beech trees (of course) peppering the site.

The sites toward the end of Area A are more secluded and scenic. Site 15 is small but private and open to the sky. Site 16 is very sunny. It's a bit open and encircled by a loose forest of beech and spruce.

There's a line of spruce that frames site 18, which is also spacious and has a canopy of beech overhead. There's a steep bank off to the right of the site that leads down into a small ravine. Site 17 is moderately sized and secluded from the road by several large spruce trees. Site 19 is at the end of the loop. This site is fairly small, but it's nicely enshrouded by maples. It's open just enough to the sky so that plenty of sunlight filters down to the site.

Between the site A loop and the B loop is a short strip with sites 20 through 23. Even though they're far from the rest of the sites, there's not much of a sense of seclusion from the road or from each other, but if you wanted some sites side-by-side, these would be just fine.

There's a campground host at site 27 (on the left as you enter Area B) and a small playground next to site 28. Nearby, site 29 and the Tamarack lean-to are both set up for wheelchair access. Both sites 32 and 34 abut the steep hillside behind the sites, which adds to the sense of seclusion. Site 36 is also isolated and set up against the hillside.

Sites 35, 37, 38, and 39 are in their own little neighborhood. These are very spacious sites with a dark canopy of conifers overhead. They're open to each other, but they make for a fantastic quartet of

MAP

LEAN-TOS

1. FIR	9. LOCUST	17. ELM	25. HAZELNUT	33. PLUM
2. WILLOW	10. ASH	18. HICKORY	26. SUMAC	34. APPLE
3. CEDAR	11. SPRUCE	19. PINE	27. DOGWOOD	35. GINKGO
4. CHERRY	12. POPLAR	20. ASPEN	28. BASSWOOD	36. JUNIPER
5. BIRCH	13. MAPLE	21. TAMERACK	29. CHESTNUT	37. YEW
6. LARCH	14. BEECH	22. HOURBEAM	30. BUTTERNUT	
7. HEMLOCK	15. WALNUT	23. HAWTHORN	31. MULBERRY	
8. OAK	16. ALDER	24. SYCAMORE	32. PEAR	

sites. A stone wall encircles the back of sites 38 and 39, which adds to the sense of seclusion. Of this group of sites, site 39 is probably the most secluded.

Sites 43 and 44 are across the road from each other, but very well hidden on the sides from neighboring sites. Site 43 is also up against the hillside. Site 49 is spacious, fairly secluded, and set within a grove of very young, slender maples. It also has the steep hill against its back, and a trail leading up Dorset Mountain is right next to it.

Moving through the lower end of the B loop brings you to the lean-to sites. The Plum, Ginko, and Apple lean-tos are set in a trio. They're nicely secluded on the sides, but set close to each other. A bit more road noise from US 7 is noticeable here, but only during the day. Dogwood is very nicely secluded, as it's set down off the road at the end of a longer driveway.

GETTING THERE

From Interstate 91 north, take Exit 2 and follow VT 30 toward Manchester. Take US 7 north and follow this to the park.

Sumac is as well, although it's not quite as far off the road. Hazelnut is set off the road on a small rise and is enshrouded in a dark spruce grove.

There are two tent sites mixed in here as well. Site 40 is huge. The bathroom building is behind it, but a small hill behind the site creates a sense of seclusion. It's also across from site 41, which is small but private. This site, too, is surrounded by a small hill, almost as if it were landscaped, and nestled within a mixed forest of spruce and maples.

Farther up on this part of the loop, there's a trail leading down to the lake across from site 42 and the Sycamore lean-to. The sites and lean-tos here share the ambiance of a waterfall in the background.

Moving into Area C, the Yew lean-to is on a small but private site. Sites 50 and 51 are close to each other, but beautifully secluded from the other sites in this part of the campground. They're both open to the sky overhead and surrounded by young maple and beech trees. Sites 52 and 53 face the steep hill that runs along most of the northern side of the campground. They're open to the road but secluded on the sides. The trail leading down to Emerald Lake is right next to site 53.

Deeper into the Area C campsites, there are many that are rather small, not too private, and close to the restroom. There are also some spacious and spectacularly secluded spots. Set up on a short loop of this part of the campground road and encircled by slender beech, maple and birch, site 63 enjoys a shimmering green effect when the sun shines through the trees. It's open to this short loop, but very well secluded on the sides. Site 62 is a bit smaller and more hidden, surrounded by a picturesque mix of spruce and birch. Both of these sites are fairly close to the restroom, but set off by the stand of trees in the center of the loop.

As you near the far end of the campground road, you'll find site 66, which is an absolutely beautiful site surrounded by a grand, mixed grove of mature beech, spruce, birch, and maple trees. It's open to the sky just enough for a glimpse of the sun and stars. Site 67 is also a large site surrounded by spruce for a cooler, shaded feel and a sense of seclusion. Sites 68 and 69 are at the absolute end of the campground road. They're fairly close to each other but marvelously secluded, carved out of dense spruce forest. These last few sites share that a cool, dark, sylvan feeling. There are many exquisite sites at Emerald Lake State Park, but these more remote sites are among the best.

GIFFORD WOODS STATE PARK

GIFFORD **W**OODS is a perfectly situated spot from which to launch your adventures into the Green Mountains and the Killington area. Whether you're here for late-season skiing or mountain biking at Killington, or hiking along Vermont's spine, especially portions of the Appalachian Trail or Vermont's Long Trail, this is a great, centrally located base camp.

The Appalachian Trail passes right through the park, and it forms the right border for site 12 within the campground. I happened to stay there one night, and found it fascinating to be perched right on that fabled footpath. Turn left from this site and head for the summit of Katahdin or turn right for Amicalola Falls, Georgia.

Like other Vermont state parks, the site arrangement at Gifford Woods State Park is a loosely spaced combination of tent sites and lean-tos named for tree varieties. There are two distinct areas within the campground, the Upper Loop and the Lower Loop. The whole upper area of the campground is set beneath a truly mixed woodland with deciduous and coniferous trees as well as old and new forest. Sites 1 and 2 are tucked in together right across from the playground, which is also off the Upper Loop's campground road. These are great if you need a pair of contiguous sites for a larger group. Conversely, you will definitely meet your neighbors if you arrive previously unacquainted.

Site 3 is spacious, but it's right next to the playground, so it's not quite as private and could be noisy if there are a lot of kids on the swings and slide. This would be a great site to secure if you are camping with small kids and plan on spending time at the playground. Besides the playground, kids will like the footpath and self-guided nature tour that winds through the woods behind the playground and picnic area.

> *Gifford Woods State Park is exceptional both as a relaxing destination and a base camp for Green Mountain hiking adventures.*

RATINGS

Beauty: ☆ ☆ ☆ ☆ ☆
Privacy: ☆ ☆ ☆ ☆
Spaciousness: ☆ ☆ ☆ ☆
Quiet: ☆ ☆ ☆ ☆
Security: ☆ ☆ ☆ ☆
Cleanliness: ☆ ☆ ☆ ☆

ADDRESS: Gifford Woods State Park
34 Gifford Woods
Killington, VT 05761

OPERATED BY: Vermont Agency of Natural Resources, Department of Forests, Parks, and Recreation

INFORMATION: Gifford Woods State Park, (802) 775-5354 (in season), (888) 409-7579 (October–May)

OPEN: Mid-May–Columbus Day

SITES: 27 tent sites, 21 lean-to sites

EACH SITE HAS: Fire ring or brick hearth, picnic table

ASSIGNMENT: First come, first served or by reservation: (888) 409-7579

REGISTRATION: At ranger station

FACILITIES: Coin-operated hot showers, flush toilets, playground, picnic area

PARKING: At sites

FEE: $14 for tent sites, $21 for lean-tos

RESTRICTIONS: Pets: Dogs on leash only
Fires: Fire rings only
Alcohol: Sites only
Vehicles: Parking at sites only
Other: Reservations require 2-night minimum stay; check-in after 2 p.m., check-out by 11 a.m.; quiet hours 10 p.m.–7 a.m.; maximum 8 people per site

Sites 4 and 5 are well-isolated sites with a solid sense of privacy. Site 4 is a pretty, isolated site, even though it's set right at the intersection where the one-way, upper campground loop road rejoins itself. Site 5 is tucked off on its own in the woods, set back from the road.

Sites 6 and 7 are set a good distance off the road, but they're quite close to each other. Sites 9 and 10 are right across the campground road from each other. They're more open, so they aren't quite as private. Like sites 1 and 2, this pair would be fine for a group needing two sites.

Site 8 is fairly well isolated. It's located next to the Ash lean-to. Site 11 isn't bad, but it's also a bit more open than some of the other sites in the Upper Loop. Site 11 is right across from the Appalachian Trail.

Aside from also being right on the Appalachian Trail, site 12 is otherwise another of Gifford Woods's top-notch tent spots. It has plenty of space and is fairly well isolated. Site 13 is a spacious site, set back a bit from the road, but it has a water spigot located right outside, so you'll get lots of visitors. If you want to meet a bunch of your campground neighbors, this is the site for you.

The lean-tos are interspersed among the individual tent sites. The Birch lean-to is in a pleasant, isolated spot. This one would be worth getting just for the privacy of the site. Apple is similarly off on its own. Maple and Beech are set right next to each other, and would be a fun pair of shelters for larger groups.

Spruce is fairly well isolated on the inside of the loop. Hemlock is across from the frequently visited water spigot at site 13, but it's in the woods a ways, so it's more private. The Elm lean-to also has a decent distance between the site and the road.

Overall, the upper campground sites are quieter than the lower sites. The surrounding forest is thicker, and you're that much farther from VT 100. Still, there are some attractive spots on the lower loop as well. The lower loop includes sites 14 through 27.

Site 27, the first site you come to, is open and quite spacious, but consequently not very private. The same could be said about the first three lean-to sites within

MAP

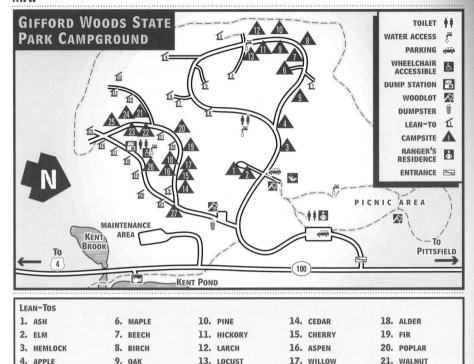

GIFFORD WOODS STATE PARK CAMPGROUND

TOILET	♦♦
WATER ACCESS	♂
PARKING	🚗
WHEELCHAIR ACCESSIBLE	♿
DUMP STATION	🔲
WOODLOT	🪓
DUMPSTER	🗑
LEAN-TO	🏠
CAMPSITE	▲
RANGER'S RESIDENCE	🏠
ENTRANCE	✉

N

PICNIC AREA

MAINTENANCE AREA

KENT BROOK

To U.S. 4

—To PITTSFIELD

100

KENT POND

LEAN-TOS

1. ASH	6. MAPLE	10. PINE	14. CEDAR	18. ALDER
2. ELM	7. BEECH	11. HICKORY	15. CHERRY	19. FIR
3. HEMLOCK	8. BIRCH	12. LARCH	16. ASPEN	20. POPLAR
4. APPLE	9. OAK	13. LOCUST	17. WILLOW	21. WALNUT
5. SPRUCE				

this loop: Oak, Walnut, and Poplar. The Willow, Aspen, and Cherry lean-tos are grouped closely together as well. There aren't many trees between these sites. If you're having a camping family reunion or some other confluence of friends and family, securing either troika of lean-tos would give you the perfect venue.

The Fir lean-to is set off on its own, and it's right across from the restrooms. Site 26 is also conveniently located near the facilities, but it isn't very private. The Alder lean-to is set up for wheelchair access.

Moving farther along the loop and back into the tent sites, site 25 is smaller but nicely isolated—a worthwhile trade-off in my book (so to speak). Actually, sites 21 through 25 are all moderately spaced and well isolated. Next to site 21, there's a short road leading up to another trio of lean-tos—Cedar, Locust, and Larch.

GETTING THERE

Gifford Woods State Park is located right off VT 100, just north of the access road for Killington Ski Area.

(Larch? I had never heard of that kind of tree before! It is a hardy, alpine conifer that flourishes at altitudes up to 5,000 feet. It has slender, soft needles that actually turn somewhat golden in fall.) If you have a very large group that wants to bunk out in a trio of lean-tos, Gifford Woods State Park is clearly where you want to be, specifically the Lower Loop, where most of the lean-tos are situated. It sometimes makes you wonder about the naming conventions of these lean-tos. What happens if they start running out of tree varieties? I can see it: If they built another loop full of lean-tos in one of the larger Vermont State Park campgrounds, we might end up with Mangrove, Eucalyptus, and Joshua!

Site 20 is open and spacious, but not as private or set into the woods as some of the others. Sites 15 through 19 are larger sites, but you run the risk of having an RV set up nearby. The woods here are moderately dense, but you'll still have one in view if it moors next door. Similarly, site 14 is very open and has plenty of room to spread your wings (or your tarp and your tent's rainfly), but you'll give up a little privacy.

Perhaps the nicest aspect of Gifford Woods State Park is that you don't have to travel far outside the park, or even inside the park, before you run across some hiking trails. The Appalachian Trail runs right through the park, and reconnects with the Long Trail approximately 1.5 miles north of the park. Another spectacular sight to see is the seven-acre stand of old-growth hardwoods, located right across VT 100 from the campground. This pristine wilderness has some massive sugar maple, beech, birch, and ash trees. Tread lightly, and enjoy this grand old forest.

GROUT POND
RECREATION AREA

THIS IS NO SANITIZED, drive-in, drive-out campground. The campsites at Grout Pond are spread out along a hiking trail that winds around the western shores of the pond. You have to hike your gear in to your tent site. This extra effort will give you a huge payoff, though.

You hike in to any of the 12 tent and lean-to sites via the Pond Loop Trail. This trail cuts through a dense forest, through which you can catch tantalizing glimpses of the pond as you start out. As its name implies, the Pond Loop Trail brings you all the way around Grout Pond. The campsites are spread liberally along the first mile of the trail. No camping is permitted beyond site 12, the last "developed" tent site. Since you hike into the sites, parking is in the small lot past the campground host cabin.

Don't expect to happen upon the campsites as soon as you set out from the parking area. The first site is just under a 0.5-mile hike in. Carry a manageable amount of gear, or better yet, have a wagon or some sort of wheeled cart to transport your stuff. If you're hauling gear without wheeled assistance, start out by bringing your tent to stake your claim on your site. These sites are first come, first served. You can't make reservations, so it's a good idea to have a backup plan if they are full.

This is very rustic, primitive camping. There's a true wilderness feel to these sites that is usually reserved for backcountry backpacking trips.

At 0.1 mile down the Pond Loop Trail, you'll come to a trailhead for the 3.2-mile East Trail, the 1-mile hike to the Kelley Stand parking area, and the 2-mile hike to the Somerset Reservoir. Shortly after passing this trailhead, you'll come to another trailhead for the Camp Trail, which follows a shorter loop out from the pond than the winding East Trail. Stay on the Pond Loop Trail to get to the campsites.

> *These hike-in campsites give a sense of wilderness isolation typically reserved for extended backpacking trips—they are as remote as it gets.*

RATINGS

Beauty: ✿ ✿ ✿ ✿ ✿
Privacy: ✿ ✿ ✿ ✿ ✿
Spaciousness: ✿ ✿ ✿ ✿
Quiet: ✿ ✿ ✿ ✿ ✿
Security: ✿ ✿ ✿ ✿ ✿
Cleanliness: ✿ ✿ ✿ ✿ ✿

ADDRESS: Grout Pond
Recreation Area
Fire Road 262
Arlington, VT 05250

OPERATED BY: Green Mountain
National Forest

INFORMATION: Green Mountain
National Forest
Manchester Ranger
District
2538 Depot Street
Manchester Center,
VT 05255
(802) 362-2307

OPEN: Year-round

SITES: 12 hike-in tent sites
and lean-to sites
around pond, sev-
eral day-use or
trailer sites

EACH SITE HAS: Fire ring with grate,
picnic table, tent
platform or pad

ASSIGNMENT: First come, first
served

REGISTRATION: Register by occupying site

FACILITIES: Pit toilets

PARKING: At trailhead to
campsites

FEE: Donations accepted

RESTRICTIONS: Pets: Dogs on leash
only
Fires: Fire rings only
Alcohol: Sites only
Vehicles: In main
parking area only
Other: Day-use areas
open 6 a.m.–10 p.m.;
quiet hours 10 p.m.–
7 a.m.; maximum 8
people per site; 14-
day maximum stay

Site 1 is set down off the trail on the shore of Grout Pond. It's an incredibly spacious site where you'll get breezes blowing in off the pond and a decent amount of sunlight filtering through the moderately dense forest. The site is hidden in a very subtle way from the Pond Loop Trail by a stand of trees and a short stone wall. Down in the site, you'll have a clear view of the pond, as well as access to it for your canoe or kayak.

That brings up another point about getting to your site. Once you've marked your site with your tent, you could go back to your car and haul your gear in, taking four or five or however many trips. Or, you could load up your canoe or kayak and paddle to the site. Then you've got your vessel right there at your campsite and can explore the crystalline waters of Grout Pond after you've set up camp. You could also haul your gear inside your canoe or kayak atop a wheeled cart.

The next site on the Pond Loop Trail, site 2, is very isolated from the trail. Standing on the Pond Loop Trail, you can barely see it. There's a twisting, 50-foot path down to the site, which is a bit smaller than site 1, but just as open to the pond, and extremely secluded.

If privacy is more important to you than being right on the pond, site 3 is a perfect choice. This site is set up in the woods away from the pond. You'll cross over a series of short footbridges put there to minimize trail erosion. Please use the bridges; don't step off or around them. The site is set within a very dense forest of deciduous trees, with a lot of maple and beech. It's moderately spacious, but site 1 is clearly the largest at Grout Pond if that's an important factor.

Right across the trail—but extremely secluded from it—on the pond side is site 4. Follow a 50-foot path down toward the pond to the site. It's smaller than site 1 or 2, but very sunny and open to the water.

Just past sites 3 and 4, there's a picnic area next to the pond. If you're waiting for someone to finish packing up before you occupy a site, this is a great spot to rest and have a bite. When I first walked the Pond Loop Trail, I mistook this for a campsite, but it's clearly marked as a no-camping and no-fires area.

Another superbly secluded site is site 5, set up in the woods on the opposite side of the trail from the

MAP

pond. The spur trail to the site is approximately 70 feet long. It gets dark early here, as very little evening sunlight penetrates the extremely dense, mostly deciduous forest. Between the distance from the Pond Loop Trail and the woods encircling site 5, you will feel a complete sense of solitude.

It may be fairly small, but site 6 is also well isolated from the Pond Loop Trail and the neighboring campsites. It's set about 25 feet off the trail. It's a fairly small site, but it has a tent platform, is very open to the sun, and is encircled by a dense grove of young maple trees.

If you would rather be way off in the woods, check out site 8. This is a lean-to site accessed via a 150-foot spur trail. The site is set within a grove of moderately spaced beech and ash trees with dense undergrowth.

Site 7 is actually past site 8, and it's located on the pond side of the trail. This is another small site, but it's buffered by dense undergrowth for a solid sense of seclusion. It's also very sunny and open to the pond. Site 9 is a lean-to set up in the woods away from the pond in a fairly open part of the forest.

GETTING THERE

From VT 100, take the Stratton/Arlington road in Wardsboro, just north of Mount Snow. Follow this to the brown Forest Service sign for Grout Pond on the left (heading north).

If ever there were a near-perfect site, it would have to be site 10. This site is very isolated by virtue of its remote location on the Pond Loop Trail and the distance from its nearest neighbors. It's a moderately sized site set beneath a loose stand of maples and spruce. There's a nice, flat, grass-and-moss-covered area for your tent carved out of the dense undergrowth. There's also a tree hanging out over the pond, which adds some character to this site.

There is a complete sense of isolation to site 11. It's on the pond side, about 70 feet from the Pond Loop Trail and distant from any neighbor. This is a moderately spacious site, set within a relatively dense forest of mostly deciduous trees and encircled by dense undergrowth.

The last of the crown jewels right on the shores of Grout Pond is site 12, also about a 70-foot hike in from the Pond Loop Trail. This site is set in a grove of mixed deciduous and coniferous trees. It's on the smaller side, but its seclusion more than compensates for that. The dense undergrowth and surrounding forest, the distance from the Pond Loop Trail, and the distance from the nearest site make for a complete wilderness camping experience.

These last few sites along the Pond Loop Trail— sites 10, 11, and 12—are as secluded and wild as just about any you will find in New England. The layout and character of site 10 make it my favorite. It has a Japanese garden feel to it, with the moss cover, the artful spacing of the trees, the one tree growing out over the pond, and its open flow. From site 10, you have a full view of the pond, and the openness allows you to enjoy the breezes and the sunlight, or the moonlight once dusk has fallen.

When you arrive at Grout Pond, you'll see some sites up near the campground host cabin, near the day-use area. These are likely spots for RVs. Pitch your tent here only as long as you have to wait for one of the pondside sites to open up.

HALF MOON STATE PARK

THE CONTIGUOUS Bomoseen and Half Moon state parks are essentially a string of ponds, marshlands, and abandoned quarry sites, all interconnected by several hiking trails ranging in length from 0.3 to 4.5 miles. From the sheltered enclave of Half Moon Pond, you could hike the Half Moon Pond Trail to the Glen Lake Trail, follow this through Beaver Meadow, and pass Moscow Pond to Glen Lake. From Glen Lake, the Slate History Trail will bring you to Lake Bomoseen.

The campground at Half Moon State Park is divided into two areas along either side of the pond. The loop with sites 1 through 35 is off to the left as you enter the camping area, and the rest of the sites, 36 through 60, are off to the right. Both sides of the campground have sites perched right on the shore of Half Moon Pond. These are the best sites.

As you enter the 1 through 35 loop, sites 1 and 2 sit immediately on your left. They are spacious and set within a loose grove of maples and other deciduous trees. Located right where the campground road splits, site 2 is very open.

Sites 4 and 6 are both situated on the shore of Half Moon Pond. Site 4 is spacious and has a partially grass-covered surface upon which to pitch your tent. It's a bit close to site 6, which is on the left as you look at the pond. Still, this is a key spot if you've brought along a canoe or kayak. You could launch your boat right from your campsite. Site 6 is smaller than site 4, but it's also shadier. Paddlers and anglers should reserve sites 4 and 6, as they're perfectly suited for either activity.

There is a deeper sense of seclusion to site 3. It's set up in the woods off the campground road, opposite but overlooking the pond. Site 5 is too open. The back side of the site faces the restrooms, and the front opens to site 6.

> *Half Moon Pond is pristine, and the campground that wraps around either side provides some spectacular pondside camping.*

RATINGS

Beauty: ✿ ✿ ✿ ✿ ✿
Privacy: ✿ ✿ ✿ ✿
Spaciousness: ✿ ✿ ✿ ✿ ✿
Quiet: ✿ ✿ ✿ ✿ ✿
Security: ✿ ✿ ✿ ✿
Cleanliness: ✿ ✿ ✿ ✿

ADDRESS: Half Moon State Park
1621 Black Pond Road
Fair Haven, VT 05743

OPERATED BY: Vermont Agency of Natural Resources, Department of Forests, Parks, and Recreation

INFORMATION: Half Moon State Park, (802) 273-2848 (summer), (888) 409-7579 (October–May)

OPEN: Mid-May–Columbus Day

SITES: 60 tent sites, 10 lean-to sites

EACH SITE HAS: Stone hearth, picnic table

ASSIGNMENT: First come, first served or by reservation: (888) 409-7579

REGISTRATION: At ranger station

FACILITIES: Coin-operated hot showers, flush toilets, water spigots, dump station

PARKING: At sites

FEE: $16 for tent sites, $23 for lean-tos

RESTRICTIONS: **Pets:** On leash only
Fires: Fire rings only
Alcohol: Sites only
Vehicles: Parking at sites only
Other: Reservations require 4-night minimum stay; check-in after 2 p.m., check-out by 11 a.m.; quiet hours 10 p.m.–7 a.m.; maximum 8 people per site

The sites on the forest side of the campground loop road—sites 7, 10, and 11—are very spacious and open, but they still offer mild seclusion because they are surrounded by moderately dense deciduous forest. Sites 8, 9, 12, 13, and 14 are right on the pond, but are bunched in close together. They are all super sites, separated by small stands of deciduous trees; however, they're smaller, more closely packed, and less private.

Site 15 is large and well isolated on the sides and back of the site, but it's open to the road. Sites 14 and 16 are right on the pond. Site 16, however, feels jammed in between the other sites. These open sites may not provide as much privacy, but then again, they are on the water. Site 17 is also right on the pond, but it's slightly larger, more private, and right next to the small beach area.

Sites 20 and 21 are well secluded on the sides, if not from the front. Site 19, however, is very open. It's also right next to the restrooms. There's a similar, exposed character to sites 23 and 24. These spacious sites are nestled within a grove of mixed hardwoods.

The 25 through 35 section of the loop generally gives you a choice between smaller pond side sites or larger, open, wooded sites. There's a cool, dark feel to the forest here, as the canopy is high and dense, but at the ground level, the campsites in the low 30s are very open. One plus in this section is a trailhead for the Nature Trail between sites 30 and 31.

Heading off to the right as you enter the campground brings you to its more secluded section with sites 36 through 60. The boat-rental facility is also on this side of the pond. There are several fabulous pond-side sites in this area. If you can, try to land in site 48, 50, 58, or 60—more on them in a moment.

The location of site 36 provides isolation on all sides. It's tucked into the contours of a small hill to the left of the campground road as you head in. There's no pond view, but it's spacious, scenic, and private. The hill on which site 36 is perched is in the center of a small loop where most of the lean-to sites are located, but you can't see them from the site. The seclusion of this site is marvelous.

MAP

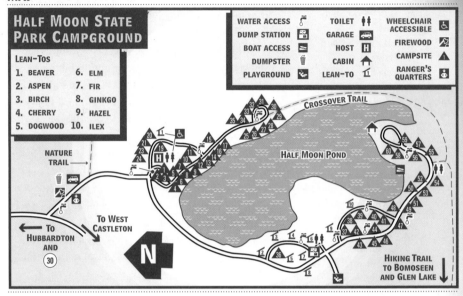

HALF MOON STATE PARK CAMPGROUND

	WATER ACCESS	TOILET	WHEELCHAIR ACCESSIBLE
	DUMP STATION	GARAGE	FIREWOOD
	BOAT ACCESS	HOST	CAMPSITE
	DUMPSTER	CABIN	RANGER'S QUARTERS
	PLAYGROUND	LEAN-TO	

LEAN-TOS

1. BEAVER	6. ELM
2. ASPEN	7. FIR
3. BIRCH	8. GINKGO
4. CHERRY	9. HAZEL
5. DOGWOOD	10. ILEX

CROSSOVER TRAIL

NATURE TRAIL →

HALF MOON POND

← To HUBBARDTON AND 30

To WEST CASTLETON

N

HIKING TRAIL TO BOMOSEEN AND GLEN LAKE ↓

There's a beautiful, open grove of pine trees across from site 38. The dark, slender pines poke up through the rich, brown carpet of pine needles. There's a silent, sylvan feel to this site. It's small but very well isolated. Site 37 shares a similar character, although it's a bit larger. It's also right across from the Hazel lean-to. Site 39 is small, but secluded and right across from the Ilex lean-to.

Just outside site 40 across the road, there's a short footpath that leads to the pond, so it's the next best thing to being on the water. Site 40 is also isolated and shady, as it's set within a grove of young, mixed deciduous trees. Site 41 is narrow and on the small side, but it's carved out of a grove of young deciduous trees whose brilliant green leaves brighten the whole site.

Sites 42 and 43 sit opposite each other across the campground road. Site 42 is smaller and set in young mixed forest. Site 43 is very spacious and secluded on all sides, but it's open to the road and site 42. There's a similar layout and arrangement to sites 44 and 45. Site 44 is smaller than 45 and set within a grove of conifers and hardwoods. Site 45 is a little bigger and more secluded in a dense coniferous grove.

GETTING THERE

From VT 4 in Castleton Corners, take Exit 4 for VT 30 north. Follow this to Hubbardton. Turn left on Hortonville Road. Follow this to Black Pond Road. Turn left and follow this to the park.

Site 46 is very spacious and secluded, set off the road in a dense, mixed forest. Sites 47 and 49 are moderately spacious, but very open. These two are on either side of an open, grassy area surrounding the water spigot.

The trade-off of spaciousness and seclusion for a waterside setting is one I am usually quite willing to make. Site 48, for example, is small but right on the pond. There aren't many trees filling in the forest canopy directly overhead, so it has an open view to the sky and easy access to the water.

Site 50 is very spacious and provides a nice sense of seclusion. It's set among towering spruce trees right on the pond.

While it's not on the pond and doesn't offer a clear pond view, site 51 does offer excellent seclusion, with dense forest on all sides. It's also set up off the campground road.

Just before the boat-launch area is site 52, which is set within a spruce grove and is relatively roomy and private. Site 53 is a bit smaller than 52, and it's very open to the road. Site 55 is of decent size, but it's also very open to the road. It's right next to the restrooms and a trailhead for the Glen Lake Trail. It's also directly across the road from the boat-rental facility. You can rent a canoe for $5 an hour, $15 for a half day, or $30 for a full day.

Dense undergrowth and a stand of trees isolate site 56 from the campground road. Site 57 is also quite private, set within a grove of mixed deciduous and coniferous trees, and moderately spacious. Site 58 is very spacious and fairly well secluded, but the best aspect is its location right on the pond. Site 59 is also large and near the pond, but not right on the shore. It's very well secluded on the loop at the end of the campground road.

Site 60 is also set on this short loop. This site is large and set in a loose grove of spruce overlooking the pond. It's next to the Tall Timbers Cottage, which is also part of the campground and available for rent, but there's enough forest between the site and the cottage that it's not much of a bother.

JAMAICA STATE PARK

DON'T EVEN THINK of coming here without a reservation on one of the river-release weekends. When the West River swells to its banks, the campground at Jamaica State Park swells with whitewater kayakers. If you want to score a site for one of those biannual weekends (one in the spring and one in the fall), you'll have to plan way ahead. Even for the rest of the year, Jamaica State Park's campground is heavily reserved. They do take first-come, first-served campers, but open sites can sometimes be hard to come by. Do yourself a favor and plan ahead for this one.

There are 43 tent sites and 18 lean-tos. There are several lean-tos arranged in a small loop at one end of the campground, but most sit in a line facing the West River. I can only imagine the scene during river-release weekends: These lean-tos packed with camping and paddling gear and the river surging along, dotted with brilliantly colored kayaks and thrilled paddlers.

Generally, the campground and the surrounding park are very quiet. There are no major highways nearby, so there isn't much in the way of road noise. The campsites are situated beneath a moderately spaced forest of towering spruce and shorter, younger hardwoods. The dense undergrowth provides a nice sense of seclusion between most of the individual sites. The sites themselves are spacious and have a hard, sandy surface that's perfect for holding down tent stakes.

The loop heading off to the right as you enter the camping area brings you to sites 1 through 11. There's a cathedralesque feel to the forest on this side of the campground, with the towering spruce trees presiding over the woodland. Sunlight and breezes flow easily through the forest to the sites.

Sites 1 and 2 are set back in the woods among the loosely spaced forest. Site 1 is open and fairly spacious. Site 2 is larger and set up off the campground loop

> *The atmosphere at Jamaica State Park mirrors that of the river: calm and serene most of the time, but wild when the whitewater is up.*

RATINGS

Beauty: ✿ ✿ ✿ ✿
Privacy: ✿ ✿ ✿ ✿
Spaciousness: ✿ ✿ ✿ ✿
Quiet: ✿ ✿ ✿ ✿ ✿
Security: ✿ ✿ ✿ ✿
Cleanliness: ✿ ✿ ✿ ✿

road. It has an open feel without sacrificing its sense of privacy.

The added elevation of sites 3 and 4 makes them more secluded. These sites, roomy and clean, are set on a small rise off the campground-loop road. Site 3 is opposite the volleyball net in the day-use area, which you can see through the woods. It's cool to be close to the action, but it could get noisy during the day. Site 4 is located next to the restrooms. Site 5 is a little smaller than most of the other sites in this loop, but it's set off the campground loop road, which adds privacy.

Nearby, the Briar lean-to is set up for wheelchair access. The rest of the lean-tos within this part of the loop are positioned facing out from or perpendicular to the loop road, which increases their privacy.

The lean-tos are spread out beneath the loosely spaced forest and against a good-sized hill that is peppered liberally with loosely spaced pine and spruce, and coated in a soft blanket of pine needles. The effect is captivating. The Hackberry and Ironwood lean-tos are set at the base of the hill. The forest is open enough here so that there's plenty of room to pitch tents at the lean-to sites.

A spruce grove and a small embankment give site 6 a pleasant sense of privacy from the lean-tos behind the site. However, site 6 is open to the Ironwood and Hackberry sites facing the hill. Site 7 is very spacious and airy, but also secluded by a deep spruce grove and young deciduous trees on one side. This is helpful because it's also right next to the restrooms.

The added elevation of site 8 enhances its privacy. This spacious site is set up on a platform off the campground road and surrounded by loosely spaced spruce and dense, young deciduous trees and undergrowth. Site 9 is set at the base of the hill behind the Hackberry and Ironwood lean-tos. This site is very isolated on both sides, but open to site 8 across the road. Site 9 is large, and there's a handsome, open character to the forest here. Site 11 is roomy yet very secluded on all sides, framed by towering spruce trees. Site 10 also is very spacious and private.

The campground loop is split by a short road, on which sites 12 and 13 are located. These sites are

MAP

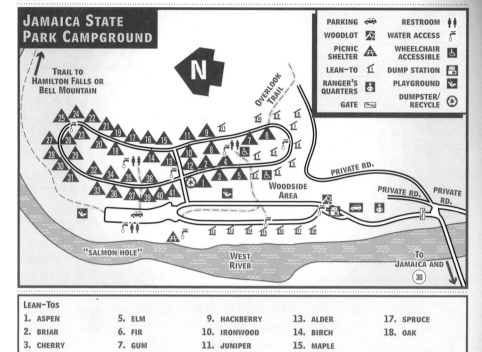

JAMAICA STATE PARK CAMPGROUND

Legend:
- PARKING
- WOODLOT
- PICNIC SHELTER
- LEAN-TO
- RANGER'S QUARTERS
- GATE
- RESTROOM
- WATER ACCESS
- WHEELCHAIR ACCESSIBLE
- DUMP STATION
- PLAYGROUND
- DUMPSTER/RECYCLE

TRAIL TO HAMILTON FALLS OR BELL MOUNTAIN

N

OVERLOOK TRAIL

PRIVATE RD.

WOODSIDE AREA

PRIVATE RD.   PRIVATE RD.

"SALMON HOLE"

WEST RIVER

To JAMAICA AND 30

LEAN-TOS

#	Name	#	Name	#	Name	#	Name	#	Name
1.	ASPEN	5.	ELM	9.	HACKBERRY	13.	ALDER	17.	SPRUCE
2.	BRIAR	6.	FIR	10.	IRONWOOD	14.	BIRCH	18.	OAK
3.	CHERRY	7.	GUM	11.	JUNIPER	15.	MAPLE		
4.	DOGWOOD	8.	BEECH	12.	ASH	16.	PINE		

roomy but very exposed and close to the road. Site 12 is open to the sky, so the site itself receives lots of sunlight filtered through the forest. The sites don't offer much in the way of privacy, though.

The forest is dense along the larger loop to the left as you enter the campground, which has sites 14 and up. The forest's character adds seclusion and privacy to these sites, most of which are moderately to very spacious. Site 14 is huge but doesn't provide much privacy, as it's very open on the sides. Sites 15 and 16 are similar in size and shape. They are both moderate in size and fairly well isolated.

Even though it's right across from the restrooms, site 17 does have dense undergrowth on all sides. It is also set up on a small rise, so it strikes a balance of moderate privacy and convenience to the facilities. Site 18 is spacious and open, but not too private. Site 19 is a bit smaller and secluded on both sides, but it's open to the road.

There's a deep sense of privacy to site 20 because it's set down off the campground road. There's also a

GETTING THERE

Follow VT 30 into Jamaica. Head east on Depot Street for a half mile to the park.

big rock in the center that you could use as a small table. This site is framed by spruce and dense undergrowth. Sites 21, 22, and 23 are all similar in size, shape, and spaciousness. Site 22 is set up off the campground road, and site 23 is down off the road. These sites are all fairly secluded and moderately spacious.

Sites 24 and 25 are close together and a bit smaller than sites 21 through 23. Site 24 is set off the road a bit. Site 27 is huge, but very open to the road. This site would be good for a larger group. It's framed on the sides by dense undergrowth and spruce trees, and it abuts the back of site 26. Site 29 is set down off the road and otherwise nicely secluded. It's very spacious and surrounded by dense, young undergrowth broken by towering spruce. Sites 28, 30, and 31 are similar in character in that they are moderately spacious and well isolated on the sides. Site 32 sits off the road in the dense undergrowth. It's smaller but nicely secluded.

If you're camping with kids, site 33 is a good choice, as it's right near the playground. It's also a great site if you plan to do a lot of hiking. There's a trailhead behind the playground that leads you to the gentle, 2.5-mile Railroad Bed Trail that follows the West River to the Ball Mountain Dam, the 2-mile Overlook Trail that takes you up and over the summit of Little Ball Mountain, and 3-mile Hamilton Falls Trail that brings you to the dramatic, 125-foot cascade of Hamilton Falls.

At sites 38 and up, the forest opens quite suddenly. These sites are separated by narrow stands of spruce and white pine. These are roomy but open sites. It's up to you how you feel about a site with this character, but I prefer sites that are more densely wooded.

There's a mixed sandy and grassy surface at site 39, which is framed by loose pines and spruce. This site is also right along the day-use parking area, separated by a relatively dense stand of trees.

Sites 39, 40, and 41 are all increasingly vast. These sites would work well for larger groups needing two or three contiguous sites. They're also great for stargazing or sunbathing, as they are wide open to the sky, and there's plenty of room to pile up paddling gear for those wild river-release weekends.

MOUNT ASCUTNEY STATE PARK

DIFFERENT PEOPLE associate Mount Ascutney with different things. For some, it's the ski area they think of first (although it is not officially part of Ascutney State Park). For others, it may be the hiking. For a select group of people, hang gliding comes to mind. Mount Ascutney is one of the premier spots in New England from which to launch a hang glider. For those activities (well, at least the hiking and hang gliding), spending the night camped out in the state park at the base of Mount Ascutney is a great way to start.

There are two distinct camping areas within Mount Ascutney State Park. Sites 1 through 18 are off to the right as you enter the park. Sites 19 through 39 are in the loop off to the left. The auto road to the summit is directly ahead of you when you enter the park here.

I particularly like the sites in the 1 through 8 loop off to the right. They are spread out, so most provide solitude and seclusion. The forest here is a dense mix of primarily coniferous trees. The only caveat is that this side of the campground is fairly close to VT 44A, so you will hear a bit of road noise during the day, but not too much at night.

The first cluster of sites includes sites 1 through 5. The road on this side of the campground is a straight in-and-out, two-way road. The other side has a one-way loop. Site 1 is fairly small, and is located right off the campground road. Site 2 is set off the road and is more isolated. Sites 3, 4, and 5 are grouped together, but site 5 has a long driveway leading into the site that adds to its privacy. Sites 3 and 4 would be good for a large group, as they are close together. The mixed forest gives the individual sites a shaded solitude.

Site 10 is spacious, but open to the road and right across from the restrooms. Sites 9, 11, and 12 are set in a small group, much like sites 3, 4, and 5. Site 9 is too open and close to the road. Sites 11 and 12 are tucked

> *Mount Ascutney has an elaborate network of hiking trails, easily accessible from the southern end of the campground.*

RATINGS

Beauty: ✿ ✿ ✿ ✿
Privacy: ✿ ✿ ✿ ✿
Spaciousness: ✿ ✿ ✿ ✿ ✿
Quiet: ✿ ✿ ✿
Security: ✿ ✿ ✿ ✿
Cleanliness: ✿ ✿ ✿ ✿

ADDRESS: Mount Ascutney
State Park
1826 Back Mountain
Road
Windsor, VT 05089

OPERATED BY: Vermont Agency of
Natural Resources,
Department of
Forests, Parks, and
Recreation

INFORMATION: Mount Ascutney
State Park, (802) 674-
2060 (summer), (888)
409-7579 (October–
May)

OPEN: Mid-May–October 15

SITES: 39 tent sites, 10 lean-
to sites

EACH SITE HAS: Stone hearth or fire
ring, picnic table

ASSIGNMENT: First come, first
served or by reser-
vation: (888) 409-
7579

REGISTRATION: At ranger station

FACILITIES: Coin-operated hot
showers, flush toi-
lets, water spigots

PARKING: At sites

FEE: $14 for tent sites, $21
for lean-tos

RESTRICTIONS: Pets: On leash only
Fires: Fire rings only
Alcohol: Sites only
Vehicles: Parking at
sites only
Other: Reservations
require 2-night mini-
mum stay; check-in
after 2 p.m., check-
out by 11 a.m.; quiet
hours 10 p.m.–7
a.m.; maximum 8
people per site

around a corner off the campground road, so they offer a deeper sense of privacy. Again, all these sites are a stone's throw from VT 44A through the woods, so at times there will be some road noise.

The next group of sites you'll encounter as you move down the campground road are sites 6 through 8. These three sites are also set in a cluster. Site 8 is near the restroom, which is a good thing for some people and not so good for others. Site 7 sits on a short spur off the campground road. Its added elevation gives it a little more privacy. These sites are all moderately spacious.

As you walk up to site 7, on your right you'll see the short footpath leading to site 6. Site 6 is very well isolated, with about a 50-foot hike into it. Site 6 has a fire ring instead of a hearth, which I generally prefer. Although the stone hearths are aesthetically pleasing, the iron fire rings seem to be safer, containing the fire, ashes, and coals on all sides.

The forest surrounding site 6 is relatively dense, but thins directly above the site to let in lots of sunlight during the day and give you a clear view of the sky at night. There are shadowy spruce trees spread on all sides of the site, giving it a pleasant, dark, cool feel, even on the warmest of summer days. There's still a bit of road noise from time to time, which is my only complaint about this otherwise excellent spot.

There's a dense spruce grove with lots of fern ground cover surrounding site 13, so there's a considerable sense of isolation from all sides, but it's still open to the road. Site 14 is small but set down off the road, which makes it fairly secluded.

There's a small loop at the end of the campground road where sites 15 through 18 are set up. There's a stand of towering spruce trees growing out of the center of the circle. Sites 15 and 16 are large but open to the road. Site 17 is located on a small rise above the campground road. This site is good-sized and fairly secluded. The best site within this loop is site 18. There's about a 25-foot path leading up to it from its parking space. The site is set within a relatively dense grove of mixed deciduous and coniferous trees, but its distance from the road gives it an exquisite air of seclusion.

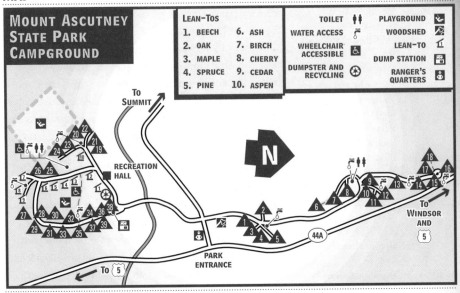

MOUNT ASCUTNEY
STATE PARK
CAMPGROUND

LEAN-TOS	
1. BEECH	6. ASH
2. OAK	7. BIRCH
3. MAPLE	8. CHERRY
4. SPRUCE	9. CEDAR
5. PINE	10. ASPEN

TOILET	PLAYGROUND
WATER ACCESS	WOODSHED
WHEELCHAIR ACCESSIBLE	LEAN-TO
DUMPSTER AND RECYCLING	DUMP STATION
	RANGER'S QUARTERS

To SUMMIT

RECREATION HALL

N

To WINDSOR AND 5

44A

PARK ENTRANCE

To 5

Now on to the other side of the campground, where the second loop contains sites 19 through 39 and the lean-tos. Site 22 sits near the trailhead for the Futures Trail. From here, you'll have access to a 1-mile hike to Bare Rock Vista, a 3.4-mile hike to the Steam Donkey overlook, a 4.1-mile hike to the junction with the Windsor Trail, and a 4.5-mile hike to the summit of Mount Ascutney.

There's a solitary quality to site 22. It's roomy and buffered on all sides by woods. I like site 22 the best on this side of the campground. Site 21 is also very spacious, but the side of site 21 is the back of site 19. You can see right through one site to the other. Site 20 is spacious and more open than these two, and it's set within fairly dense forest. The arrangement of sites 19 and 21 makes them a good pair for a group.

A low canopy of spruce trees adds to the solitude at site 23. It's a bit on the small side, though. Site 24 is tucked off to the left, and it's also isolated on the sides, but it opens in the back to the sites behind it and to the lean-tos set around an open area. Most of the lean-tos at Mount Ascutney State Park sit in an open field and a

GETTING THERE

Take Interstate 91 to Exit 8. From there, follow US 5 almost 2 miles to VT 44A. Follow VT 44A about 1 mile until you see signs for the park.

loose grove of spruce and maple. The Oak and Beech lean-tos are the most exposed and the least private. The Maple lean-to is set up for wheelchair access and is right across from the restroom and the campground host site. The Pine lean-to is nicely isolated and set within a tall grove of spruce.

Sites 25 and 26 are both moderately spacious and set within a loosely spaced grove of spruce with dense undergrowth. These two sites are well secluded on the side, but somewhat open to each other. The White Birch and Cherry lean-tos are set up at the end of a short spur off the campground road. They are close to each other, but great for a larger group.

A grove of maples and other mixed deciduous varieties surrounds the spacious site 27, which is open to the sky and set off the campground road. Sites 29 and 31 are spacious, but open to the road. You'll still hear occasional road noise from VT 44A on this side of the campground, especially in this part of the loop.

Set back from the campground road, sites 28 and 30 feel isolated. Site 30 is exceptionally spacious. Site 33 is open to the road but separated from neighboring sites. A loose grove of spruce borders the back of the site, and a wall of deciduous trees and dense undergrowth defines the sides. There's a short footpath right next to this site that leads up to the playground area and the restroom.

There is a slightly longer entryway leading to site 35, buffering it from the campground road. Sites 34 and 37 are across the road from each other but buffered on either side. Site 34 is moderately spacious, while site 37 is huge and very open above.

Site 36 is just like site 34 in size and shape. Site 38 is also similar, but it's a bit more vast and very open to the sky. Site 39 is set off the campground road, making it private. It's also set within a dense grove of mixed conifers and hardwoods with lots of underbrush.

Whether it's the hiking or the hang gliding that brings you to Mount Ascutney State Park, a night in one of the campground's secluded sites will be a night well spent.

MOUNT MOOSALAMOO CAMPGROUND

Ripton

WANT TO FEEL LIKE you're really out there? Mount Moosalamoo offers an incredibly remote wilderness atmosphere. To get to the campground, you turn off the paved road (actually VT 7), and start heading down a long and winding dirt road. This is called the Goshen Road, as it will eventually lead you to the town of Goshen. Several miles down on the right, you'll come to the road leading into Mount Moosalamoo Campground. If our campground ratings judged seclusion, this would easily get six stars.

Moosalamoo is the Abenaki Indian word thought to mean "the moose departs" or "he trails the moose." The Abenakis frequently traveled through and stayed in this region, and their history and legacy linger.

The entire campground and all of the campsites within are shaded by a mixed forest of hardwoods, with lots of maple and birch. The brilliant green leaves at the height of spring and summer cast a glow over the campground. The forest is young and spaced loosely enough to let generous amounts of light reach the campsites.

There are a total of 19 sites at Moosalamoo. They're set on both sides of the short campground-loop road. The sites are large and spaced well apart. There's plenty of room at each to accommodate the group limit of eight campers per site. Mount Moosalamoo campground would also score six stars for site spaciousness if the scale went that high!

The campground host is in site 1, which is off to the left as you come into the campground loop. Behind site 1, you'll catch your first glimpse of the big, open field in the center of the campground. There's also a little arboretum out there with a variety of deciduous and coniferous trees. The sign in front of the arboretum calls it a Backyard Wildlife Habitat. The evergreens within were planted in memory of former campground hostess Sarah Foster.

> *When you're camping at Mount Moosalamoo Campground, you are truly out in the wilderness.*

RATINGS

Beauty: ✪ ✪ ✪ ✪ ✪
Privacy: ✪ ✪ ✪ ✪ ✪
Spaciousness: ✪ ✪ ✪ ✪ ✪
Quiet: ✪ ✪ ✪ ✪ ✪
Security: ✪ ✪ ✪ ✪
Cleanliness: ✪ ✪ ✪ ✪

ADDRESS: Mount Moosalamoo
Campground
VT 32
Ripton, VT 05766

OPERATED BY: Green Mountain
National Forest

INFORMATION: Green Mountain
National Forest
Middlebury Ranger
District
1007 VT 7 South
Middlebury, VT
05753-8999
(802) 388-4362

OPEN: Memorial Day–
Labor Day

SITES: 19

EACH SITE HAS: Fire ring, picnic
table

ASSIGNMENT: First come, first
served

REGISTRATION: Pay at self-serve fee
station

FACILITIES: Pit toilets, hand
water pumps

PARKING: At sites

FEE: $5

RESTRICTIONS: **Pets:** On leash only
Fires: Fire rings only
Alcohol: Sites only
Vehicles: Maximum
2 vehicles per site
Other: Check-out by
2 p.m.; quiet hours
10 p.m.–6 a.m.; max-
imum 8 people per
site; 14-day maxi-
mum stay; Green
Mountain National
Forest is closed to
ATVs (yeah!)

As you get deeper into the campground loop past site 4, the forest becomes denser, and the sites have an even greater wilderness sense and isolated feel. Sites 7, 9, 11, and most of the other odd-numbered sites on the inner side of the campground loop abut the central open field. If you camp on one of the inner loop sites, you'll be able to walk out the back of your site into this field, which is perfect for a game of Frisbee, lying in the sun, or stargazing.

Most of the sites are fairly uniform in size, but sites 10 and 14 are extra large. They each have two picnic tables. Site 16 and 17 are pretty big sites as well, but they are only equipped with one table apiece. Any of these are worth investigating if you're camping with a larger group or family.

Site 19 is right next to the arboretum, a pleasant aspect. It's also quite close to the recycling station.

Mount Moosalamoo Campground is small, inti-mate, and has a wonderful sense of remoteness. I can think of only one caveat, although it certainly isn't unique to this campground alone: Bring whatever bug spray works best for you. You'll be deep in the woods here, and the insects can be ravenous.

There are plenty of hiking trails within easy access of Mount Moosalamoo Campground. You'll see trail-heads for the Mount Moosalamoo and North Branch trails as you enter the campground. The blue-blazed trails are the local hiking trails. The white-blazed trails are the Appalachian Trail and the Long Trail, which overlap through the Moosalamoo region. There's also a trailhead right outside the campground for the Voter Brook Overlook.

Any of these trails intersect with other trail net-works that wind throughout the forest in this part of Vermont. Try to get your hand on a trail map, because the trail network is extensive, and it wouldn't be too difficult to wander off a bit farther than you intended.

MAP

MOUNT MOOSALAMOO CAMPGROUND

GREEN MOUNTAIN NATIONAL FOREST

Mt. MOOSALAMOO TRL.

To FS-32 AND 7

FS-24

NORTH BRANCH TRL.

To VOTER BROOK OVERLOOK

N

VAULT TOILET	👥
WATER ACCESS	🚰
PARKING	🚗
RECYCLING CENTER	♻
PAY STATION	S

GETTING THERE

Follow VT 7 west, past the Middlebury College Snow Bowl and Breadloaf campus. Turn left on Road #32 (Goshen Road). Follow this dirt road for 4 miles and look for the campground signs on the right.

QUECHEE GORGE STATE PARK

> *There are numerous short hikes in and around Quechee Gorge— you could spend countless hours gazing up into the dramatic formations of the gorge.*

IN A STATE FULL of incredible natural spectacles, Quechee Gorge has got to be one of Vermont's most amazing and unique sights. Plunging 165 feet down to the Ottauquechee River (whew, I'm glad they shortened that to name the gorge), Quechee Gorge looks like the scene in *Butch Cassidy and the Sundance Kid* where Robert Redford and Paul Newman, when cornered by the "good" guys, jump off their perch on a sheer cliff into a raging river. Seen from the US 4 bridge that passes over it, the gorge's depth looks almost surreal. You'll be able to tell when you're there, even if you miss the signs for the gorge and the state park. There are always a bunch of people who have stopped to look over the bridge.

Just before you get to the gorge (if you're heading north on US 4), you'll come to Quechee Gorge State Park Campground, quietly tucked off on the left amid the tourist shops selling T-shirts and maple syrup lining the other side of the road. For the most part, the campground is set beneath a loosely spaced forest of conifers without much undergrowth. That factor, combined with the spacing and height of trees, gives the forest a statuesque presence. Visitors feel protected and secluded beneath the forest canopy. The spicy scent of coniferous trees, mixed in with the musty aroma of woodsmoke, instantly brings you into the deep wilderness. These olfactory delights abound here.

Overall, the sites are large and somewhat open. You could land a space shuttle in site 2, yet it still feels fairly isolated from the neighboring sites by the forest and a bit of undergrowth. You'll hear some road noise from nearby US 4, but it's not too bad. At night, it's guaranteed to lessen. Also, the road noise is reduced the farther back you go in the campground.

While most of the more spacious sites would be suitable for wheelchair access, site 3 is specifically

RATINGS

Beauty: ✫ ✫ ✫ ✫ ✫
Privacy: ✫ ✫ ✫ ✫
Spaciousness: ✫ ✫ ✫ ✫
Quiet: ✫ ✫ ✫
Security:✫ ✫ ✫ ✫
Cleanliness: ✫ ✫ ✫ ✫

configured that way. Site 6 is right across from the restroom and shower building. There's a small playground behind the restroom building. Whether or not you want to be close to these is your call.

There's a steep embankment that falls away from the campground behind sites 7 through 14. This is not part of Quechee Gorge per se, but perhaps the river flowed this way many moons ago. This feature of the landscape makes for dramatic scenery, but you'll need to be extra cautious if you have kids running around. A tumble down this embankment would be grim.

The Birch lean-to is also located along the steep drop-off by sites 7 through 14. Additionally, you'll find a horseshoe pit near the Birch lean-to. Didn't bring your own horseshoes? No problem—visit the host site (to the right of the shower building) to check out a set.

There isn't much of a sense of privacy at site 8, and it's a bit too exposed for my taste. Site 9 is huge. It's shielded overhead by the forest canopy, although it's very open at the ground level. You find these same characteristics at sites 12 and 10. These two sites are also close to each other, which is particularly appealing for a larger group that might want two adjoining sites. Site 16 is another site that is almost too vast.

The Walnut and Ash lean-tos are located right next to each other—also a good pair for a group large enough to need two lean-tos. The Hickory and Hackberry lean-tos are also adjacent. With the lean-tos in the Vermont state park campgrounds named for tree varieties, a new species is just one more thing you might learn while camping here.

Another good pair of sites for a larger group would be sites 18 and 19. These two are very open and close together. What the sites lack in privacy, they make up for in spaciousness. Close to a large, open field in the center of the campground, these are good sites to consider if you're camping with a tribe of kids and need a place for them to run around and burn off some energy. The swing set and slides are located in this field. There also is a trailhead for the Quechee Gorge Trail located nearby at the intersection of the campground roads. This short trail is perfect for a quick walk after dinner.

KEY INFORMATION

ADDRESS: Quechee Gorge State Park
764 Dewey Mills Road
White River Junction, VT 05001

OPERATED BY: Vermont Agency of Natural Resources, Department of Forests, Parks, and Recreation

INFORMATION: Quechee Gorge State Park, (802) 295-2990 (summer), (888) 409-7579 (October–May)

OPEN: Mid-May–October 15

SITES: 47 tent sites, 7 lean-to sites

EACH SITE HAS: Fire ring, picnic table

ASSIGNMENT: First come, first served or by reservation: (888) 409-7579

REGISTRATION: At ranger station

FACILITIES: Coin-operated hot showers, flush toilets, playground

PARKING: At sites

FEE: $14 for tent sites, $21 for lean-tos

RESTRICTIONS: Pets: On leash only
Fires: Fire rings only
Alcohol: Sites only
Vehicles: Parking at sites only
Other: Reservations require 2-night minimum stay; check-in after 2 p.m., check-out by 11 a.m.; quiet hours 10 p.m.–7 a.m.; maximum 8 people per site

MAP

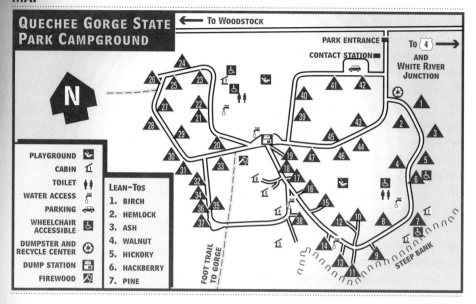

QUECHEE GORGE STATE PARK CAMPGROUND

To Woodstock

PARK ENTRANCE
CONTACT STATION
To 4
AND
WHITE RIVER JUNCTION

PLAYGROUND	
CABIN	
TOILET	
WATER ACCESS	
PARKING	
WHEELCHAIR ACCESSIBLE	
DUMPSTER AND RECYCLE CENTER	
DUMP STATION	
FIREWOOD	

LEAN-TOS
1. BIRCH
2. HEMLOCK
3. ASH
4. WALNUT
5. HICKORY
6. HACKBERRY
7. PINE

FOOT TRAIL TO GORGE

STEEP BANK

GETTING THERE

From Interstate 89 in Vermont, follow US 4 north toward the town of Quechee. The signs for the campground are right before Quechee Gorge itself.

Set against the woods bordering the central field, sites 20 through 22 are moderately spacious and have easy access to the field. The Pine lean-to is also located on the field. It is open and not too private, but it is configured for wheelchair access. The campground also winds around a bit closer to US 4 here, so between the proximity to the road and the field, it can get a little noisy.

There will be a bit of road noise at sites 23 through 28. Site 23 lacks privacy. Site 24 is close to the road. In fact, you can see the store on the other side of US 4 through the woods. However, site 24 does have a nice amount of dense forest on either side.

Site 26 is huge but wide open. This site is also right next to part of the Quechee Gorge Trail, which is a mere 0.21 miles. Site 27 is spacious and set within a spruce grove. Site 29 is roomy and open, and the back of the site widens to the field and restroom. Site 30 is set within a grove of mixed deciduous and coniferous trees. This site also faces the gorge, so through openings in the forest, there's a view as the gorge drops away below. Site 31 is vast, and set beneath a coniferous grove, so the site floor is covered with a blanket of pine needles upon which you can pitch your tent.

There's a steep drop-off facing sites 31 through 37. The scenery is nothing short of dramatic, but in these sites there are numerous additional reasons to keep a close eye (or a short leash) on the kids. Sites 32 and 34 are airy but not quiet as private as the rest. Site 35 is very open; the back of the site opens to the back of the lean-to sites.

At the end of this spur off the campground loop road, site 37 is set in a quiet grove of conifers and offers isolation. Site 37 is an incredible campsite. It's very spacious, framed by conifers, and open to the sky to get lots of sunlight. It is also right next to the Quechee Gorge Trail, which is a short hike down to the gorge from the campground.

Site 38 is located between the Walnut and Ash lean-tos. It's framed by dense woods, but exposed in front. Within the 42 through 47 loop, site 47 is huge and somewhat open in front and above, but dense forest isolates the site on the sides. Site 45 is also huge and airy. It's set within a pine grove. Sites 44 and 46 are a little smaller but still secluded. Site 43 is huge and open. This site, set within a grove of pines, is closer to the road and the recycling station, however.

It's a bit smaller than some of its neighbors, but site 39 is still rather roomy. It is carved out of a grove of loosely spaced white pines. Site 40 is open, spacious, and set within pine grove. It's a beautiful site, but it's also on the US 4 side of the campground, so you'll hear some road noise. Sites 42 and 43 are closer to the campground loop road, so they're not as quiet as the more secluded sites.

Stowe

SMUGGLERS NOTCH STATE PARK

> *Settled high in the Green Mountains, Smugglers Notch Campground is quiet and secluded, and has easy access to some of the best hiking in Vermont.*

EVER WONDER WHERE the "smugglers" in Smugglers Notch comes from? Apparently, when President Thomas Jefferson passed an embargo forbidding trade with Great Britain and Canada in 1807, it was especially hard on the folks living in northern Vermont. So most of those industrious, independent Vermonters kept right on trading with Montreal, moving cattle and other goods up through the narrow passage between the towering, 1,000-foot cliffs. They established a grand tradition of smuggling that continued with abolitionists helping slaves head north to seek liberation in Canada and rumrunners bringing liquor south into the country from Canada during prohibition.

These days, things are a bit quieter in the notch. The campground at Smugglers Notch State Park is across the street from part of Stowe Mountain Resort ski area, so you get glimpses of the towering mountain through the trees. You're also surrounded by Mount Mansfield State Forest, so the hiking opportunities are virtually limitless. The campground is set beneath a mixed, mostly deciduous forest, with a field in the center. It is very quiet, especially at night. Even during the warmest periods of summer, the air is crisp and cool this high up in the Green Mountains.

There's a dense grove of mixed deciduous trees and lots of undergrowth surrounding the moderately spacious site 1. That solid wall of forest provides the site with seclusion. The sites here have either a brick or cobblestone hearth for a fireplace. Site 1 has a charming stone hearth. The site abuts site 2 to the back, but it still has a nice sense of isolation.

A small stand of trees with a spruce and two maples guards the entrance to site 2. Mixed forest with dense undergrowth surrounds the fairly spacious site, which is otherwise relatively open to the campground

RATINGS

Beauty: ✪ ✪ ✪ ✪ ✪
Privacy: ✪ ✪ ✪ ✪ ✪
Spaciousness: ✪ ✪ ✪ ✪
Quiet: ✪ ✪ ✪ ✪
Security: ✪ ✪ ✪ ✪
Cleanliness: ✪ ✪ ✪ ✪

road. It has an isolated feel, as do most of the sites in the small, intimate campground.

There's a trailhead for a nature trail leading to Mountain Brook right next to site 3. Sites 3 and 4 are large and airy. They are situated right across the campground loop road from each other, but both are surrounded by dense forest.

Site 5 is moderately spacious and isolated on the sides by the dense forest. There's also a huge stump in the middle of the site, suitable for use as a table or chopping block. It may be huge, but site 6 is right next to the restroom buildings, set within a loosely spaced deciduous grove.

A dense forest pleasantly surrounds site 7. It's open to the sky above, and near the grassy field at the center of the campground. Site 8 is set up for wheelchair access. This site is moderately spacious and has an open feel to it. The restroom building is right behind the site for easy access to the facilities.

Site 9 is huge but open to the road. It would be perfect for a larger group or a family with small children, since it is also right next to the field. About two-thirds of the surface of site 9 is covered with grass, and it has a wooden, split-rail fence with a flower box separating the site from the campground road. There's also a huge maple growing on the right side of the site, so what it may lack in woodland seclusion, it more than makes up for with its pastoral feel.

There's a decent amount of spaciousness and seclusion at site 10, but it is close to the restroom buildings. There's a small stand of deciduous trees at the entrance to the site, which gives it a nice, closed-off feel.

A spur off the campground road to the right brings you to sites 17 through 11, in descending order. Site 17 is vast and set within a dense deciduous forest. It's also open to the sky, so lots of sunlight filters down to the site. This is a pleasant combination of privacy and openness. Site 16 is small, but it's secluded by a dense wall of deciduous trees, which it needs since it's also right across from the restroom building. The site is open to the sky above, and it takes on a green hue when the sun reflects off the leaves of the maples, birch, and beech trees framing it.

KEY INFORMATION

ADDRESS: Smugglers Notch State Park 6443 Mountain Road Stowe, VT 05672

OPERATED BY: Vermont Agency of Natural Resources, Department of Forests, Parks, and Recreation

INFORMATION: Smugglers Notch State Park, (802) 253-4014 (summer), (888) 409-7579 (October–May)

OPEN: Mid-May–October 15

SITES: 21 tent sites, 14 lean-to sites

EACH SITE HAS: Stone hearth, picnic table

ASSIGNMENT: First come, first served or by reservation: (888) 409-7579

REGISTRATION: At ranger station

FACILITIES: Hot showers, flush toilets

PARKING: At sites

FEE: $14 for tent sites, $21 for lean-tos

RESTRICTIONS: Pets: On leash only
Fires: Fireplaces only
Alcohol: Sites only
Vehicles: Parking at sites only
Other: Reservations require 2-night minimum stay; check-in after 2 p.m., checkout by 11 a.m.; quiet hours 10 p.m.–7 a.m.; maximum 8 people per site

SMUGGLERS NOTCH STATE PARK CAMPGROUND

PRIVATE PROPERTY

MOUNTAIN BROOK

PRIVATE PROPERTY

FIELD

LEAN-TOS	
1.	BALSAM
2.	SPRUCE
3.	HEMLOCK
4.	PINE
5.	ASH
6.	ELM
7.	BEECH
8.	MAPLE
9.	BIRCH
10.	OAK
11.	CHERRY
12.	ASPEN
13.	CEDAR
14.	LARCH

SHOWERHOUSE	
CABIN	
TOILET	
WATER ACCESS	
GARAGE	
WHEELCHAIR ACCESSIBLE	
PUBLIC PHONE	
DUMPSTER	
DUMP STATION	
WOODLOT	

TO SMUGGLERS NOTCH ← 108

TO STOWE AND 100 →

N

GETTING THERE

Follow VT 100 north to VT 108. Follow VT 108 past Stowe Mountain Resort to the state park on the right, across the road from the northeastern part of the ski area.

You can see Stowe Mountain Resort ski area through the forest surrounding the large site 15, marked by a small stump at its entrance. A quiet little brook flows to the right of the site.

A mixed grove of deciduous and coniferous trees surrounds site 14. It's very spacious and has a grassy surface on which to pitch your tent. The back of the site is exposed, and you can see some buildings outside the campground. This site is also right next to the Cherry lean-to site. This would be a perfect site if the forest right behind it were a bit more dense and grown in, as it's buffered on the sides and open to the sky.

There's a combined sense of seclusion and spaciousness to site 13. It's walled in by the dense forest on the sides and to the back, but feels very open in the center. There's a huge hemlock right at the entrance to the site. The canopy from that tree and a couple of others give the site a "roof." There's a very open feeling both at and above site 12. There are grassy areas to the right and left within the site, and mixed deciduous trees surround it, lending a decent sense of seclusion. Site 11 is set at the end of the campground road across from the Larch lean-to. It's secluded on all sides and open in the front facing the lean-to. It's also got a great sky view, making it the sort of site that allows sunlight in during the day, and brilliant moonlight at night.

A stately pair of maples guards site 18 on the left, and one tall, narrow maple on the right. The huge and private site winds around to the right and is set within a dense deciduous grove. It's not as open to the sky as some of the other sites on this side of the campground along the 11 through 17 loop, but the configuration of the site and the dramatic view of the ski area through the trees earn this site high marks. Also, the forest floor drops off and the woods open up as you look into the site, giving you a deeper view into the forest and a more secluded, wilderness feel. There will be some sporadic road noise from VT 108, but practically none at night.

The back of site 19 is isolated by thick, deciduous forest. It's a fairly large site that sits close to the Elm lean-to. It feels exposed to the campground road along the front of the site, although there is a sparse, narrow stand of young deciduous trees along the road.

There is a similar open feel to site 20. This U-shaped site abuts the field in the center of the campground. The proximity to and view of the field is perfect if you have some younger campers who need to run around and burn off some excess energy before you zip them into the tent at night. Like site 19, a narrow stand of maples separates this site from the road. I love the cobblestone hearths you'll find in most of the sites here. Site 21 is a bit smaller than sites 19 and 20. The back of the site is wide open to the field.

Camping at Smuggler's Notch puts you directly across the road from Mount Mansfield. This is Vermont's highest peak and home to some of the world-class hiking for which Vermont is renowned. There are 35 miles of hiking trails winding up and over Mount Mansfield, so plan your hike and pay attention. It wouldn't do to inadvertently come down on the other side of the mountain.

Test yourself on classics like the aptly named Profanity Trail and Subway, or you can opt for any of a variety of routes that connect to the Long Trail. Even below the summit, this ridgeline hike passes overlooks with stunning views of the Green Mountains.

UNDERHILL
STATE PARK

> *Underhill State Park's campsites are mostly hike-in sites. This design and its remote mountainside location add to the campground's deep wilderness feel.*

THE AIR IS CLEAR AND COOL as you approach Underhill State Park. Perched on the western flanks of Mount Mansfield—Vermont's highest peak—this is the spot for launching your hiking adventures on and around the mountain. You can literally begin a hike up Mount Mansfield from your campsite.

Underhill State Park itself feels remarkably isolated. At night, the silence and solitude is complete, and the darkness absolute. Most of the sites are hike-in sites, which adds to the seclusion.

Sites 8 through 11 are spread the farthest from the rest of the campground. These hike-in sites are located past the park shelter, an open log cabin–type structure in the day-use and picnic area. Sites 8 through 11 all require a hike-in of between 50 and 70 feet, so they are very secluded. The only other people you'll see from within one of these sites are your immediate neighbors, and at night, all you'll see are glimmers of their campfires through the forest.

This cluster of sites is set within a moderately dense forest of young deciduous trees, with lots of beech and maples. They are not especially huge sites, especially since much of the center of each is occupied by a large stone hearth. However, the sense of solitude here more than makes up for these sites' modest size.

There is a separate parking area for the hike-in sites, so you won't have to lug your gear quite as far as if you parked down by the ranger station. This parking area is also used by day hikers going up Mount Mansfield, so if it's full when you first arrive, be patient and try again later.

Across the campground road from this small parking area is the Pine lean-to, which is also accessible via a short hike. It would be worth getting this site just for its privacy. You won't see anyone or anything but the surrounding deciduous forest.

RATINGS

Beauty: ✿ ✿ ✿ ✿ ✿
Privacy: ✿ ✿ ✿ ✿ ✿
Spaciousness: ✿ ✿ ✿ ✿
Quiet: ✿ ✿ ✿ ✿ ✿
Security: ✿ ✿ ✿ ✿ ✿
Cleanliness: ✿ ✿ ✿ ✿ ✿

You can also get to sites 8 through 11 by hiking past the park shelter. On the way up to site 9, you'll pass a water spigot. Fortunately, the site is farther up the trail, so you won't have people walking by on the way to fill their canteens for the hike up Mansfield.

I love these kind of hike-in sites because they really add to the feeling of being out in nature. There are wheeled carts available for use down by the ranger station to help you haul your camping gear into the sites. Sites 6 and 7 are also hike-in sites, spread out along a walking path that winds out in a short loop from the ranger station. These two sites are a bit larger than sites 8 through 10. Site 7 is moderately spacious but fabulously shrouded in dense forest.

There's a decent sense of isolation to site 6, which has a short wooden retaining wall that keeps the tent platform level. This site is set beneath a grove of tall spruce trees that lend a woodsy, cool atmosphere to the site. The forest is spaced loosely enough that it lets lots of sunlight down through the woods. This, too, adds to the site's unique character. It's relatively close to the restrooms, but not too close.

The Cedar lean-to, on the other hand, is right behind the restrooms—a bit close for me. Site 5 and the Ash lean-to are tucked down behind Cedar. Site 5 is set within a moderately dense forest at the edge of the woods. Both site 5 and the Ash lean-to are also at the edge of a fairly steep bank, which requires that you be extra cautious if you're camping here with kids.

There is an open, grassy picnic area right across the parking lot from the ranger station. Sites 1 through 4, and the Maple, Birch, and Beech lean-tos are set around the periphery of this small field. These sites are a bit too exposed, but it is so quiet and dark here at night that it wouldn't matter much as evening fell. These sites also face a steep embankment.

Tucked at the edge of the picnic area is the tiny site 4. You'd have trouble pitching a tent here designed for more than two people. Sites 1 through 3 are moderately spacious and a bit more set off from the road. Site 1 is set higher than the others. All three are carved out of fairly dense forest surrounding the open field

ADDRESS: Underhill State Park
P.O. Box 249
Underhill Center,
VT 05490

OPERATED BY: Vermont Agency of
Natural Resources,
Department of
Forests, Parks, and
Recreation

INFORMATION: Underhill State Park,
(802) 899-3022 (sum-
mer), (888) 409-7579
(October–May)

OPEN: Mid-May–
Columbus Day

SITES: 11 tent sites, 14 lean-
to sites

EACH SITE HAS: Stone hearth, picnic
table

ASSIGNMENT: First come, first
served or by
reservation:
(888) 409-7579

REGISTRATION: At ranger station

FACILITIES: Flush toilets, water

PARKING: At either of two central parking areas

FEE: $14 for tent sites, $21
for lean-tos

RESTRICTIONS: Pets: On leash only
Fires: Fire rings only
Alcohol: Sites only
Vehicles: Parking in
either of 2 small lots
near groups of sites
Other: Reservations
require 2-night mini-
mum stay; check-in
after 2 p.m., check-
out by 11 a.m.; quiet
hours 10 p.m.–7
a.m.; maximum 8
people per site

MAP

UNDERHILL STATE PARK CAMPGROUND

TOILET	LEAN-TO	RANGER'S QUARTERS	WATER ACCESS	
PIT TOILET	SPRING	FIREWOOD	WHEELCHAIR ACCESSIBLE	
PARKING	GATE	GROUP FIRE PLACE	PARK SHELTER	

GETTING THERE

Follow VT 15 to Underhill Center. Turn onto Pleasant Valley Road. Follow this through the town of Underhill to Mountain Road. Turn onto Mountain Road and follow the signs to the park.

and the picnic area. Since all of the other sites here are hike-in sites, these sites are the most easily accessible at Underhill State Park.

Wherever you land at Underhill State Park, you won't be far from the trails that follow the spine of the Green Mountains and bring you to the highest point in Vermont.

MASSACHUSETTS

BEARTOWN
STATE FOREST

BEARTOWN STATE FOREST is a beautiful, intimate campground set along the shores of Benedict Pond, a good-sized pond ready to accept anglers, swimmers, and paddlers. There are only 12 sites, but if there were a rating for perfect sites, Beartown would be way out in front.

Camping here is by reservation only, so plan ahead, call ahead, and try to get yourself one of the spectacularly secluded and superbly scenic pondside sites. The Appalachian Trail passes right through the forest and next to the campground. If I were hiking the Appalachian Trail, I would think it worth the effort to plan for a night at Beartown State Forest, especially if I could secure site 11.

Sites 1 and 2 are spacious. Site 1 is huge in fact, and it has a large, grassy area where you could place your tent. The sites themselves are surrounded by fairly dense forest. Sites 3 and 4 are in a small grassy field that separates the parking area from the state forest road. These sites are wide open and quite spacious, but not very private. They are also close to the pit toilets, which are the only facilities at this primitive campground. Even though sites 3 and 4 are right off the small parking area, they can still offer seclusion, especially since there isn't going to be any road traffic later in the evening.

Site 6 is also a very spacious site. It's set just to the left of the restrooms. If you're going to camp closer to the road, though, (i.e. if you couldn't score a pond site), choose site 5. There's a very short lug-in from the parking area, which gives this site a pleasant, isolated feel. It's also set within a dense grove of mixed deciduous and coniferous trees that shield it from the state forest road.

Site 7 is a roomy and private site off to the left as you start to wind down the short road that leads to the

> *Whether you're into hiking, biking, paddling, or horseback riding, you won't run out of things to do at Beartown State Forest*

RATINGS

Beauty: ✩ ✩ ✩ ✩ ✩
Privacy: ✩ ✩ ✩ ✩
Spaciousness: ✩ ✩ ✩ ✩
Quiet: ✩ ✩ ✩ ✩ ✩
Security:✩ ✩ ✩ ✩ ✩
Cleanliness: ✩ ✩ ✩ ✩

KEY INFORMATION

ADDRESS: Beartown State Forest
69 Blue Hill Road
Monterey, MA 01245

OPERATED BY: Massachusetts Department of Environmental Management

INFORMATION: Beartown State Forest, (413) 528-0904

OPEN: Mid-May–mid-October

SITES: 12

EACH SITE HAS: Fire ring, picnic table

ASSIGNMENT: October–April: first-come, first-served. May–September: reservations, (877) I-CAMP-MA (422-6762) or www.reserve america.com

REGISTRATION: At ranger station

FACILITIES: Pit toilets

PARKING: At sites or in central parking area

FEE: Massachusetts residents, $5; nonresidents, $6

RESTRICTIONS: Pets: On leash only
Fires: Fire rings only
Alcohol: Prohibited
Vehicles: Maximum 2 per site
Other: Motorized vehicles must check in at forest headquarters

pond sites. It is also right across from the water fountain. The dense wall of woods surrounding the site gives it a wilderness feel.

All of the sites have at least one picnic table and a fire ring. From both sites 8 and 12, you'll have easy access to the footpath leading to the shore of Benedict Pond. Site 8 is more open than the other sites in the pondside neighborhood. Like site 12, it's near but not directly on the pond.

From site 12, you'll still have a good pond view from your table over the waterfront sites, but you probably won't see the water through your tent's front flaps. Site 12 is also set up on a small rise, which gives it good drainage as well as being a better vantage point. Sites 9 through 11 are situated right along the edge of the pond. Site 11 is the primo pond spot. This really is a perfect, dramatically sculpted site. It sits on a small rise that looks out onto the placid waters of Benedict Pond and the rolling hills that frame the water. The pond access trail runs by the right of the site, but that's no bother. Besides offering a view filled with dramatic scenery, the site is also well isolated. With its pond-facing orientation and the ring of wildflowers and maples surrounding it, this site offers the best of both the pond and the woods.

Since you're bound to spend lots of time just sitting and drinking in the view (and who knows, you may make some new friends happy to share the experience), there are two picnic tables at this site. You could take this site for a week and never have to leave once. You can paddle, swim, and fish right from your campsite. Even doing nothing in a site like this is spectacular.

Sites 9 and 10 have equally dramatic pondside locations. The two sites individually are a bit smaller than site 11, and they're a bit close together, but this would be a perfect pair for a group, and you couldn't ask for two more scenic sites. All in all, sites 9, 10, and 11 are classic pondside campsites. It's worth planning way ahead for a few nights in one of these sites.

Beartown State Forest is a very quiet campground, even during the day. The only sounds you'll hear are the woodland birds talking back and forth, the soft splash of a canoe or kayak paddle out in the

GETTING THERE

pond, and perhaps the whiz of a line being cast into the water.

With all this solitude, there's still plenty to do within Beartown State Forest. There's a larger beach and day-use area up the state forest road before you get to the campground. To hit the hiking trails right from the campground, follow the Benedict Pond Road (the paved road running through the forest and past the campground) to the Wildcat Trail, the Turkey Trail, the Sky Peak Trail, and the Airplane Trail. I've never ridden it before, but I've heard from mountain-biking buddies out in this neck of the woods that the Airplane Trail is one you won't want to miss.

All the above trails are multi-use trails, so you'll see hikers and bikers. Be careful, be aware, and share the trails. Horses are allowed on these trails as well, but you might not see as many, since there is a separate bridle trail. The blue-blazed trails are the hiking trails, the red-blazed trail is the bridle trail, and the white blazes indicate the Appalachian Trail. The orange-blazed trails are open to everyone—hikers, bikers, horses, and off-road vehicles.

From Great Barrington, follow MA 23 east toward Monterey. Turn left on Blue Hill Road, and follow this to Beartown Road and signs for the park.

CLARKSBURG STATE PARK

> *The campground at Clarksburg State Park has a dark, cool, sylvan feel even on the most brilliant summer days.*

CLARKSBURG STATE PARK is up in the absolute northwestern corner of Massachusetts, right along the Vermont border. The sites at this moderately sized campground are carved out of a dense forest of pines, spruce, and hemlock that gives the woods a dark, cool feeling. Even on the most brilliant, sunny days, the whole campground is immersed in the shade of the verdant forest.

The coniferous roof of the campground covers most of the sites with a velvety blanket of pine needles. The sites are spread out along a large, central campground loop road bisected by a crossroad. Sites 9 through 14 are situated along the crossroad. The rest are on the outer loops.

You can reserve most of the sites through Reserve America. Sites 1, 4, 10, 11, 12, 14, 18, 23, 25, and 29 are the first-come, first-served sites. Those located along the inner side of the campground loop and the crossroad have the most densely forested feel. The sites facing Mauserts Pond, although they are still quite a ways back from the water's edge and carved out of the forest, offer a bit more light coming through the trees and occasional glimpses of the pond.

Sites 1 and 2 are very spacious and have an isolated feeling. Even though the woods here are thick, you can catch a glimpse of Mauserts Pond from site 2. Sites 6 and 7 are pleasant and set down from the road, which adds to their privacy and sense of isolation. Sites 10 and 11 are smaller than most of the other sites at Clarksburg State Park, and they are close to the facilities.

Along the stretch of the campground loop where sites 16 through 23 are located, the sites are large, and they are isolated from each other and from the rest of the sites. These are all decent sites for tent camping, as you'll enjoy a sense of solitude here. There are more hardwoods mixed into the forest along this portion of

RATINGS

Beauty: ✿ ✿ ✿ ✿
Privacy: ✿ ✿ ✿ ✿
Spaciousness: ✿ ✿ ✿ ✿
Quiet: ✿ ✿ ✿ ✿
Security: ✿ ✿ ✿
Cleanliness: ✿ ✿ ✿ ✿

the campground loop road. The brilliant green leaves of the maples in summer brighten the forest.

Moving farther along the one-way campground loop road, you'll come to site 23, which is tremendous. It is set way back from the road, it's rather large, and it has a calming sense of wilderness seclusion. The forest directly overhead is clear, so you'll also get light filtering down to the site floor, as well as glimpses of the night sky for stargazing (once you've put your campfire out and your eyes adjust to the dark).

Sites 25 and up are a bit smaller than most of the others, particularly those situated along the outside of the campground loop road, but they're still attractive and offer a private atmosphere, as they're set within the dense coniferous forest. The walls of pine and spruce here form an effective barrier between the individual sites. Site 29 is the exception, but this is a large site well suited for a group or family.

Site 31 is set within its own clearing. This is a good spot if you have smaller kids, as it will be easier to keep an eye on them. Site 33 looks much the same, but is a bit smaller.

It seems that site 36 has vanished from the Clarksburg State Park campground loop. In its place is a trailhead that leads off in the direction of the Mauserts Loop Trail. Perhaps the site was sacrificed to make a spot for the trailhead—not a bad trade-off if you ask me.

Finishing up the campground loop road, sites 35 through 44 are smaller than some of the other isolated, larger sites and those located along the outer loop. However, thanks to the deep, dense nature of Clarksburg's forest, they still provide privacy and isolation.

Overall, the sensation here is one of being sequestered in a dense forest. There's a hushed silence about the place, even during daylight hours. In the evening, all you're likely to hear is the snap and crackle of campfires.

During the day, you'll definitely want to check out Mauserts Pond. There's a footpath leading to the pond right across from site 25. If you bring a canoe or kayak, it might be easier to head over to the day-use area, which has a boat launch and beach.

There are several fairly lengthy hiking trails wind-

KEY INFORMATION

ADDRESS: Clarksburg State Park
1199 Middle Road
Clarksburg, MA
01247

OPERATED BY: Massachusetts Department of Environmental Management

INFORMATION: Clarksburg State Park, (413) 664-8345 (summer), (413) 442-8928 (mid-October–mid-April)

OPEN: Mid-May–mid-October

SITES: 44

EACH SITE HAS: Fire ring, picnic table

ASSIGNMENT: First come, first served or by reservation: (877) I-CAMP-MA (422-6762), www.reserve america.com

REGISTRATION: At ranger station

FACILITIES: Flush toilets, beach area, boat launch

PARKING: At sites

FEE: Massachusetts residents, $10; nonresidents, $12

RESTRICTIONS: Pets: Dogs on leash only
Fires: Fire rings only
Alcohol: Prohibited
Vehicles: Maximum 2 per site
Other: Reservations require 2-night minimum stay; campground office hours 8 a.m.–7 p.m.; 14-day maximum stay

MAP

CLARKSBURG STATE PARK CAMPGROUND

To MAUSERTS POND

CONTACT STATION

To 8, CLARKSBURG, AND NORTH ADAMS

HOST FAMILY

N

RESTROOMS
WATER ACCESS
PARK HEADQUARTERS

GETTING THERE

Follow MA 8 through Clarksburg heading toward Vermont until you see the signs for Clarksburg State Park on the left.

ing through Clarksburg State Park. The Mauserts Loop Trail leads from the campground and crosses over Beaver Creek, then brings you up toward Vermont. The Horrigan Road Trail veers off to the west about two-thirds of the way to the Vermont border, after which the trail is called (appropriately enough) the Vermont Line Trail. The Bog Trail winds around the northern end of the pond and brings you to the beach and boathouse.

GRANVILLE STATE FOREST

YOU'LL FIND Granville State Forest in the southwestern corner of Massachusetts. The southern edge of the forest is actually right on the Connecticut border. There used to be two separate camping areas here, Hubbard River and Halfway Brook. While the Hubbard River area had a more remote, wilderness feel, it has been closed for several years. If you're interested in this area, contact the ranger station and ask when it may reopen.

The Halfway Brook campsites are a bit farther up the road from where the Hubbard River sites sat. The Halfway Brook sites are nestled within a fairly dense forest of mostly hardwoods. It's a relatively small camping area, with only 22 sites that sit deep within the borders of the state forest, so it's nice and quiet here. In the evening, all you'll hear are the birds as they settle down for the night, the soft rush of Halfway Brook, and the crackle of your campfire.

Most of the sites at the Halfway Brook camping area are available by reservation. Only sites 8, 11, 12, 13, and 16 at Granville State Forest are available on a first-come, first-served basis.

Sites 1 through 5 are definitely worth a look if they're available. These are set off from the main campground and face West Hartland Road. Site 1 couldn't be any closer to Halfway Brook, which makes this site particularly attractive. The site sits right next to a small pond formed by the intersection of Halfway Brook and Small Brook. Sites 1 and 2 are very private, as there is plenty of forest between them and the rest of the campground. Adding to the sense of seclusion, sites 1 and 2 are set farther back off the road. Any other sounds you might hear from the rest of the campground are obscured by the light whisper of Halfway Brook tumbling by in the background.

Sites 3, 4, and 5 are also nicely isolated, but a bit

> *When you're camping at Granville State Forest, you'll fall asleep to the sounds of the forest and the soft whisper of Halfway Brook.*

RATINGS

Beauty: ✿ ✿ ✿ ✿
Privacy: ✿ ✿ ✿ ✿
Spaciousness: ✿ ✿ ✿ ✿ ✿
Quiet: ✿ ✿ ✿ ✿
Security: ✿ ✿ ✿ ✿
Cleanliness: ✿ ✿ ✿ ✿

ADDRESS: Granville State
Forest
323 West Hartland
Road
Granville, MA 01034

OPERATED BY: Massachusetts
Department of
Environmental
Management

INFORMATION: Granville State
Forest, (413) 357-6611

OPEN: Mid-May–
mid-October

SITES: 22

EACH SITE HAS: Fire ring, picnic
table

ASSIGNMENT: First come, first
served or by reser-
vation: (877)
I-CAMP-MA (422-
6762), www.reserve
america.com

REGISTRATION: At ranger station

FACILITIES: Flush toilets, hot
showers, pay phone

PARKING: At sites or in central
parking area

FEE: Massachusetts residents, $10; nonresi-
dents, $12

RESTRICTIONS: **Pets:** On leash only
Fires: Fire rings only
Alcohol: Prohibited
Vehicles: Maximum
2 per site; off-road
vehicles prohibited
Other: Reservations
require 2-night mini-
mum stay; camp-
ground office hours
8 a.m.–10 p.m.; quiet
hours 10 p.m.–7 a.m;
14-day maximum
stay; Hubbard River
area closed until fur-
ther notice

closer to the rest of the campsites in the main loop.
The rear border of these sites abuts the borders of sites
6, 8, and 9 in the main campground loop. These sites
are set within more open forest, so they're spacious but
a bit less private—even though they're still accessed via
West Hartland Road, and not via the campground
loop. Parking for sites 1 through 5 is also separate from
the rest of the campground.

Adjacent sites 6 and 7 are very large. There's a
fair degree of privacy between these sites and the rest
of the campground, but the forest is loosely spaced
between them. This would be a good pair of sites for a
larger group. Site 8 is nicely isolated, nestled into the
forest right where you turn off the campground road to
the parking area. It is surrounded by fairly dense forest, so there is a strong sense of seclusion from the rest
of the campground.

The rest of the sites provide a blend of seclusion,
spaciousness, and privacy, as they are set amid the
dense, mixed forest that shelters the campground. Site
11 is quite secluded. There's a short drive down to the
site off the primary parking area in the center of the
campground. Sites 10 and 11 are both close to the gently murmuring Halfway Brook.

Sites 12 and 14 are very spacious. They are also
set up to be wheelchair accessible, with a wheelchair-
accessible parking spot close to site 14. Site 16 is nicely
isolated, set at the very end of the campground loop
road on the other side of the campground opposite
sites 10 and 11. Sites 19, 20, and 21 are all fairly close
to each other, and they are a bit more open than some
of the sites at Granville State Forest. Sites 15 and 19 are
near a small, grassy field, out behind the restrooms.
Sites 13 and 21 are bit too open for my tastes, and
they're situated right on the campground loop road.

There is an elaborate network of hiking trails winding through the rest of the forest. Across the street from
the campground are trailheads for the Ordway Trail and
the Civilian Conservation Corps Trail. From the CCC
Trail, you can loop around on the Corduroy Trail, which
heads out past the forest headquarters and travels
through a wetland before reconnecting with the CCC
Trail. The hiking trails on this side of West Hartland

MAP

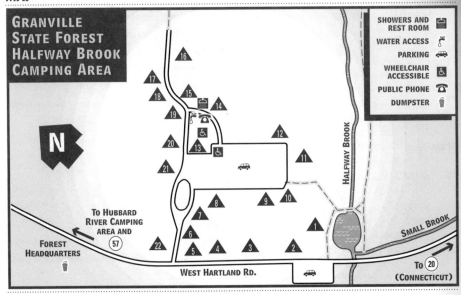

GRANVILLE
STATE FOREST
HALFWAY BROOK
CAMPING AREA

SHOWERS AND REST ROOM
WATER ACCESS
PARKING
WHEELCHAIR ACCESSIBLE
PUBLIC PHONE
DUMPSTER

N

To HUBBARD RIVER CAMPING AREA AND 57

FOREST HEADQUARTERS

HALFWAY BROOK

SMALL BROOK

WEST HARTLAND RD.

To 20 (CONNECTICUT)

road are fairly flat.

On the same side of the road as the campground, there's the Halfway Brook Trail and the Hubbard River Trail, which leads down to where the Hubbard River Campground used to be. You can also access the Woods Trail, which travels up and over a small ridge-line, and the Ore Hill Trail, which follows the eastern border of the forest. The trails on this side of the road travel either along or up and over Ore Hill. The afore-mentioned trails are all multi-use trails, so you can hike, mountain bike, and ride horses. Keep this in mind and exercise appropriate caution and courtesy. Even though you might feel like you're out in the mid-dle of nowhere at Granville State Forest, you may find that is just the sensation you were seeking.

GETTING THERE

From the intersection of MA 8 and MA 57 in New Boston, follow MA 57 west to West Hartland Road. Head south on West Hartland Road until you see signs for the forest and the campground.

North Andover

HAROLD PARKER STATE FOREST

> *Harold Parker is unique in its feeling of remoteness and its proximity to Boston. It's great when you need a quick escape.*

THE FOREST ENSHROUDING the campsites at Harold Parker is relatively uniform in its character, at least among the older trees. There are sections where the undergrowth thins out, and others where it grows so dense it looks primeval. The forest is composed primarily of tall white pines and low deciduous trees. Huge, open sites characterize the campground itself.

Sites 7, 8, and 9 are all exposed and close to the restroom. Site 8 is also wheelchair accessible, as are many others at Harold Parker State Forest. Even though site 10 is moderately spacious, it pales in comparison to the massive clearing where sites 9 and 11 sit. You could practically build a house atop this pair of sites.

Site 13 is absolutely enormous, and quite secluded. Several 80-foot-tall white pine and maple trees punctuate the site. A low wall of young pines, which must be the big white pines' progeny, encircles the site. The younger pines surrounding the site fill in the forest and provide an air of complete seclusion.

Although it's open to the road and sky, site 14 feels secluded by virtue of its location on the campground road. There are several hiking trails winding throughout the campground, two of which lead off into the woods just past site 14.

Site 15 is another massive site. It's set within a grove of short white pines and is elevated from the road, which adds privacy. Sites 17 and 19 are small, but set within a grove of white pines. The ground is covered with pine cones and a soft blanket of pine needles. Moderate undergrowth and young white pines surround these sites.

All these conifers give the forest a wonderful scent and make the forest a very quiet place. Usually, all you'll hear is the wind rushing through the soft needles atop the forest's elder statesmen. Now is another good

RATINGS

Beauty: ✿ ✿ ✿ ✿
Privacy: ✿ ✿ ✿ ✿
Spaciousness: ✿ ✿ ✿ ✿ ✿
Quiet: ✿ ✿ ✿ ✿
Security: ✿ ✿ ✿ ✿
Cleanliness: ✿ ✿ ✿ ✿

time to remind yourself that you're less than an hour from Boston.

Set at the corner of the campground road, sites 21 and 23 are open to the road on two sides. Like sites 17 and 19, they're set in a pine grove, but 21 and 23 are more exposed to the road. Another road just past site 21 leads down to Frye Brook.

The first site within the B loop gives you an idea of what to expect from the rest of the sites in this section. Site B1 is huge, but it's right across from the restroom. Site B3 is similar.

Both sites B5 and B6 are wide open to the road, but they're just far enough from each other on opposite sides of the road to provide a mild sense of seclusion. Sites B7 and B8 are very spacious. B7 is set up off the road, and B8 is set down from the road. The way the weather usually ends up when I'm camping, I'd go for higher ground. Site B10 is moderately spacious and isolated at the top of a little hill on the campground road.

There's a uniform, moderately dense character to the forest in this part of the campground. There's also a thick understory of deciduous trees and young pines, with towering white pines filling in the upper layers of the forest.

Site B12 is colossal and punctuated by several massive white pines. B11 is also rather large. Nearby, you can see two former sites that were closed for restoration, part of the regular maintenance of this heavily used campground. The forest is slowly and steadily filling in the old sites.

A large, granite boulder guards site B16. This site is also speckled with a stand of towering white pines, and nicely isolated by the boulder and its location along the road. Right across from the G1 group sites, it could get a bit noisy.

While site B18 is much smaller than B16, it has a high degree of privacy, as it's encircled by dense undergrowth. B21 is also a massive, open, sunny site well removed from neighboring sites. Site 22 is similarly secluded.

Towering, 100-foot-tall pine trees surround site B23. There's a cathedral quality and stately feel to the forest. This site is gigantic and very open. Site B24 is

KEY INFORMATION

ADDRESS: Harold Parker State Forest
1951 Turnpike Street
North Andover, MA 01845

OPERATED BY: Massachusetts Department of Environmental Management

INFORMATION: Harold Parker State Forest, (978) 475-7972 (office), (978) 686-3391 (forest headquarters)

OPEN: Mid-April–mid-October

SITES: 90

EACH SITE HAS: Metal fire box, grill, picnic table

ASSIGNMENT: First come, first served or by reservation: (877) I-CAMP-MA (422-6762), www.reserveamerica.com

REGISTRATION: At ranger station

FACILITIES: Flush toilets, water spigots, playground, showers

PARKING: At sites and 3 additional parking areas

FEE: Massachusetts residents, $10; nonresidents, $12

RESTRICTIONS: Pets: On leash only
Fires: Fire rings only
Alcohol: Prohibited
Vehicles: Maximum 2 per site
Other: Reservations require 2-night minimum stay; quiet hours 10 p.m.–7 a.m; 14-day maximum stay

MAP

HAROLD PARKER STATE FOREST CAMPGROUND

RESTROOM
WATER ACCESS
PARKING
WHEELCHAIR ACCESSIBLE
CAMP OFFICE
SWIMMING
PLAYGROUND
BASKETBALL HOOP
DUMPSITE

To 125

HAROLD PARKER RD.

FRYE BROOK

N

FRYE POND

JENKINS RD.

To 62

GROUP SITE G1

GETTING THERE

Follow MA 114 through Middleton into North Andover. Continue for several miles until you see Harold Parker Road and signs for the park. Drive through the park, following signs for the campground.

also large, but it's smaller than B23. Of course, that's like saying Mount McKinley isn't quite as big as Mount Everest.

Sites 29 and 30 are situated across the road from each other. They're very spacious, but they don't offer much in the way of privacy. Site 28 is like 29, in that it's open to two sides of the road—too open for my tastes. Most of these sites are massive and set amongst stately white pines. That's certainly the case with site 38.

The few sites along the short C road, including sites C2 through C5, are exposed to each other but very spacious and spread out. On the A-loop road, sites A2 through A6 are roomy but exposed to each other and to the road. Farther up the A loop, sites A7, A8, and A13 are exposed to the restrooms.

Sites A15 and 48 are close neighbors and are open on two sides at an intersection of the campground road. Site 46 is huge—it's a bit secluded by the forest on one side, but it's exposed on the other to site 48.

Site 41 is roomy and surrounded by an understory of young white pines and huge, older white pines and maples. It's secluded by its location, and it's just a bit open to site 44 across the road. Sites 43 and 44 feel a bit more nestled into the forest due to the absence of neighboring sites on either side. A dense understory and huge white pines surround site 45, but the site is small, which gives it a cozy feel.

The loose trio of sites 52, 54, and 56 sits off on its own. The campground road leading past them cuts through a dense, mixed forest with equally dense understory and ferns filling in the ground cover and thickening up the forest. Sites 52 and 54 are outrageously huge, open, and exposed to the sky.

Then you come to what is most likely the premier site at this campground. Site 56 is unbelievable. It is completely secluded, massive, and encircled by dense, younger white pines, huge maples, and older white pines. It is far from any other site, so the sense of solitude is absolute.

There's a funky bend in the campground road farther down, so even though sites 59, 61, 62, and 63 are moderately spacious, they're all open to this road where it cuts back at almost a 45-degree angle. From this intersection, the sites along the right side of the campground road, including sites 63 and up, face Frye Pond. Sites 61 through 68 are exposed and don't offer much privacy, but they are close to the pond. Site 68 is set up off the road, right next to the playground area.

Of the pondside sites, site 69 is the prettiest, set within an open forest that rolls gently down to the shore. The loose pines and maples give this site a dark, cool character.

Sites 79 and 81 are smaller and open to the restrooms, parking area, and basketball net. Sites 85, 86, and 87 are extremely spacious and open. There are more wheelchair-accessible sites in this part of the campground, including sites 61, 74, 77, and 78.

Harold Parker has some of the largest sites I have ever seen, yet many are well secluded. While this would seem remarkable and welcome at any campground, it's all the more amazing when you consider this campground is closer to Boston than any other profiled in this book.

MOHAWK TRAIL STATE FOREST

> *The towering forest at this campground's entrance is breathtaking. If that doesn't get you, wait until you see the campsites along Cold River.*

A SENSE OF REVERENCE overcomes you upon entering Mohawk Trail State Forest. The woods here have a "cathedralesque" quality. Take a moment as you drive in to get out of your vehicle. Gaze at the tall, nicely spaced spruce and pine forest towering over you and forming a canopy that preserves both the "wise silence of the forest," with apologies to Ralph Waldo Emerson, and the delightful scent of conifer.

This is an older-growth forest, as the trees are all at least 100 feet tall, with some reaching considerably higher than that. At the forest floor, the tree trunks are quite massive; there isn't much in the way of an understory, so the forest has an open feel to it. The sunlight filters down through the giant conifers in broken shafts, and most breezes are captured by the long arms of the trees. Parts of the forest are also interspersed with mixed maple, birch, and other hardy deciduous trees, as well as the offspring of the giant evergreens.

The sites in the first cluster are set close together, but remain fairly open for such a densely forested area. These sites are clean and spacious, but not quite as private as you might expect when you first see the forest.

In the loop with sites 36 through 56 down near the Cold River, you hear the sounds of the forest birds and the rushing water. The sites located right along the river are the best. They are set within a beautiful, loose grove of mixed hardwoods and conifers. RVs are allowed in the Mohawk Trail State Forest, but you won't find any in this part of the campground, primarily because they are not able to negotiate the extremely tight turn at the end of the road.

The riverside sites are spectacular. Sites 45 through 48 all sit right on the riverbanks at the end of the loop, so they are even more isolated than the other sites in this cluster. Sites 46 and 47 are the perfect riverside sites. Across the river from site 47 is the

RATINGS

Beauty: ✿ ✿ ✿ ✿ ✿
Privacy: ✿ ✿ ✿ ✿
Spaciousness: ✿ ✿ ✿ ✿
Quiet: ✿ ✿ ✿ ✿ ✿
Security: ✿ ✿ ✿ ✿
Cleanliness: ✿ ✿ ✿ ✿ ✿

Mohawk State Forest picnic area, but the day-trippers will be gone by the time you're lighting up your campfire to cook dinner.

The sites numbered in the 30s are spacious, but they are also exposed and set on a hard, dirt surface.

Sites 14 through 22 sit off a short road from the upper campground loop. Sites 15 and 16 are small but sweet riverside sites set up on the riverbanks a bit higher than the sites in the 40s and 50s. Site 22, at the end of this small loop, is the key site in this cluster, as it is very spacious and private.

The whole 14 through 22 loop is set beneath a grove of enormous spruce trees, so there's plenty of shade and that earthy, deep-woods scent. And of course, there's the Cold River rushing right by the campsites, so all your senses are satisfied.

The main section of the campground with sites 1 through 12 and 23 through 33 is a decent section, but the sites offer minimal privacy. There's a developed forest canopy, so this area gets a lot of shade, but the minimal undergrowth doesn't give the sites much of a sense of seclusion.

When you come to camp at Mohawk Trail State Forest, look for the sites in the upper 40s and lower 50s at the end of the campground and near the Cold River. That's where you'll want to be. If that doesn't work, go for the 14 through 22 loop.

Remember, this is black bear country, so all the appropriate precautions apply with food, garbage, and even clothes upon which you may have spilled food. When you're turning in for the night, place anything that may retain food scents safely in your car.

KEY INFORMATION

ADDRESS: Mohawk Trail State Forest
P.O. Box 7
MA 2
Charlemont, MA
01339

OPERATED BY: Massachusetts Department of Environmental Management

INFORMATION: Mohawk Trail State Forest, (413) 339-5504

OPEN: Mid-May–mid-October

SITES: 56 sites, 7 cabins, group-camping area

EACH SITE HAS: Fire ring, picnic table

ASSIGNMENT: First come, first served or by reservation: (877) I-CAMP-MA (422-6762), www.reserve america.com

REGISTRATION: At ranger station

FACILITIES: Flush toilets, water spigots, showers, wheelchair-accessible restrooms

PARKING: At sites

FEE: Massachusetts residents, $10; nonresidents, $12

RESTRICTIONS: Pets: Dogs on leash only
Fires: Fire rings only
Alcohol: Prohibited
Vehicles: Parking at sites only
Other: Reservations require 2-night minimum stay; campground office hours 8 a.m.–10 p.m.; quiet hours 10 p.m.–7 a.m; 14-day maximum stay

MAP

GETTING THERE

Follow MA 2 east from North Adams until you see the signs for Mohawk Trail State Forest on the left.

MOUNT GREYLOCK STATE RESERVATION

YOU WON'T FIND MANY other campgrounds with a deeper sense of wilderness and seclusion than the Sperry Road campground on Mount Greylock. This is true, primitive, mountainside camping. Sure, you can still drive your car to the campsite, but you are literally up on the side of a mountain within the deep forest. The campground is 6 miles up the auto road leading to the Bascom Lodge at the summit of Mount Greylock. Bear left off the auto road onto Sperry Road, which leads into the campground.

Each of these sites feels remote and rustic. There are 34 individual sites and 5 group sites. Most are available by reservation; the rest are first come, first served. The sites here are private and spread out. Some are a bit on the small side, but their rustic nature and deep wilderness seclusion is perfect. The sites are spread out along the main campground road and a short loop branching off to the left after you enter the campground. Each is nestled within the dense forest of mixed deciduous and coniferous trees.

Located where the short loop heads off the campground road to the left, site 8 is open on both sides. It's less private than the other sites, as it has road on two sides, but it's spacious and easily accessible. Sites 6 and 17 are smaller than the others on this loop, but they're still pleasant and surrounded by fairly dense woods. Site 17 is set within a grove of young hardwoods and is close to the pit toilets. Site 18 is set off the road, so the sense of seclusion is intense. Site 21 is very spacious and has a small grassy area for your tent. Site 22 is too open for my tastes, but it is close to the restroom if that's a priority.

Several of the sites farther down the campground road are lug-in sites. These are my favorites, as the wilderness air and privacy predominate. You truly feel as if you have the woods to yourself, even though

> *Here you'll be deep in the woods, perched on the mountainside, and close to a massive network of hiking and biking trails.*

RATINGS

Beauty: ☆ ☆ ☆ ☆ ☆
Privacy: ☆ ☆ ☆ ☆ ☆
Spaciousness: ☆ ☆ ☆ ☆
Quiet: ☆ ☆ ☆ ☆ ☆
Security: ☆ ☆ ☆ ☆ ☆
Cleanliness: ☆ ☆ ☆ ☆

ADDRESS: Mount Greylock
State Reservation
P.O. Box 138
Rockwell Road
Lanesborough, MA
01237

OPERATED BY: Massachusetts
Department of
Environmental
Management

INFORMATION: Mount Greylock
State Reservation,
(413) 499-4262

OPEN: Mid-May–
mid-October

SITES: 35 sites

EACH SITE HAS: Fire ring or stone
hearth, picnic table

ASSIGNMENT: First come, first
served or by reser-
vation: (877)
I-CAMP-MA (422-
6762), www.reserve
america.com

REGISTRATION: At ranger station

FACILITIES: Pit toilets

PARKING: At sites

FEE: Massachusetts residents, $5; nonresi-
dents, $6

RESTRICTIONS: Pets: On leash only
Fires: Fire rings only
Alcohol: Prohibited
Vehicles: Parking at
or near sites
Other: Reservations
require 2-night mini-
mum stay; quiet
hours 10 p.m.–7 a.m;
14-day maximum
stay

you're still car camping. Sites 23 and 26 are classic walk-in sites. They require about a 50-foot hike-in, making them quite secluded. When you set up in one of these sites, you won't even see your car from your campsite, much less any neighbors.

Site 30 is small but very isolated and private. Sites 25, 26, 27, and 29 are also lug-in sites that provide a tremendous amount of privacy. Site 28 is right off the road—not quite a lug-in site—but still isolated from its neighbors. The walk-in sites offer the deepest sense of solitude imaginable. You won't see or hear anyone else around you.

Site 33 is another lug-in site on the other side of the road. You can barely see it from the campground road. Overall, Mount Greylock's Sperry Road camp-ground is absolutely silent, save for the natural sounds of the forest and your own campfire.

Sites 34 and 35, at the campground road's end, are also walk-in sites. These are quite spacious and dis-tant from the rest of the campsites. They are remark-ably secluded and set within a dense forest of mixed hardwoods and conifers, younger trees and old, so the variety of the forest is visually stunning. After the sun goes down, the thick forest reflects the light from your campfire, making the trees look like a wall surrounding your site.

During the day, there is plenty to do here. Camped right on the side of Mount Greylock as you are, you're right in the midst of a giant network of trails for hiking and mountain biking. The Appalachian Trail cuts through here, so you may run into some through-hikers up on and around Greylock.

A number of trailheads lead right out of the camp-ground. There's a Nature Trail loop that leads behind sites 13, 14, and the Chimney group site. It eventually intersects with the Hopper Trail and the March Cataract Trail. The Hopper Trail starts right next to site 16. Down by the end of the loop with sites 4 and 5, there's the Roaring Brook Trail and the Deer Hill Trail.

Then there's always the classic Thunderbolt Trail on the other side of the mountain, one of New Eng-land's earliest ski trails cut by the Civilian Conserva-tion Corps. I've only descended the mighty

MAP

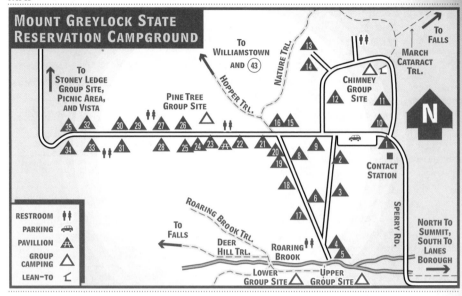

MOUNT GREYLOCK STATE RESERVATION CAMPGROUND

To WILLIAMSTOWN AND (43)

To FALLS

MARCH CATARACT TRL.

To STONEY LEDGE GROUP SITE, PICNIC AREA, AND VISTA

PINE TREE GROUP SITE

NATURE TRL.

HOPPER TRL.

CHIMNEY GROUP SITE

35 32 30 29 27 26
34 33 31 28 25 24 23 22 21
16 15
12 11
10
20
19
18
9
8
2
6 3
17

ROARING BROOK TRL.

CONTACT STATION

N

SPERRY RD.

NORTH TO SUMMIT, SOUTH TO LANES BOROUGH

To FALLS

DEER HILL TRL.

ROARING BROOK

4
5

RESTROOM
PARKING
PAVILLION
GROUP CAMPING
LEAN-TO

LOWER GROUP SITE   UPPER GROUP SITE

Thunderbolt once, and I have somewhat fond memories of the trail. It was in the late winter, so I brought out my telemark skis for the occasion. It was downright ugly—the dense late winter snow grabbed my skis and refused to let go. The mountain won that day, but it was a blast nevertheless.

GETTING THERE

Follow MA 7 and MA 20 north through Lanesborough, then follow signs to the Mount Greylock State Reservation headquarters. The campground is located on Sperry Road, which is several miles up the auto road heading toward the summit.

NICKERSON STATE PARK

> *Nickerson State Park is quite large, but it's also one of the few spots on the Cape where you can find a slice of wilderness for yourself, even during the busy summer season.*

IT'S NO SECRET that Cape Cod gets packed during the summer. Just look at MA 3 leading toward the Sagamore Bridge or MA 495 and MA 25 leading toward the Bourne Bridge on a Friday night in summer, and you'll see lines of cars waiting to get on the Cape. What may be a secret, though, is that you can still find solitude and wilderness on the Cape. Nickerson State Park is one of those rare and remote spots.

Part of the reason Nickerson is such an incredible refuge amidst the Cape Cod crowds is its size—it's huge. At 1,955 acres with 418 campsites, you can find all sorts places to quietly lose yourself in the rolling pine forests that blanket the park. This is one of the most densely forested areas on the Cape. The forest itself is beautiful, with loosely spaced balsams, firs, and pines. Once you've decided on a spot to pitch your tent, take a moment and inhale deeply. When there's an onshore breeze, you can smell the earthy scent of the coniferous forest and the salty tang of the nearby ocean in the same breath.

There aren't any sites within Nickerson set aside specifically for tent campers, but several of the eight camping areas lend themselves particularly well to tents. Look for sites in areas 2, 3, 5, or 7. Areas 2 and 3 are about a mile from the main entrance and are set up in open loops. Each has its own restroom and several drinking-water spigots.

Area 5 is about a half mile from the entrance on the way to Flax Pond. Several of the sites here are open and loosely spaced, especially 12, 14, and 16 through 18. A few pathways lead off the bluff down to Flax Pond, where you can swim, fish, paddle, or just enjoy a few moments walking along the water.

There are also some loosely spaced sites in area 7. Of the 46 sites in area 7, the clusters of 27 through 29 and 30 through 36 are particularly isolated, especially

RATINGS

Beauty: ✰ ✰ ✰ ✰
Privacy: ✰ ✰ ✰
Spaciousness: ✰ ✰ ✰
Quiet: ✰ ✰ ✰ ✰
Security: ✰ ✰ ✰ ✰
Cleanliness: ✰ ✰ ✰ ✰

if you're with a group and can secure them all. The sites in the low 30s are closest to Higgins Pond. Some of these sites (especially those closest to the water) have some sandy areas, so if you have a set of those extra-large tent stakes for securing your nylon dome in loose surfaces, bring them along.

Several sites are reservable from late May through early September. These include sites 24 through 67 in area 1, sites 113 through 122 in area 2, sites A through 83 and 93 through 104 in area 3, sites 30 through 78 in area 4, sites 16 through 23 in area 5, sites 46 through 98 in area 6, sites 110 through 144 in area 6X, and sites 8 through 17 and 27 through 44 in area 7. All other sites are first come, first served.

Even if you take the last site in the park (which is not outside the realm of possibility if you come in July or August), you're still in for some sweet tent camping. And even on those sticky summer nights when the weather is hot and muggy, there are often cool breezes blowing through the forest and over the bluffs.

The several kettle ponds (glacial ponds fed by groundwater or precipitation) dotting the park are among Nickerson's main attractions, especially for day-use visitors. Cliff Pond is the largest, and it's the only pond in which waterskiing is allowed. Nevertheless, it still makes for beautiful paddling and swimming. Electric trolling motors are allowed in Flax Pond, if you want to drop a hook in the water in hopes that you'll find a hungry trout. The others, Higgins Pond, Eel Pond, Little Cliff Pond, Ruth Pond, Keeler's Pond, and Triangle Pond are just for paddling, swimming, fishing, or pond-gazing (for information on fishing licenses, see Appendix C, page 224).

You could spend days exploring the trails that wind throughout Nickerson before you crossed them all. You can hike, bike, in-line skate (on the paved paths), and in the winter, you can cross-country ski and snowshoe. It's an amazing network of trails, and even on the busiest summer weekend, you can still discover a little piece of wilderness solitude. Some of the trails end up in the park's neighbor's backyards, so if you end up on something that looks like private property, be respectful, turn around, and hike back into the park.

KEY INFORMATION

ADDRESS: Nickerson State Park
3488 Main Street
MA 6A
Brewster, MA
02631-1521

OPERATED BY: Massachusetts Department of Environmental Management

INFORMATION: Nickerson State Park, (508) 896-3491

OPEN: Mid-April–Mid-October

SITES: 418 in 8 areas

EACH SITE HAS: Fire ring, picnic table

ASSIGNMENT: First come, first served or by reservation: (877) I-CAMP-MA (422-6762), www.reserve america.com

REGISTRATION: At ranger station

FACILITIES: Restrooms with flush toilets, hot showers, pay phone

PARKING: At sites and day-use areas

FEE: Massachusetts residents, $12, nonresidents, $15

RESTRICTIONS: Pets: On leash only
Fires: Fire rings only; do not leave unattended
Alcohol: Prohibited
Vehicles: Parking at sites only
Other: Reservations require 2-night minimum stay; quiet hours 10 p.m.–7 a.m; 14-day maximum stay

MAP

NICKERSON STATE PARK CAMPGROUND

6A

LINNELL RD.

MAIN ENTRANCE

AREA 5

AREA 1

HIGGINS POND

LITTLE CLIFF POND

FLAX POND

FLAX POND RD.

AREA 2

AREA 3

AREA 4

CLIFF POND

AREA 6

AREA 7

AREA 6x

MILLSTONE RD.

FIRE TOWER

MILLSTONE RD.

SILAS RD.

FREEMAN WAY

N

BOAT RAMP	
SHOWERS	
RESTROOM	
PARKING	
PUBLIC PHONE	
PICNIC AREA	
PICNIC PAVILLION	
GATE	
CAMPGROUND	
DUMPSITE	
PARK HEADQUARTERS	
BIKE RENTAL	

HIKING TRAIL – – – – –
EQUESTRIAN TRAIL - - - - -
BIKING TRAIL • • • • • •
BIKE/SKI TRAIL ||||||||||||
POWER LINE •—•—•—•

GETTING THERE

Follow MA 6 east to MA 6A west. Follow MA 6A west for a mile or so to the entrance to the state park and campground on your left.

More than 8 miles of the 25-mile Cape Cod Rail Trail pass through the park, making it the perfect launch pad for trips on the trail. You can pedal all the way to Dennis to the west of Nickerson State Park or South Wellfleet to the east. There are several businesses along the trail that rent bikes and helmets, if you didn't bring your own.

The Namskaket Sea Path also runs along the shoreline where Nickerson State Park faces Cape Cod Bay. It extends for 2 miles from Linnell Landing in Brewster to Skaket Beach in Orleans. This is well worth exploring, especially at low tide, when you can walk across the mouth of Namskaket Creek. The Namskaket Sea Path passes through an intertidal zone, where you'll see seashells, hermit crabs, sea birds, and all sorts of seaweed and driftwood at the high-water mark.

SAVOY MOUNTAIN STATE FOREST

YOU COULD SEPARATE the 45 campsites at Savoy Mountain State Forest by character into two very different groups. Most of the campsites are set within the woods bordering the campground, but many are found atop a hill covered by an open, grassy field punctuated by several large oaks, apple trees, and lilac bushes. This orchard-like field in the center of the campground affords a nice view of the sky that even extends to most of the sites set into the woods on the outer perimeter of the campground loop road.

The first three sites at Savoy Mountain State Forest are tucked off on their own short road leading to the right after you pass the ranger station at the campground entrance. Sites 1 through 3 are quite isolated from the rest of the campground. They are considerably more private than most of Savoy's sites, especially site 1, which is located at the end of this short road. Site 3 is very spacious, set on a slight rise at the beginning of the short road leading down to its cluster. Sites 1 and 2 are the best sites in this part of the campground, however. They are roomy and isolated from each other, as well as from the rest of the campground. They're also set in a grove of tall maple trees.

The forest framing the campground at Savoy Mountain State Forest is a dense mix of mostly deciduous trees, so there's a strong sense of shade and privacy to the wooded sites. In these sites, light filters down to the forest floor in fractured shards.

The sites set on the grassy hilltop at the center of the campground, including sites 34 through 45, are breezy, vast, and open, but not quite as private as the wooded sites. While I'm almost always a fan of more secluded forested sites, many of these central sites have a fabulous pastoral feel to them. They are perfect for some intense stargazing, or even for leaving the tent

> *Savoy Mountain State Forest has a fascinating blend of sites, some tucked into the woods, some set on a grassy hill, and others nestled among apple trees.*

RATINGS

Beauty: ✪ ✪ ✪ ✪
Privacy: ✪ ✪ ✪ ✪
Spaciousness: ✪ ✪ ✪ ✪
Quiet: ✪ ✪ ✪ ✪ ✪
Security: ✪ ✪ ✪ ✪ ✪
Cleanliness: ✪ ✪ ✪ ✪

KEY INFORMATION

ADDRESS: Savoy Mountain State Forest 260 Central Shaft Road Florida, MA 01247

OPERATED BY: Massachusetts Department of Environmental Management

INFORMATION: Savoy Mountain State Forest, (413) 663-8469 or (413) 664-9567

OPEN: Mid-May–Columbus Day

SITES: 45 sites, 4 cabins

EACH SITE HAS: Fire ring, picnic table

ASSIGNMENT: First come, first served or by reservation: (877) I-CAMP-MA (422-6762), www.reserve america.com

REGISTRATION: At ranger station

FACILITIES: Flush toilets, showers, water spigots

PARKING: At sites

FEE: Massachusetts residents, $10; nonresidents, $12

RESTRICTIONS: Pets: On leash only Fires: Fire rings only Alcohol: Prohibited Vehicles: Parking at sites only Other: Reservations require 2-night minimum stay; quiet hours 10 p.m.–7 a.m; 14-day maximum stay

packed and sleeping under the stars. What sites 34 through 45 may lack in seclusion and privacy, they more than make up for in the meadow setting—perfect for a remake of *The Sound of Music.* On the outside of the campground loop road, sites 29 through 31 are set within the forest at the edge of the field, and these sites enjoy the benefits of both.

If these sites had nicknames, site 32 would be called the orchard site, as it is framed by several small apple trees. Site 31 is also quaintly isolated by a couple of apple trees maintaining vigil at the entrance. If those are the orchard sites, then site 39 is the lilac site, set high on the open field right next to a huge lilac bush.

Sites 8 through 21 are spaced out along the other side of the campground loop road. These sites are close enough to the forest to provide solitude, but also face the field and offer a dramatic view of the hilltop, wildflowers, trees, and a sweeping expanse of sky—and in some cases, of South Pond. The trail to the South Pond Beach starts between sites 17 and 18.

The spacious site 21 is tucked into a clearing in the dense forest at the end of this part of the campground loop road. Its position at the end of the road and the thick forest encircling the site provide seclusion. The forest is also clear directly overhead, giving you a view of the night sky.

Perched on the corner where the campground road loops around, site 22 is roomy and pleasant. Site 23, next door, is large and scenic. A grand old maple hovers overhead, offering the site a comfortable roof.

Nestled into a grove of small apple trees and wildflowers off the outer perimeter of the campground loop road, site 29 also has an orchard feel. The other sites along this stretch of road are spacious and accessible, but set apart and tucked into the woods enough to offer a bit of privacy.

The day-use area, just down the road from the campground, has a beach and boat launch, providing access to North Pond. Because of this, expect North Pond to be more crowded than its sibling to the south. While there is a small beach area on South Pond, you can only get there through the campground. Both ponds have excellent hiking trails that loop around

MAP

them and toward the rest of Savoy Mountain State Forest's trail network.

GETTING THERE

Follow MA 2 east into Florida. Turn right onto Central Shaft Road and follow the signs to Savoy Mountain State Forest.

WAQUOIT BAY NATURE PRESERVE

> *Washburn Island feels as wild and remote as the South Pacific— but getting there is much easier.*

REMOTE, UNCROWDED, QUIET—not words often associated with Cape Cod, especially during the crazy summer season. Washburn Island may change the way you look at the Cape. It certainly did for me. The island is located right at the mouth of the Childs River. When you paddle or motor out there, you're never too far from shore. Plus, these are protected waters that rarely get too rough, so it would be a relatively easy trip if you plan to arrive by canoe or kayak. As such, this is a perfect spot for your first island camping experience.

The beach is a long, sweeping, flat sandy beach that opens to a shallow bay with gentle waves. This would be a very safe place for kids to spend the day in and out of the water. The water also tends to be a bit warmer here as it is so shallow.

The 11 campsites on Washburn Island are all spectacularly secluded. There truly is not a bad site here. This is a pack-in, pack-out camping area, meaning you have to take back all your trash with you. Also, there are no open fires or fire rings. You'll have to do your cooking on a portable hibachi or camping stove. You'll also have to bring all your own water, as there is no water source on the island.

Hiking up toward the manager's tent just behind the informational signs posted on the beach as you arrive, turn to the right on the trail to get to sites 1 through 6, and left to get to sites 7 through 11. All the sites here are marked both from the inland side and from the beach by small painted stones.

Sites 1 and 2 would be perfect for a group wanting two contiguous sites. Site 1 is a bit smaller than site 2, but similar in character, in that a dense wall of forest encircles it to the back and sides, with an open view of the beach to the front.

Set on a small bluff overlooking the beach, site 2

RATINGS

Beauty: ✩ ✩ ✩ ✩ ✩
Privacy: ✩ ✩ ✩ ✩ ✩
Spaciousness: ✩ ✩ ✩ ✩ ✩
Quiet: ✩ ✩ ✩ ✩ ✩
Security: ✩ ✩ ✩ ✩ ✩
Cleanliness: ✩ ✩ ✩ ✩ ✩

has a truly dazzling view of the beach and bay. There's also a calming sense of seclusion to this site, as it is framed by dense forest, and undergrowth on the sides. Site 2 is fairly close to site 1, but both maintain a sense of solitude from the rest of the campsites, if not from each other.

Site 3 is a good-sized site. It's relatively close to the bathroom building on the eastern side of the campground, but not too close. As it is a larger site, this would make a fine site for a large family or group. Sites 4, 5 and 6 are all fairly open to each other, but still quite spectacular. Sites 5 and 6 are moderately spacious with lots of trees sprinkled throughout. They are both very open to the beach.

Spread out along the southwestern shore of the island, sites 7 through 10 all open to the beach. Sites 7 and 8 are a bit closer too each other, but that certainly doesn't detract from their magnificence. They remain secluded by the forest, and are perched a bit higher off the beach. Sites 7 and 8 are moderate in size, similar to site 10, though site 10 is more isolated.

If stargazing is your thing, check out site 9. This spacious site has few trees blocking your view of the sky, and it funnels right down to the beach. There is plenty of room to set up your tent practically anywhere you want within this site. Its size makes it perfect for a larger group or family.

Site 10 feels incredibly remote. It's surrounded by 50-foot-tall scrubby white pines and maples. The ground on this site, and most of the others, is a firm, sandy surface covered by a blanket of pine needles. The loosely spaced forest opens to the bay for a million-dollar view of the water and cool sea breezes. This is truly a magical combination.

Site 11 is a larger group site, and it's the only site on Washburn Island that isn't located right on the beach. It is situated a bit farther inland within the forest. It's also fairly close to one of the two composting toilets on the island. Although it's set back from the shore, you'll still feel some clean, cool breezes blowing in off the water.

The paths within the sites and the hiking trails leading around the island are all well marked with

KEY INFORMATION

ADDRESS: Waquoit Bay National Estuarine Research Preserve 149 Waquoit Highway Waquoit, MA 02536

OPERATED BY: Massachusetts Department of Conservation and Recreation

INFORMATION: Waquoit Bay National Estuarine Research Preserve, (508) 457-0495

OPEN: Mid-May–late October

SITES: 11 sites

EACH SITE HAS: Incredible beauty

ASSIGNMENT: Reservations via Waquoit Bay Preserve office; or Reserve America, (877) I-CAMP-MA, www.reserve america.com

REGISTRATION: Permit required

FACILITIES: Composting toilets, no water available

PARKING: On the beach

FEE: Massachusetts residents, $5; nonresidents, $6

RESTRICTIONS: Pets: Dogs on leash only; prohibited on beach
Fires: No open fires; portable grills or stoves only
Alcohol: Prohibited
Vehicles: Pull up your canoe or kayak on the beach
Other: Check-in after 1 p.m.; check-out by 11 a.m.; maximum 5 people per site (25 for group site); pack out all trash

MAP

RESTROOM

ISLAND MANAGERS

WAQUOIT BAY

N

GETTING THERE

From Falmouth, head south on MA 28 and park at the White's Landing boat launch, located next to Edward's boatyard. Paddle out of the Childs River, bear left, and follow the shoreline of Washburn Island to the campsites.

neatly arranged limbs that have fallen from the trees. Please stay on the paths when walking about the island to preserve its fragile ecology. You'll also reduce the danger of picking up a tick—a real possibility here. Make sure to check yourself and your kids thoroughly. If you find a tick, don't panic. They have to be embedded for about 24 hours to transfer the toxins that cause Lyme disease. If you check yourself every day, you should be fine.

The openness to the beach, the incredible views, and the sense of seclusion found in most of the campsites here is a powerful combination of attributes. The peaceful silence is remarkable, especially for the Cape. Were the pines and beech trees on Washburn Island suddenly replaced by palm trees, you'd swear you were somewhere in the South Pacific.

CONNECTICUT

DEVIL'S HOPYARD STATE PARK

East Haddam

I F YOU'RE WONDERING HOW this state park came by its name, you're not alone. There are a variety of "theories" as to how the name Devil's Hopyard came to be. One thing folks do agree on is that the name refers to the numerous holes bored into the rock at the base of Chapman Falls. The most oft-repeated explanation is that these are the result of the Devil hopping from rock to rock to avoid getting his hooves wet, burning holes in the rocks with each hop. If you can think of a better or more entertaining theory, feel free to share it with your fellow campers.

The Chapman Falls campground at Devil's Hopyard State Park has 21 sites spread out in a wooded grove right near the campground's namesake. The falls provide not only a beautiful spot to relax and enjoy the view right outside the campground, but the constant rush of the water is a welcome addition to the forest's soundtrack.

The 21 wooded sites at this cozy little campground are arranged on either side of the short campground road. The sites are spacious, but not too private. They are set along a barrier of scrub brush that separates the campground from the waters above Chapman Falls on one side, and on the other are set against the woods.

The sites along the water are the pleasant. Those at the end of the loop are nicer still, plus they have the added benefit of being a bit more private. Site 8 is one of the most secluded sites in the campground. Sites 10 and 11 are also set off from the rest of the campground, but not from each other. This would be a good pair of sites for a group.

Site 15 is desirable, as it's situated right along the water leading to the falls. Sites 16, 17, and 18 are all incredibly peaceful places to camp right along the water. Site 16 is the key spot for anglers—you could fish

> *Devil's Hopyard is small and scenic, with a cozy group of campsites located just a few steps from Chapman Falls.*

RATINGS

Beauty: ☆ ☆ ☆ ☆ ☆
Privacy: ☆ ☆ ☆
Spaciousness: ☆ ☆ ☆ ☆
Quiet: ☆ ☆ ☆ ☆ ☆
Security: ☆ ☆ ☆ ☆
Cleanliness: ☆ ☆ ☆ ☆

ADDRESS: Devil's Hopyard
State Park
366 Hopyard Road
East Haddam, CT
06423

OPERATED BY: Connecticut
Department of
Environmental
Protection

INFORMATION: Devil's Hopyard
State Park, (806) 873-
8566

OPEN: Mid-April–
Labor Day

SITES: 21

EACH SITE HAS: Fire ring, picnic
table

ASSIGNMENT: First come, first
served or by reser-
vation: (877)
668-CAMP (2267),
www.reserve
america.com

REGISTRATION: At ranger station

FACILITIES: Pit toilets

PARKING: At sites

FEE: $11

RESTRICTIONS: Pets: Prohibited
Fires: Fire rings only
Alcohol: Prohibited
Vehicles: Maximum
2 per site
Other: Check-out by
noon; visitors
allowed 8 a.m.–
sunset; quiet hours
11 p.m.–7 a.m.; no
swimming in river

right from your campsite (for information on fishing licenses, see Appendix C, page 224).

Because of its small size and remote location, the campground is very quiet except for the welcome sounds of the woodland birds and the light, incessant rushing of Chapman Falls. The loosely spaced forest of mixed deciduous and coniferous trees lets a lot of light down to the campsites. The forest at the border of the campground and within the rest of the park is much more densely packed.

Chapman Falls is a spectacular series of waterfalls that cascade downward for nearly 60 feet, continuing on as the Eight Mile River. The river flows past the Devil's Hopyard picnic area a bit farther downstream from the campground. This day-use area is popular with anglers. It's also a scenic place to walk around or to just relax by the river. Except for the campground, Devil's Hopyard State Park is closed from sunset to 6 a.m.

This area of Connecticut is just north of the town of Lyme. If that name sounds familiar, it should. Lyme has the unique and unwelcome distinction of being home to the first diagnosed cases of Lyme disease. While the area in which Lyme disease has been reported has spread over the last several years, it's still worth paying extra attention to ticks in this area. Deer ticks are the culprit. The nymph (or baby) deer ticks are particularly nasty. They're also extremely small and difficult to find. This doesn't mean you should stay inside all summer long. Just check yourself over very carefully, especially your head and hair. If you do find a tick, don't panic. Generally, the tick has to be embedded for 24 hours to pass on the toxins that cause the disease. Just remove the tick completely with a pair of tweezers, and sterilize the bite with Bactine or any antiseptic first-aid ointment.

MAP

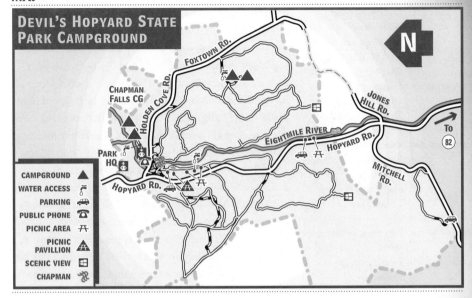

DEVIL'S HOPYARD STATE PARK CAMPGROUND

CHAPMAN FALLS CG

FOXTOWN RD.

HOLDEN COVE RD.

JONES HILL RD.

PARK HQ

EIGHTMILE RIVER

HOPYARD RD.

To 82

MITCHELL RD.

HOPYARD RD.

N

CAMPGROUND	▲
WATER ACCESS	
PARKING	
PUBLIC PHONE	☎
PICNIC AREA	🛆
PICNIC PAVILLION	▲
SCENIC VIEW	⊞
CHAPMAN	

GETTING THERE

From the intersection of CT 82 and CT 156, follow Hopyard Road north for approximately 3 miles. Turn right on Helon Cove road to the campground.

HOUSATONIC MEADOWS STATE PARK

> *Between the high forest canopy and the riverside setting, Housatonic Meadows is a beautiful spot.*

THE STATUESQUE FOREST and the Housatonic River flowing by make for a dramatic setting at this western Connecticut campground. Many of the sites at Housatonic Meadows are spread along the banks of the river. There are two main areas within the campground: the Riverside Area off to the left as you enter the campground, and the large loop off to the right where the majority of the sites are located.

The Riverside sites are very open and set directly on the riverbank beneath a loosely spaced forest of tall conifers. They're also packed in fairly tight. These sites are beautiful. It's a delight to camp next to the river, but you'll be as close to your neighbors as you are to the river. What the sites offer in peaceful, relaxing scenery and proximity to the river, they lack in seclusion and privacy. You run the risk of being near a trailer or RV, but you could also set up your tent so that the first thing you see and hear in the morning is the Housatonic cascading by.

There are a few sites in the Riverside Area that are more private than the others. Sites 23 and 24, at the end of the Riverside Area road, are the most private in this section. They're at the end of the cul de sac, and being off on their own little loop provides them with more isolation. Sites 1 and 2, at the beginning of the Riverside Area road, also offer a welcome sense of solitude. This is especially true of site 1, which is separated from the rest of the row of sites by a short line of brush.

The forest here is a beautiful mix of tall pines and maples. Closer to the river, the forest is mostly pines, so there's a deep shade over this part of the campground. Between the shade of the forest canopy and their proximity to the river, these campsites remain cool even on the steamiest summer days.

While the sites here are close together, they are large and very neat. You might not have much privacy,

RATINGS

Beauty: ✿ ✿ ✿ ✿
Privacy: ✿ ✿ ✿
Spaciousness: ✿ ✿ ✿ ✿
Quiet: ✿ ✿ ✿
Security: ✿ ✿ ✿ ✿
Cleanliness: ✿ ✿ ✿ ✿

but you are right on the river. You can fly-cast or launch canoes and kayaks from your campsite, although it's probably best to drive upriver and launch from there. Then you can enjoy a leisurely paddle back to the campground. The Housatonic is fairly wide here, and the water moves right along rapidly. It's relatively safe for these activities, but as always, be prudent when entering the river, especially if you are with children. Swimming here is not permitted, as the current is often swift.

The Knob Hill Area is off to the right as you enter the campground. The loop to the left within this area has some very pleasant sites perched high along the riverbank. These sites afford a somewhat obscured view of the river through the forest. They are fairly open, but set on the border between the woods and a grove of tall conifers that shade the rest of the sites.

Generally speaking, most of the sites along the left side of this loop (the side facing the river) are the best for tents. These sites are tucked neatly into the forest, and while they're not right on the riverbank like the sites in the Riverside area, they offer more seclusion, and you can still catch glimpses of the river through the loosely spaced forest. You can also walk down through the forest to just sit and watch the river flow by—one of my favorite things to do.

In the first part of the loop on this side, sites 25 through 27 are too exposed, set facing the ranger station. Sites 31, 32, and 33 are isolated sites, set within a dense pine grove. If you're going to set up your tent on this side of the campground, check to see if any of these sites are available.

The farthest end of the loop on this side is called the Pine Bluff Area. The sites numbered in the 80s here are attractive. They face the river and sit on the edge of both the forest and the meadow. They're more secluded than the other sites in this area, particularly those set within the grassy field. The sites in the meadow (numbered in the 60s, 70s, and 90s) are spacious but not too private. The rest of the Pine Bluff sites are too open; they're set on a grassy hill without much privacy and no woods separating the camping area from views of CT 7.

KEY INFORMATION

ADDRESS: Housatonic Meadows State Park Campground CT 7 Sharon, CT 06754

OPERATED BY: Connecticut Department of Environmental Protection

INFORMATION: Housatonic Meadows State Park, (860) 672-6772 (camp office), (860) 927-3238 (park office)

OPEN: Mid-April–Labor Day, off-season camping offered until December 31; call for site and facility availability

SITES: 97

EACH SITE HAS: Fire ring, picnic table

ASSIGNMENT: First come, first served or by reservation: (877) 668-CAMP (2267)), www.reserve america.com

REGISTRATION: At ranger station

FACILITIES: Flush toilets, showers, water spigots, pay phone, dump station

PARKING: At sites

FEE: $13

RESTRICTIONS: Pets: Prohibited
Fires: Fire rings only
Alcohol: Prohibited
Vehicles: Maximum 2 per site
Other: Check-out by noon; quiet hours 11 p.m.–7 a.m.; no swimming in river

MAP

HOUSATONIC MEADOWS
STATE PARK CAMPGROUND

RESTROOM	👫
WATER ACCESS	🚰
PUBLIC PHONE	☎
DUMP STATION	🅿
MANAGERS OFFICE	🛈

HOUSATONIC RAILROAD

HOUSATONIC RIVER

STONES

N

GETTING THERE

Follow CT 7 north, approximately 2 miles north of the intersection of CT 7 and CT 4. Look for the campground signs on the right, heading north.

The river is clearly the main attraction, but there's also some fun hiking nearby. You can hike up and over the 1,120-foot-high Pine Knob from the campground. You can pick up the trail across CT 7 from the campground, or drive south a short distance to the trailhead. Follow the blue blazes and hike the entire 2.5-mile loop over Pine Knob and Ridge Crest. You'll also be on the Appalachian Trail for a time. The southern leg of this loop follows the Hatch Brook back down to the river, which makes for a cool, relaxing hike.

MACEDONIA BROOK STATE PARK

Kent

> *Macedonia Brook State Park is magically scenic, with many isolated sites along the river that are perfect for fishing or just watching the river flow.*

DEEP IN THE FORESTS of western Connecticut, Macedonia Brook State Park is grand in both size and character. Following the long access road leading into the campground (or more accurately, campgrounds, as there are several distinct areas within the park), you'll pass some stellar picnic areas set beneath the towering forest and right next to the pristine waters of Macedonia Brook. You'll also pass the sites of the Old Furnace, the Gorge, and the Lower Falls. Myriad twists and turns in the brook invite you to spend hours casting a line in the tumbling water to coax out a brook trout.

There are several separate camping areas within Macedonia Brook State Park: Birch, Hickory, Red Pine, Overlook, and Maple. Some of these areas are further subdivided, and they are spread out along the long and winding road leading through the campground. The remote wilderness character of the forest combined with the widely dispersed camping areas give the entire campground a quiet, secluded feeling.

You'll pass the day-use pavilion and volleyball net as you drive toward the camping areas, and the Silver Birch Area is the first group of campsites you'll come to. Sites 1 through 4 in Silver Birch are open sites within a grassy loop right by Macedonia Brook. While these sites don't offer much privacy from one another, they are completely separate from the rest of the campground. Their riverside location is their most compelling characteristic. You could fly-fish right from your site (for information on fishing licenses, see Appendix C, page 224).

The Upper Birch Area includes sites 7 through 12, which are open, spacious, and neat, but not particularly private. They're set on a grassy hillside with sporadic trees, but the whole area is surrounded by dense woods. Many of the sites are set against the bordering forest. The field offers sweeping views of the night sky

RATINGS

Beauty: ✰ ✰ ✰ ✰ ✰
Privacy: ✰ ✰ ✰ ✰
Spaciousness: ✰ ✰ ✰ ✰
Quiet: ✰ ✰ ✰ ✰ ✰
Security: ✰ ✰ ✰ ✰
Cleanliness: ✰ ✰ ✰ ✰ ✰

ADDRESS: Macedonia Brook
State Park
159 Macedonia
Brook Road
Kent, CT 06757

OPERATED BY: Connecticut
Department of
Environmental
Protection

INFORMATION: Macedonia Brook
State Park, (860) 927-
4100 (campground),
(860) 927-3238 (park
office)

OPEN: Mid-April–
September 30

SITES: 83

EACH SITE HAS: Fire ring or stone
hearth, picnic table

ASSIGNMENT: First come, first
served or by reser-
vation: (877)
668-CAMP (2267),
www.reserve
america.com

REGISTRATION: At ranger station

FACILITIES: Pit toilets

PARKING: At sites

FEE: $11

RESTRICTIONS: Pets: Prohibited
Fires: Fire rings only
Alcohol: Prohibited
Vehicles: Parking at
sites only
Other: Check-out by
noon; quiet hours
11 p.m.–7 a.m.; no
swimming in river

for an intense stargazing experience. The constant
whoosh of the stream rushing by is peaceful and relaxing. There is a water pump located between sites 11
and 12, which also have huge stone hearths for your
campfire instead of the typical fire ring.

The Lower Hickory Area includes sites 13 through
17. These sites are close to the river and fairly isolated,
although the forest is open within this area. Upper
Hickory is home to sites 21 and 22. These sites are
even more exposed, set on the border between the forest and an open, grassy area.

The Red Pine Loop, with sites 24 through 27, is a
pleasantly isolated loop. I especially like this corner of
the campground; there's not a bad spot in it. The
woods are a bit denser, so these sites offer a great sense
of seclusion. There are more deciduous trees mixed
into the forest, and the added shade gives these spots a
deep-woods feel. Site 24 is tucked off on its own at the
top of the loop, and site 25 is nicely isolated.

Perched on the banks of Macedonia Brook, sites
28 and 29 would be well suited for a group of fly-fishermen. These two sites sit together on a small grassy
field right next to the brook. They're exposed, set
between the brook and the campground road—but
they're actually quite private later in the day, as they're
entirely separate from the rest of the campground.

The Overlook Area includes sites 31 through 42.
The upper sites on this wide, grassy hillside have a
spectacular view of the forest, sky, and the surrounding
hillsides of South Cobble and Chase Mountain. The
sites within this loop are large but not too private.

The Maple Area is quite spread out, and it
includes sites 43 through 51. These sites are beautifully
isolated in a dense grove of varied tree species. These
loops are just past the Overlook Area as you drive
along the campground road.

The camping areas within Macedonia Brook State
Park seem to offer a choice between seclusion and
sweeping views. The sites on the grassy hillsides are
more open to breezes, so they are often cooler and less
buggy than the sites set deep within the woods.

There are numerous hiking trails winding
throughout the state park, and there are plenty of

MAP

places to drop a hook in the water. Most of the trails are called (and marked) simply by colors. The Blue Trail follows a ridgeline to the east of the camping areas. The Yellow Trail intersects the Blue Trail just west of the pavilion. The Green Trail, leading out from the Upper Birch Area, also intersects with the Blue Trail. The Orange Trail runs from the Upper Birch Area to the Maple Area. Lastly, The White Trail takes you from the pavilion to the top of nearby Cobble Mountain.

GETTING THERE

From Kent, follow CT 341 north to Macedonia Brook Road on the right. Turn right here and follow this until you see signs for the park.

SELDEN NECK
CAMPGROUND

> *Selden Neck has some of the most spectacular and accessible island camping in New England.*

THERE IS ABSOLUTELY NO WAY you'll find an RV at the Selden Neck Campground in Gillette Castle State Park. There are no designated tent-only areas, and no inherent rules or regulations prohibiting them, but until someone invents an RV that floats, Selden Neck is just for tent camping. You can only reach the park and the campground by boat.

This fabulously peaceful little state park sits perched on the northern corner of a small island separated from the banks of the Connecticut River by Selden Creek. The campsites are right on the river, and there are no docks, moorings, or facilities other than fireplaces and pit toilets. You'll have to approach the campsite with a small watercraft. Whether you choose a sailboat or motorboat, or better yet, a canoe or kayak, is entirely up to you.

There are four discrete camping areas on Selden Neck: Hogback, Springledge, Quarry Knob, and Cedars Camp, listed roughly in order of my personal preference. The first three areas are situated along the banks of the Connecticut River. The main channel runs down the river right next to Selden Neck, so on a busy summer day, there will be lots of boat traffic, including some ferry boats and sizable powerboats. Consequently, it can be a bit busy during the day, and there may be some chop on the river and splashing up against the banks of Selden Neck. Secure your boat adequately, or pull your canoe or kayak up onto the shore to keep it from getting bashed around—or worse, slipping off into the river without you.

The Hogback, Springledge, and Quarry Knob areas are similar to each other in character. There are small, grassy areas upon which to pitch your tent. You'll be fairly close to the riverbanks, and behind the sites there's a short, steep hill that rises in the center of the island. Hogback is the smallest of these areas, with

RATINGS

Beauty: ✿ ✿ ✿ ✿
Privacy: ✿ ✿ ✿ ✿ ✿
Spaciousness: ✿ ✿ ✿ ✿ ✿
Quiet: ✿ ✿ ✿ ✿
Security: ✿ ✿ ✿ ✿ ✿
Cleanliness: ✿ ✿ ✿ ✿ ✿

room for six campers. Springledge accommodates eight campers, and Quarry Knob has room for twelve.

You can really immerse yourself in wilderness and solitude here, despite the fact that you're camping right on the Connecticut River, which can sometimes feel like the maritime equivalent of an interstate. The small, densely forested camping areas, the way they are set off from each other, and the fact that you're on an island all contribute to the atmosphere of isolation on Selden Neck. This becomes even more apparent toward the end of the day as the river traffic quiets down.

The Cedars Camp area attracts a lot of day use, as it's tucked into a corner of Selden Creek off the main branch of the river. If the weather or winds are rough, this would be a good choice because the small beach where you arrive is more protected. It's also a good choice if you happen to be camping with a larger group, as this area of Selden Neck can accommodate up to 20 people.

The nearest boat ramp is the Deep River public boat launch, which is right across the river from Selden Creek and the island on which the campground is located. It's a fairly short paddle in a canoe or kayak, and a snap in a small motorboat or sailboat. The only trouble is parking at the boat launch. Parking right at the boat launch is only for Deep River residents who have purchased a sticker. Get dropped off or park just outside the boat launch parking area, if there's room.

Keep this in mind as you're preparing for your trip: You are traveling to an island to camp. There are no stores on this island. You need to bring with you everything you will use—all your food, water, and camping supplies. Running out to a store because you forgot batteries or hot dogs is not impossible, but it's not going to be easy. The flip side of that coin is that you must also pack out everything you've used as well as any trash you've generated. The camping areas have pit toilets, but there aren't any garbage cans. Live by the pack-it-in, pack-it-out mantra.

One trick that I've always appreciated for packing meals when kayak camping (equally applicable for canoes or other small boats) is to prepare something you can freeze. Take a frozen Tupperware container

KEY INFORMATION

ADDRESS:	Selden Neck Campground c/o Gillette Castle State Park 67 River Road Haddam, CT 06423
OPERATED BY:	Connecticut Department of Environmental Protection
INFORMATION:	Gillette Castle State Park, (860) 526-2336
OPEN:	May 1–September 30
SITES:	4 sites, accommodating 46 people total
EACH SITE HAS:	Fire pit, pit toilet
ASSIGNMENT:	Reservations required; make at least 2 weeks prior to visit by mail to Gillette Castle State Park Supervisor, address above; include full payment by check or money order made out to Treasurer, State of Connecticut
REGISTRATION:	Claim your site
FACILITIES:	Pit toilets
PARKING:	Boats only
FEE:	$4 per person per night
RESTRICTIONS:	Pets: Prohibited Fires: Fire pits only Alcohol: Sites only Vehicles: Boats only Other: Visitors must leave by 8 p.m.; campers must pack out all trash

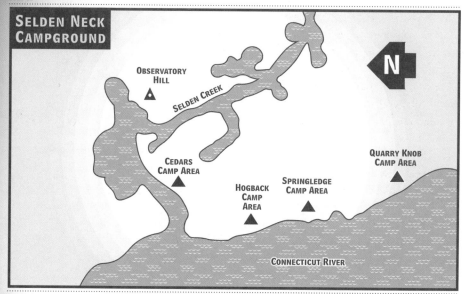

GETTING THERE

To get to the Deep River boat ramp, take Exit 4 off CT 9. Follow CT 154 into Deep River. Turn right at the four-way intersection downtown (CT 80 heads off to the left). Follow this road to Deep River boat launch.

with you, and by the time dinner rolls around, your meal will have mostly defrosted. Then all you have to do is heat it up, and dinner is served.

Once you make landfall and set up your camp, you'll probably want to take off in your boat to do a little exploring. Selden Creek, which winds its way around Selden Neck Island, is an absolutely delightful area to paddle. The water is often as still as glass, even on days when the wind has churned the main channel of the river into a swirling froth. Selden Creek casually winds around through swampy marsh and overhanging trees past some cliffs and the forested hills of the mainland. At times it feels like you're paddling through a bayou, other times through a northern fjord, but it always feels like you're a million miles from anyone.

RHODE ISLAND

BURLINGAME STATE PARK

BURLINGAME **S**TATE **P**ARK is a megalopolis of campgrounds. The park itself encompasses 2,100 acres. Even though it's easy to get overwhelmed by Burlingame's 755 sites (and no, that's not a typo), there are lots of spots within the park that make for some fun tent camping.

Much like cities (and with a campground this huge, it's an applicable metaphor) have good areas and not-so-good areas, so, too, does Burlingame. That's not to say that there are any dangerous areas or places you shouldn't be after sunset—just some places that are better for tents than others.

There aren't any tent-specific neighborhoods within Burlingame State Park, but there are individual sites set aside for tents. These designations are based primarily on site size. There aren't any hookups within Burlingame State Park, but the open, spacious nature of the sites can be inviting to RVs as well as our tent-bound brethren. Still, there are several areas you should check out that are well suited for tent camping.

Generally speaking, the farther off the main loop you get, the more secluded and quiet your campsite will be. Most of the sites are fairly open and certainly spacious, but the airy forest doesn't provide much of a barrier between sites. Most of them are set beneath a mixed forest of pine, spruce, and balsam, with a smattering of hardy deciduous trees. The salty air and the sandy soil keep the forest from growing in densely. However, the sandy soil does make it easy to drive in tent stakes.

Near the entrance to the campground, check out the Mills Camp Area. This is your first left as you drive into the campground. Mills Camp includes sites A through U and AA through UU, all of which are fairly open and set in a loosely spaced forest of low conifers.

Continue deeper into the campground and you come to the upper-500-numbered sites. These sites,

> *The campground at Burlingame State Park is massive—the largest in New England—but there are still a few spots where you can find your own slice of wilderness.*

RATINGS

Beauty: ✿ ✿ ✿ ✿
Privacy: ✿ ✿ ✿
Spaciousness: ✿ ✿ ✿
Quiet: ✿ ✿ ✿
Security: ✿ ✿ ✿ ✿
Cleanliness: ✿ ✿ ✿ ✿

KEY INFORMATION

ADDRESS: Burlingame State Park 1 Burlingame State Park Road Charlestown, RI 02813

OPERATED BY: Rhode Island Department of Environmental Management

INFORMATION: Burlingame State Park, (401) 322-7337

OPEN: Memorial Day–Labor Day

SITES: 755

EACH SITE HAS: Fire ring or stone hearth, picnic table

ASSIGNMENT: First come, first served

REGISTRATION: At campground headquarters

FACILITIES: Flush toilets, showers, camp store, pay phone

PARKING: At sites and other parking areas

FEE: Rhode Island residents, $14; nonresidents, $20

RESTRICTIONS: Pets: Prohibited
Fires: Fire rings only
Alcohol: Prohibited
Vehicles: Parking at sites and other central areas
Other: Maximum 6 people per site; visitors must be out by 10 p.m.; quiet hours 10 p.m.–7 a.m.; 4-day maximum stay

especially site 565, are isolated and wooded. Sites 554 through 559 within this area are set up where the forest is a bit denser, which provides a deeper sense of isolation. The sites themselves are perfectly open; there's just more woods in between you and your many neighbors.

Farther along the outer campground loop road, some of the lower-400-numbered sites are well isolated, especially site 424. On this section of the road, which (looking at the campground map) is the part of the loop farthest to the left, you should check out the grouping of sites 408 through 426. This cluster offers a degree of privacy and quiet. Sites 201 through 211 are exposed and not quite as private, but they're set beneath a cathedralesque grove of spruce trees. Sites 214, 216, 218, and 219 in this area are also attractive, and they're convenient to the restrooms.

The Main Camping Area, as indicated on the map and including sites 18 through 131, is where you want to be. It's much like its own campground-within-a-campground. It's more wooded, secluded, and quiet than the rest of the sites in the campground. Site 143 is particularly pleasant, as it sits well off the loop road. The even-numbered sites in the upper 130s and lower 140s are also pretty and moderately secluded.

The 131 through 150 loop in the Main Camping Area also has many sites you'll want to check out. The outer-loop sites within this area in the 160s and 170s are worth a look. Again, here the forest is a bit thicker, although there are a few sites on the inside of the loop that are fairly exposed.

The other, more densely packed portion of the Main Camping Area, which encompasses the first 90 sites, is close to the shores of Watchaug Pond and some boat-rental facilities. The sites here are tightly packed beneath an open forest canopy, but the whole area still has a woodland feel.

There are many clusters where two or three sites will be angled in towards each other. These would be good sites for large groups or families needing a couple of sites bunched together. Mention this when making your reservation if you'd like contiguous sites.

Burlingame State Park sits on the shores of Watchaug Pond, and it's just a few miles from Rhode

MAP

BURLINGAME STATE PARK CAMPGROUND

RESTROOM/SHOWERS
PORTAJONS
WATER ACCESS
PUBLIC PHONE
PLAYGROUND
DUMPSITE
DUMPSTER

BIRD SANCTUARY

To WAKEFIELD AND PROVIDENCE

LEGIONTOWN CAMP AREA

MAIN CAMP AREA
MANAGER
CAMP STORE
VOLLEYBALL
BASKETBALL
BALL FIELD
REC HALL

WORKSHOPS

1

FISHERMAN'S CAMP AREA

400 AREA

N

500 AREA

MILLS CAMP AREA

To WESTERLY

Island's renowned beaches. You'll have plenty to do both within and outside of the park.

If Burlingame State Park was any bigger, it would practically cover the state. I can see it now: The park ranger would be running for governor. I still can't help but think it's ironic that the largest campground in this book, both in terms of acreage and number of sites, sits in Rhode Island, the smallest state in New England.

GETTING THERE

Follow Interstate 95 south to RI 4 south to US 1 south. Follow US 1 to Charlestown, and turn right at the Burlingame State Park Campground sign.

FORT GETTY RECREATION AREA

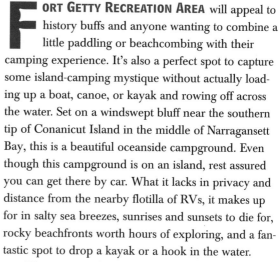

> *Fort Getty Recreation Area's campground is fairly wide open, but the panoramic vistas of Narragansett Bay and the sea breezes can't be beat.*

FORT GETTY RECREATION AREA will appeal to history buffs and anyone wanting to combine a little paddling or beachcombing with their camping experience. It's also a perfect spot to capture some island-camping mystique without actually loading up a boat, canoe, or kayak and rowing off across the water. Set on a windswept bluff near the southern tip of Conanicut Island in the middle of Narragansett Bay, this is a beautiful oceanside campground. Even though this campground is on an island, rest assured you can get there by car. What it lacks in privacy and distance from the nearby flotilla of RVs, it makes up for in salty sea breezes, sunrises and sunsets to die for, rocky beachfronts worth hours of exploring, and a fantastic spot to drop a kayak or a hook in the water.

There is a modest-sized tent-camping area, which is set off as much as possible from where the RVs roam. I say as much as possible because there isn't a whole lot of room within the campground proper. The scenery and setting compensate nicely for the forest density, though. Here's a hint: Once you've found your campsite, set up your tent so the opening faces out toward the bay. That way, when you wake up, your first views will be of the sun rising over the water.

As you drive into the park, the long access road leading into the campground passes by a couple of residences, so it feels like you're heading up someone's driveway, but keep on—this road does indeed lead to Fort Getty Recreation Area. You'll come to a pay station in the middle of the road. Check in here, then keep cruising. The road winds around to the right, and the campground is ahead on the left toward the end of the peninsula.

As you drive in, you'll pass the Fox Hill Salt Marsh on your left. This is a great place to walk around or to just find a cozy spot to take in the

RATINGS

Beauty: ✪ ✪ ✪ ✪
Privacy: ✪ ✪
Spaciousness: ✪ ✪ ✪
Quiet: ✪ ✪ ✪
Security: ✪ ✪ ✪ ✪
Cleanliness: ✪ ✪ ✪ ✪

scenery. If you're into bird-watching, you'll particularly enjoy training your eyes and binoculars on the various shorebirds found here.

You'll quickly realize this campground doesn't embody the forest-bound sense of solitude you'll find in most other New England campgrounds, but the waterfront setting can't be beat. The tent-only area is toward the top of the small hill off to the left as you reach the campsites, and includes sites 1 through 14. These sites are all very open and fairly tightly packed, but parking for them is along the periphery, so the site cluster feels like a little tent village.

Right next to the camping area is a big open field; it's a tremendous spot for picnicking, kite flying, Frisbee throwing—you name it. There's also a sand volleyball pit nearby. This space for casual play and hanging out reinforces the laid-back, island mentality that predominates at Fort Getty.

Camping with little kids? The rocky beaches surrounding the park offer endless hours of rock-hopping and beachcombing. Some of the cliffs and larger rocks are a bit steep, so you'll have to keep a sharp eye on the younger ones, but I can guarantee your kids will be tuckered out after a day spent prowling around on these rocky shores.

For the historically minded, there are a couple of bunkers remaining from when Fort Getty was an ammunition depot during World War II. These are also cool little spots in which older kids enjoy playing.

The campground's island is surrounded by several other small islands dotting Narragansett Bay. In a place like this, the environment is captivating regardless of the weather. It's brilliant on bright, sunny days, and cool and refreshing when the mainland is sweltering. The stars at night are crystal clear, and you'll see deeper into the universe since there isn't much in the way of light pollution out here. In a fog or light rain, the islands poking in and out of the mist give the place a sense of mystery, as if you'd almost expect to see a pirate ship emerging to bury its sailors' stolen treasures on one of the islands.

If you're planning a family reunion, wedding reception, or some other big bash, you can reserve the

KEY INFORMATION

ADDRESS: Fort Getty Recreation Area P.O. Box 377 Jamestown, RI 02835

OPERATED BY: Town of Jamestown

INFORMATION: Fort Getty Recreation Area, (401) 423-7211, (401) 423-7264

OPEN: May 15– September 30

SITES: 14 tent-only sites, 103 trailer sites

EACH SITE HAS: Fire ring

ASSIGNMENT: First come, first served

REGISTRATION: At ranger station

FACILITIES: Flush toilets, showers, water spigots, pay phones, boat launch, fishing dock, horseshoe pits, saltwater beach

PARKING: Near sites; additional parking at day-use area

FEE: $20

RESTRICTIONS: Pets: Dogs on leash only
Fires: Fire rings only
Alcohol: Sites only
Vehicles: Park near sites

MAP

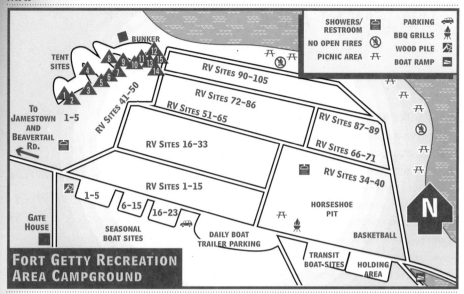

FORT GETTY RECREATION AREA CAMPGROUND

GETTING THERE

Take North Main Street to the south (toward Beavertail State Park). This road will cross Narragansett Road and turn into Southwest Avenue. Follow Southwest Avenue to Beavertail Road. After this winds around a sandy beach on the left, the entrance for the campground is on the right.

Lieutenant Colonel John C. Rembigas Pavilion for such functions. This is off to the left of the campground, the open field, and the volleyball pit; call for more information on reserving the space.

Fort Getty Recreation Area is a scenic and centrally located spot well suited to serve as your base camp for fishing (for information on fishing licenses, see Appendix C, page 224), paddling, scuba diving, and beachcombing adventures. It's also an amazing place to fly a kite. Charlie Brown would have loved it—steady winds and few kite-eating trees to be found. Those winds also make Fort Getty Recreation Area the place to be on steamy summer afternoons. While folks camping deep in the forest are sweating bullets and slapping bugs, you'll have a strong, cool breeze keeping your temperature down and the bugs away.

GEORGE WASHINGTON MANAGEMENT AREA

YOU'LL BE TEMPTED to check your map as you drive into the campground at the George Washington Management Area. Did you somehow take a wrong turn and end up in Vermont or New Hampshire? Nope, this is indeed Rhode Island, but it's far from the windswept beaches, sandy soil, short, scrubby pines, and beach roses of Rhode Island topography. As soon as you enter the campground, you are enshrouded by a canopy of conifers. The tangy pine and balsam scents mixed in with earthy wisps of wood smoke make for quite a welcome.

The entire George Washington Management Area and the contiguous Pulaski Memorial State Forest are both densely wooded areas with a gently rolling forest floor. The area is free of really steep hills, uneven terrain, and heavy undergrowth, which makes it a nice place to pitch a tent.

The campground wraps around the shores of Bowdish Lake. Down by the beach, there's a beautiful stone recreation hall built by the Civilian Conservation Corps. A plaque set in stone in front of the building honors the members of the CCC who built it. The beach is the perfect spot to go for a quick swim, spend the day with the kids, or kick back on a blanket and read a book. You could also drop a hook or a paddle in the water (or both!) if you're so inclined.

Sites 26, 27, and 28 are spacious and close to the lake. These are some of this campground's prime spots. The loop with sites 34 through 45 is another pleasant area in which to pitch your tent. These sites are a bit smaller than some of the others located along the main campground road, but they're nestled within a dense pine grove and sit fairly close to the lake—both attractive aspects. This loop is the first left off the main road once you're in the campground.

> *The entire George Washington Management Area is a lush, dense forest that is quite accessible, yet has a pleasant, remote feel.*

RATINGS

Beauty: ✿ ✿ ✿ ✿
Privacy: ✿ ✿ ✿ ✿
Spaciousness: ✿ ✿ ✿ ✿
Quiet: ✿ ✿ ✿ ✿
Security: ✿ ✿ ✿ ✿
Cleanliness: ✿ ✿ ✿ ✿

Farther down the road, sites 5 and 6 are worth investigating. They're decent sized and set off with plenty of space between them and the other sites. Sites 11 and 14 sit on the border of the campground proper and the rest of the George Washington Management Area. These sites are also pretty, as the forest becomes denser on this end of the campground. Site 12 is also particularly secluded.

Follow the main campground road past all these sites, and past the loop for Shelter 1 off to the left, and you'll head into the rest of the George Washington Management Area. This is a great area to explore when it's time for a hike or bike ride.

The entire campground has plenty of space and forest for everyone. However, several sites and sections along the main road are too open for my tastes. Sites 7, 9, 12, 17, and 18 aren't as private as some of the other sites located along the main road and those tucked off in the side loops.

If you've come with a large group, or have several members of your group who would rather not sleep on the ground, check out the two lean-to shelters. These have a wood floor and are open on one side. If you're going for one of the shelters, try to secure shelter 1. It's set on a small rise at the end of its own loop. There's a nice sense of privacy to this site. It's at the far end of the campground road, and it's right on the border between the campground and the rest of the expansive George Washington Management Area.

Shelter 2 is also in a fairly attractive spot, separate from the rest of the campground at the end of a short road leading off to the right from the main campground road. However, it's right next to a large, open, sandy lot that looks like overflow parking. While it may detract a bit from the scenery, if you have a large group all arriving in their own vehicles, you won't have any trouble finding parking. This is the site to choose if you're camping with 20 of your closest friends, all of whom insist on driving their own cars!

One restriction worth noting is that possession of alcoholic beverages is grounds for expulsion from the campground. They must have had some problems with ebullient revelers in the past, as the rangers seem quite serious about this one. This restriction is clearly stated in several spots on the campground literature. If you like to kick back with a beer or a glass of wine after dinner, wait until you get to the next campground. Try a cup of tea instead.

Another point worth mentioning is the wildlife—mostly raccoons, with the occasional black bear. Let them remain wildlife. Don't feed or otherwise tempt them by leaving food or dirty dishes around your campsite. The George Washington Management Area campground is wild and scenic, but it's also very accessible. Once otherwise-wild animals become acclimated to human presence, they often have to be relocated or exterminated, and you don't want to be responsible for that. Plus, there are safety considerations. Raccoons are occasional carriers of rabies, so report any incidences of raccoon or other animal bites or scrapes. It's also not a bad idea to report any strange or aggressive animal behavior.

GETTING THERE

From Interstate 95, follow RI 44 west through Greenville and Chepachet into Glocester. Keep an eye open for the campground sign on the right.

APPENDIXES **AND INDEX**

APPENDIX A
CAMPING EQUIPMENT
CHECKLIST

Except for the large and bulky items on this list, I keep a plastic storage container full of the essentials of car camping so that they're ready to go when I am. I make a last-minute check of the inventory, resupply anything that's low or missing, and away I go!

COOKING UTENSILS
Aluminum foil
Bottle opener
Bottles of salt, pepper, spices, sugar, cooking oil, and maple syrup in waterproof, spill-proof containers
Can opener
Corkscrew
Cups, plastic or tin
Dish soap (biodegradable), sponge, and towel
Flatware
Food of your choice
Frying pan
Fuel for stove
Matches in waterproof container
Plates
Pocketknife
Pot with lid
Spatula
Stove
Wooden spoon

FIRST-AID KIT
Antibiotic cream
Band-Aids®
Diphenhydramine (Benadryl®)
Gauze pads
Ibuprofen or aspirin
Insect repellent
Lip balm
Moleskin®
Snakebite kit
Sunscreen
Tape, waterproof adhesive

SLEEPING GEAR
Pillow
Sleeping bag
Sleeping pad, inflatable or insulated
Tent with ground tarp and rainfly

MISCELLANEOUS
Bath soap (biodegradable), washcloth, and towel
Camp chair
Candles
Cooler
Deck of cards
Duct tape
Fire starter
Flashlight or headlamp with fresh batteries
Foul-weather clothing
Paper towels
Plastic zip-top bags
Sunglasses
Toilet paper
Water bottle
Wool or fleece blanket

OPTIONAL
Barbecue grill
Binoculars
Field guides on bird, plant, and wildlife identification
Fishing rod and tackle
Hatchet
Kayak and related paddling gear
Lantern
Maps (road, topographic, trails, and so on)
Mountain bike and related riding gear

APPENDIX B
SOURCES OF
INFORMATION

MAINE
MAINE BUREAU OF PARKS AND LANDS
22 State House Station
Augusta, ME 04333
(207) 287-3821
www.state.me.us

ACADIA NATIONAL PARK
Box 177
Bar Harbor, ME 04609
(207) 288-3338
www.nps.gov/acad

NEW HAMPSHIRE
**NEW HAMPSHIRE DEPARTMENT OF
RESOURCES AND ECONOMIC
DEVELOPMENT**
Division of Parks and Recreation
172 Pembroke Road
P.O. Box 1856
Concord, NH 03302-1856
(603) 271-3628
www.nhparks.state.nh.us

**UNITED STATES DEPARTMENT OF
AGRICULTURE FOREST SERVICE**
White Mountain National Forest
P.O. Box 638
Laconia, NH 03247
(603) 528-8721
www.fs.fed.us/r9/white

VERMONT
**VERMONT DEPARTMENT OF FORESTS,
PARKS, & RECREATION**
103 South Main Street
Waterbury, VT 05671-0603
(802) 241-3655
www.vtstateparks.com

GREEN MOUNTAIN NATIONAL FOREST
231 North Main Street
Rutland, VT 05701
(802) 747-6700
www.fs.fed.us/r9/gmfl

MASSACHUSETTS
**MASSACHUSETTS DEPARTMENT OF
ENVIRONMENTAL MANAGEMENT**
251 Causeway Street, Suite 600
Boston, MA 02114-2104
(617) 626-1250
www.state.ma.us/dem

CONNECTICUT
**CONNECTICUT DEPARTMENT OF
ENVIRONMENTAL PROTECTION**
Bureau of Outdoor Recreation
State Parks Division
79 Elm Street
Hartford, CT 06106-5127
(860) 424-3200
www.dep.state.ct.us

RHODE ISLAND
**RHODE ISLAND DEPARTMENT OF
ENVIRONMENTAL MANAGEMENT**
Division of Parks and Recreation
2321 Hartford Avenue
Johnston, RI 02919
(401) 222-2632
www.riparks.com

APPENDIX C
FISHING LICENSE
INFORMATION

Note: Rates (unless indicated) are for annual passes for individuals ages 16 and older (younger kids don't need them). Call the same numbers to inquire about hunting licenses.

MAINE

(207) 287-8000

$22 for residents; $53 for nonresidents; $24 for a three-day pass

NEW HAMPSHIRE

(603) 271-3211

$35 for residents; $53 for nonresidents; $28 for a three-day pass

VERMONT

(802) 241-3700

$20 for residents; $41 for nonresidents; $20 for a three-day pass

MASSACHUSETTS

(617) 626-1600

$27.50 for residents; $37.50 for nonresidents; $23.50 for a three-day pass

CONNECTICUT

(860) 424-3000

$20 for residents; $40 for nonresidents; $16 for a three-day pass

RHODE ISLAND

(401) 789-3094

$18 for residents; $35 for nonresidents; $16 for a three-day pass

INDEX